ALSO BY T. S. MATTHEWS:

THE SUGAR PILL

Name and Address

An Autobiography by

T. S. MATTHEWS

1960

SIMON AND SCHUSTER   NEW YORK

LIBRARY OF CONGRESS CATALOG CARD NUMBER: 60-6724
MANUFACTURED IN THE UNITED STATES OF AMERICA
BY H. WOLFF BOOK MANUFACTURING CO., INC., NEW YORK, N. Y.

To Edna Gellhorn, with love

CONTENTS

Part One

Part Two

Part Three

QUESTION: What is your Name?
ANSWER: *N.* or *M.* . . .

QUESTION: What did your Sponsors then for you?
ANSWER: They did promise and vow three things in my name: First, that I should renounce the devil and all his works, the pomps and vanity of this wicked world, and all the sinful lusts of the flesh; Secondly, that I should believe all the Articles of the Christian Faith; And Thirdly, that I should keep God's holy will and commandments, and walk in the same all the days of my life. . . .

QUESTION: Rehearse the articles of thy belief. . . .

* * *

"Modern man has heard enough about guilt and sin. He is sorely enough beset by his own bad conscience, and wants rather to learn how he is to reconcile himself with his own nature—how he is to love the enemy in his own heart and call the wolf his brother."

—C. G. JUNG

Part One

QUEEN CITY

I WAS BORN IN THE CITY OF CINCINNATI, in the year 1901. Queen Victoria was still alive. Much later I discovered that Cincinnati was not the whole world nor 1901 its beginning. Last of all I learned that this old lady (who, though a Queen-Empress, apparently resembled a small, bad-tempered turtle) had presided over an age that shaped my youth.

My father was a parson. I never quite learned to think of him as a priest, which was a name he preferred. My mother was an heiress: poor dear, she would never admit it; it embarrassed her too much. From my father we learned to despise; from my mother, to be ashamed. As I have never learned to tell "the whole truth," whatever that may be, I cannot truthfully say more than this about what we learned from them. We also learned to be afraid—not only afraid of outsiders and of the outside world but most of all afraid of being judged and found wanting—although many things and people, perhaps our ancestors included, must have had a hand in that.

I was the second of six children and my parents' only son. Until my father grew old and began to weaken I was a constant disappointment to him; until my mother lay dying she would have sworn I was her dearest hope.

Cincinnati may not have been much like the rest of the world, but it was all we knew. It was frighteningly ugly and hideously dirty, but we accepted the ugliness and the dirt as natural; even children like ourselves, protected and pampered as we knew ourselves to be, took them for granted. We thought life was dirty and smelt bad and had to be washed off you several times a day. We also thought we were safe if we stayed indoors or played in our own back yard.

Our back yard, floored with sooty mud, was enclosed by the blank brick side of a warehouse and two flanking walls at least ten feet high. But nothing could shelter us from the derisive yells of the school next door. Why did we think they were derisive? Because we felt sure that all yells were directed against us; they came from the outside world, which was envious and hostile. We didn't like the back yard: it was an outpost too close to the ever-present enemy, and we had to be driven into playing there. Our lives were lived indoors, in the house.

There were three of us children then, and we lived together, in the nursery. Charlotte was seven, I was five, Mary Ann was nearly three. We were no longer regarded as babies but as children (Mary Ann had to keep up as best she could), little pack horses carrying unquestioningly the load of worries, duties, responsibilities that were piled on us. We remembered only dimly and doubtfully the pastures of infancy where we had been carefree.

Babies are neither good nor bad. They are immune from judgment so long as they are babies. But no sooner do they begin to creep than they creep into danger, and then they come under the angry shadow of the moral law. In that chrysalis-time when a baby is struggling into childhood, before he knows he's there, and before he really is there, he has to answer for his presence. The questions about his being there, at first merely blinding movement and deafening sound, later take the form of statements, warnings, accusations or outcries, all alike incomprehensible to him. He learns to distinguish between the sound of warning and the sound of encouragement. And at about this point he begins to be held accountable for his actions, actions that surprise, delight or terrify him, he never knows which it will be. He's naughty, or he is a good boy.

Painfully, with many tears and incommunicable fury, a child learns. He learns first of all to be "good": that is, to avoid pain, which is sometimes, surprisingly, punishment, and sometimes, surprisingly, not. Though he learns amazingly fast, his understanding of why he should behave in a certain way lags far behind the cunning that shapes his behavior. And often his cunning falters; sometimes what is expected of him is simply beyond him: the problem of correct behavior is too complicated or too alien, and on those dreadful occasions he collapses into naturalness.

We were "good" children.

4

The first thing I saw when I woke up in the morning was the picture. It hung on the nursery wall opposite my bed: a picture of three little boys going off to school in the rain. They were just coming out of the front door of their house; two of them were huddling together under an umbrella, and the third was struggling to open his, with his school books tucked under his arm. They had round, expressionless faces, and they were dressed in coats with little capes, round flat caps with a button on top, and rubber boots. Were they late for school? They were obviously in a hurry, but their faces, chubby and imperturbable as kittens', gave no clue to their feelings.

I had given up asking Miss Newton about them when she came in to dress us in the morning, because she got quite cross and always said the same thing. She said they were little Scotch boys and that she was tired of being asked about them. I didn't think Miss Newton really knew.

The little boys in the picture had fat legs and bodies; they were sturdy. I knew that little boys who lived in towns were not sturdy; I had heard grown-ups discussing it. Charlotte was even less sturdy than I, though she was two years older, and so of course was Mary Ann, because she was nearly three years younger. I was just about as strong as Charlotte even now, and I could put Mary Ann down so easily that she cried. When I was grown up I could probably put them both down at once, perhaps even with one hand. I liked to dream about that, and sometimes made the mistake of talking about it. That usually ended in a fight with Charlotte, or if Miss Newton heard me, in a scolding. It was naughty to boast. I asked my father what "boast" was, and he said it was making things up. I decided that boasting was a fine thing, but not to be done aloud.

The nursery windows looked out over the schoolyard next door. Sometimes the yard was filled with a yelling crowd of boys, and if they caught sight of us in the window the bedlam would concentrate against us with such dreadful insultingness that we couldn't stand up against it; we always fled from the window as soon as we were discovered. But most of the day the playground was silent and deserted.

Charlotte and I each had a real bed to ourselves; Mary Ann, because she was so small, slept in a crib. She was bad about wetting the bed, and we felt superior to her on that account.

The thing I liked best in the nursery, after the picture, was the chandelier. It wasn't really a chandelier but a brass fixture that hung from the ceiling and branched out into four gas jets that were imitation candles. They were the same color as the yellow candies we got in our Christmas stockings, that looked like kernels of corn. It was nice to lie and blink at them while Miss Newton was scolding Charlotte into bed, or in the dark of a winter morning, to wake into the sudden false brightness of illuminated night.

On either side of the fireplace there were brackets with two other gas lights; these had Welsbach burners and frosted-glass shades. When she was in a hurry Miss Newton lit them, because they were easier to reach than the imitation candles; they made a brighter, harder light. The Welsbach burners looked like hollow cones of white ashes, impossibly fragile; when they were lit they took fire with a pop and a rush and burned so fiercely that I couldn't see why they didn't burn right up or fall apart any minute. I longed to touch one to find out whether it was as gossamer as it looked, and what it felt like. Once, when I was alone in the nursery, I did—though Miss Newton had told us never to touch one or it would fall apart. I managed to get the glass shade off without breaking the mantle, and then, though I wanted very much to take hold of the cobwebby cone with my whole hand and give it a squeeze, I was afraid Miss Newton might be right, so I only touched it gently with my finger. The texture was harsh, and stiffer than I had expected. I poked a little harder, and my finger made a neat small hole. I hastily put back the glass shade, doing some further damage to the burner in the process. That night, when Miss Newton lit it, the flame shot up raggedly. I was charged with the crime, denied it, then confessed, and was put in the closet.

Miss Newton did not believe in spanking, or rather, she didn't have the heart to do it herself. But it was a rare day when one of us wasn't put in the closet "for fifteen minutes." Charlotte and I pretended loudly to each other that we did not mind the closet, and I secretly thought that Charlotte probably didn't, but I really minded it very much. It was bad enough to face the dark at night without getting an extra dose of it in the daytime. I always had to be put in by main force, weeping and struggling; but once inside I didn't make a sound. I crouched back in a corner, curling myself as small as possible against the wall, holding my breath and staring as hard as I could, in order to hear or see, or because I was afraid I might hear or see, the Something that I knew was in the closet with me. I knew that It would creep up behind me or spring suddenly unless I kept agonizingly alert, with my back to the wall.

When it was not being used as a cell of solitary confinement the closet was a perfectly normal part of the nursery, cheerfully crowded with familiar clothes, overcoats, mufflers and overshoes; but even on the brightest day the closet had the sinister quality of changeableness. When Charlotte was thrust, wailing, into it—Mary Ann was still so young she was rarely imprisoned, the mere threat was enough—I immediately remembered what it was like when you were inside, and avoided looking at the closet door, even pretending not to hear the horrifying appeals for mercy Charlotte sometimes made, pounding on the door and screaming, "Let me out! I'll be good! Let me out, let me out!"

The nursery was the heart of our world and our refuge from the rest of it; though even here safety could be overwhelmed by the illimitable power of darkness. The nursery was a place of mysteries, good ones as well as evil: the rising of the sun and its going down, winter and spring, wickedness and virtue, the gladdening fire on winter mornings, the horrible fear of the silent dark, stockings magically filled on Christmas Eve, a glimmery-white maternal angel that tucked the blankets around you when you were cold and too sleepy to do anything about it; suppers with the curtains drawn and the lights bright and the fire crackling, when the nursery was small and happy and everything big and frightening was shut outside in the night or far away downstairs at the bottom of the shadowy stair well.

7

The first prayer we learned, which we were taught to say before we went to bed, was

"Now I lay me down to sleep,
I pray the Lord my soul to keep.
If I die before I wake,
I pray the Lord my soul to take."

This implanted in my mind an associated fear of God and death, and a respect for rhyming magic.

The front door was not only latched but bolted and had a chain, always fastened at night, which checked the door from opening more than a few inches. This added precaution, we knew (how did we know? who told us? somebody did), was on account of "sneak thieves." Their technique, we imagined, was to dart into every carelessly opened door, seize whatever it was they were after, and dart out again. Had the house ever been entered by such a marauder? I don't think so; but "sneak thieves" were very real to us.

There had once been a burglar, in the house where Charlotte and I had been born and which we were too young to remember. Canon Welles had been staying with us then; he had heard a suspicious noise in the night and had cleverly called out, "Is that you, Lizzie?"—frightening the intruder so that he started to run and crashed down the back stairs. Canon Welles, in hot pursuit and without his spectacles, fell down the stairs after him. The burglar got away, empty-handed, and presumably at least as badly bruised as Canon Welles. We loved this story, which we always heard with whoops of laughter, but it gave us shivers as well.

Besides bolting and chaining the front door, the parlormaid's nightly duty was to draw the curtains in all the windows that gave on the street, and also to shut and latch the shutters. These were solid wooden panels that folded on hinges, and in daytime were tucked away into shallow cupboards at the sides of the windows. This nightly battening-down of the house increased our sense of siege.

At night the only place we felt safe was the nursery, but daylight changed everything, and then there was not a room in the house—except, of course, the cellar—where we didn't like to go exploring.

8

The third floor we had all to ourselves. There were only two rooms up there: an attic playroom, that ran almost the length of the narrow house, and a trunk room, piled with dusty boxes, trunks and things-that-had-been-put-away-for-the-winter. In the playroom was a blackboard made of real slate, and a hobbyhorse. Mary Ann was never allowed to touch the blackboard, except when Miss Newton was there to enforce fair play. Usually it was considered Charlotte's property, but once a year, on Christmas Eve, I drew a Christmas picture on it, in colored chalk. The picture was always the same—Santa Claus driving his reindeer sleigh over the roofs of a town. I had practiced drawing reindeer until I was the undisputed authority, and always carefully added a droopy triangle under their bellies to show that they were male.

In a corner stood a big chest, full of blocks, tin soldiers, dolls and games. We spent as much time in this room as we could; we hated to go outdoors. We were bookish children, and though our games were ordinary enough they somehow picked up a bookish flavor. For a while our favorite game was robbers; but we called it "blue-eyed banditti."

Nearly every day, weather permitting, we had to go for a walk with Miss Newton. We almost always went the same way, past the Cathedral down Seventh Street and the Odd Fellows Hall and the Ruud hot water heater store to Garfield Place. When we saw the sign I.O.O.F. in front of the Odd Fellows Hall we would start to chant it as if it were a silly word, but Miss Newton would hush us, and she wouldn't let us linger in front of the Ruud window, where we liked to stare at the pipes and queer-looking contraptions. Her idea was to get us to Garfield Place, though when you got there it was nothing but a dingy grass plot with sooty, dried-up grass you weren't allowed to walk on, and a statue of a man with a beard, covered with white stuff from the sparrows. Miss Newton said he was President Garfield, but he didn't interest us. After several turns around the grimy sidewalks of Garfield Place we were very glad to go home, even though we knew that the next thing would be a disagreeably thorough washing of faces, hands and ears.

The back yard was better than going for a walk, because Miss

Newton wasn't with us there. We weren't supposed to go through the kitchen, and when Miss Newton was being very responsible she saw us out through the front door, to see that we didn't go on the street—as if we would have dared. From the narrow walk that led past the side of the house we could look up at the unfamiliar windows of the nursery, or say "There's the dining room," or "I can see Daddy in his study." And when we came past the kitchen door there was the back yard, really much bigger than even the playroom and seeming even bigger because there was no roof on it and because of the tremendous walls on two sides and the great cliff at the back that was made by the warehouse building.

The back yard must have had grass once and still had patches of sparse brownish stubble, but mostly it was hard earth sifted over with coal dust. Even when it was dry, we got much dirtier there than when we went for a walk, but the washing afterwards was worth it because Miss Newton hadn't been there, nagging at us. She sometimes shouted at us from an upstairs window, "Just *look* at your face and hands!" But we knew nothing would be done about it till it was time to come in. We built fortifications by digging with sticks in the cindery mud, and I drilled Charlotte and Mary Ann. They did not make a very satisfactory army, because Mary Ann kept forgetting what she was supposed to be doing, and Charlotte would persist in talking back, although I told her again and again that a private's duty was to keep silence in the ranks. It often ended in a disaster of some sort: I would hit Charlotte with my sword, and her screams would bring Miss Newton, or Mary Ann would deliberately roll on the ground, which would let us all in for an unusually severe washing.

After a while the back yard began to pall on us; there seemed to be less and less we could do there without being either punished or washed extra hard. I brought matters to a head by climbing up the "grape arbor." This was a rickety old trellis clinging to the wall that shut off the school playground next door, and it was held together by a few withered vines. We were forbidden to climb on it, and one day I was caught in the dreadful act. I was led away to Mother-and-Daddy's room. I expected to be spanked, but it turned out to be one of those serious talks with the questions telling you what to answer ("And you wouldn't want to do *that*, would you?").

Soon after that, Mother-and-Daddy announced that something surprising was going to happen in the back yard. Workmen came and tore down the trellis, which was not really surprising; but then they dug holes and put in big posts, and one day there was a shed in the corner, with its roof stretching out from the warehouse wall. The whole thing had a new, woody smell. Under the shed they put up a swing, a seesaw, two flying rings, and a bar (Daddy called it a "parallel bar" and seemed to think that was very funny) and—this was the pleasantest surprise—a slide. Now we were even allowed to play there in rainy weather, and for a while we went there every day.

But gradually the glamour of the new back yard wore off. Mary Ann was so little that the only thing she could do was go down the slide, and finally she came to consider it her private property; she would sit at the top and refuse to budge. When I shoved her she pretended to fall and hurt herself, and that resulted in my being shut in the closet for a whole half hour. We mooned back and forth on the swing, and the seesaw was all right till you got tired of it, but the "parallel bar" was quite beyond us. By helping each other Charlotte and I managed to get up on it, but once we were there we didn't know what to do except get down again. Daddy tried to show us how to "skin the cat" but only hurt his wrist, which confirmed us in our feeling that the parallel bar was too difficult for anybody. The flying rings were too much for us also. By holding on to one with both hands I could give a run and start swinging, but I could never hold on, and Charlotte couldn't even do that much. Daddy was quite disgusted with our feeble efforts, and told us to *practice*.

On rainy days we went back to the playroom. But something seemed to have happened to it: it was somehow much smaller and dingier than before; none of us could think of any new pictures to draw on the blackboard, and the toys in the chest had become all of a sudden tiresome. Mary Ann took advantage of our mood: she found she could play with anything she liked without having it immediately taken away from her. When Charlotte and I realized what a good time she was having and how bored we were, I cuffed her, Charlotte pulled her hair, she tried to bite us and kick our shins. The howls and screams brought Miss Newton, who was unable to cope with the situation, and Mother was called in. Mary Ann was in such a state she had to be spanked, and Charlotte and I were sat on chairs and not allowed to speak.

In the calm after this storm Mother read us a wonderful new story. It was about monkeys, a tribe of them called the Bandar-log, and Mother tried to explain that these monkeys were a good deal like us. Charlotte immediately wanted to play Bandar-log. I pointed out that we would have to have tails. So Mother made us all tails; it took quite a long time, because we insisted on proper tails, with a certain amount of firmness to them and capable of being twitched. Eventually Mother made some very satisfactory ones, stuffed with cotton; they even had a curl to them at the end, and were tied around our waists with tapes.

For a long time Bandar-log was our favorite game. We began by playing it all over the house, but we made so much noise that Daddy came out of his study, and we were banished to the third floor.

The Bandar-log story led to demands for more stories like it, and they in turn led to more games. Mother made us elephant trunks, stuffed like our tails with cotton, that tied on around our heads, and we swayed and shuffled through the third floor, nodding solemnly to each other and snuffling with our trunks. I wanted to hold two knitting needles in my mouth, for tusks, but Mother said it was too dangerous; we must all be very old elephants, old and wise, who had lost their teeth. As more of the *Jungle Book* characters became real to us we no longer felt the necessity of dressing up for the part. No Mother-made imitation of Bagheera the black panther would have suited us, or of Kaa the python, or Akela the Lone Wolf. It became understood that Bagheera was my property and Akela Charlotte's. Mary Ann was half-persuaded, half-bullied into being Baloo the Bear, and once she became convinced of her role not even Miss Newton could make her drop it, though sometimes it got her into trouble, as when she was discovered searching for wild honey in the water closet.

In daylight the dining room was neutral territory; we had break-fast and lunch there with Mother-and-Daddy, but at night it was foreign ground, a grown-ups' room. When we went there to say good night we made the usual attempts to postpone going to bed, but we didn't really want to stay there, even though getting back to the nursery was a risky business. It would have been unthinkable to go through the pantry and up the winding back stairs, which were steep and pitch dark. The only way out was through the front hall, and the first thing you had to get by was the dark coat closet, whose door was almost always ajar. The only light in the hall was a dim ground-glass lantern, far away by the front door.

Charlotte and I never openly compared notes on the perils of getting back to the nursery after dark. Usually we came together, and then the coat closet and the other lurking places were not nearly so frightening. We even showed off to each other by stopping for a minute and sticking out our tongues at a dark corner where It might be. Once I slapped the wall at a place where the shadow was almost the blackest. I never repeated this foolhardy act: the instant my hand touched the wall I snatched it away as if it had been burnt, and nothing could have persuaded me that the tingling in my fingers was not due to something more than slapping the wall.

Daddy's study was the place where I felt least at home. I admired the study: I felt it was impressive, more impressive than the drawing room with its gold-framed mirror and heavy brocaded furniture, or the dining room, which had massive black walnut sideboards and towering chairs. Daddy's study was personally grand. In the recess of the bow window was his enormous flat desk, littered with fascinating but untouchable paraphernalia: his brass double inkpot, the tray for his pens and pencils, the paper cutter shaped like a Crusader's sword, the piles of papers and the squat glass jar of glue with a little brush sticking down into it, that you were sometimes allowed to borrow.

Daddy's study represented everything mysterious and foreign that we meant by the word "grown-up." This was the only room

in the house in which we felt that some kind of serious business
went on that had nothing to do with us; here, and here only, we
must never interrupt, and we intruded at our peril. To come into
the study when Daddy was "busy" was like bursting in on someone in the bathroom, but an even graver offense, we learned to
feel, against grown-up decency. And you never could tell what
sort of reception you were going to get from Daddy; you couldn't
be sure, until you had done it, whether you were interrupting or
not. If you opened the door and saw Miss Whetstone there, you
knew you were interrupting. But by that time, of course, you had
done it.

When Miss Whetstone was in the study, Daddy was always
"busy." Though it seemed to be Miss Whetstone who was really
the busy one; she sat at a little table by Daddy's desk, writing so
hard that her topknot shook, while Daddy just walked around the
room, saying things at her in a loud voice. As I came gingerly
round the edge of the door Miss Whetstone always smiled and
nodded at me, which made her topknot shake more than ever. But
Daddy would turn and stare at me and say, "What is it now?
What is it now?" or "Run along, child, can't you see I'm busy?" or
sometimes, still talking loudly at Miss Whetstone, he would stride
over and lift me out of the room as if I were a baby, and then slam
the door. This hurt my feelings, and I cried, but not loudly until
I got safely upstairs.

When I asked Mother what Daddy was doing, and what Miss
Whetstone was doing, Mother's explanations were full of grown-
up words. Miss Whetstone, it seemed, was Daddy's "secretary,"
whatever that might be. Mary Ann suggested that Miss Whetstone
was Daddy's governess, and Charlotte and I felt that there might
be something in what she said, though we told her with great scorn
that she was wrong.

I liked Miss Whetstone, and I could tell by the way her topknot
shook when she nodded at me that she liked me; but I found it was
safer to go into the study when she was not there. If I waited on
the stairs until I saw her leave, or heard the front door shut behind
her, I knew I would find Daddy in a quieter mood; he would not
be walking around the study but sitting behind his big desk, and

if he looked at me calmly over his eyeglasses I knew it would be all right to ask for the glue, or even if I might look at some of his books with pictures in them, if I did it very quietly. Charlotte could really read, and I sometimes pretended I could. All three of us had "lessons" every morning with Miss Newton in the play-room, but all of us, including Miss Newton, regarded this "school" as a pastime rather than as a serious attempt to learn.

Miss Newton was a romantic, although she didn't look it, and had romantic ideas about everything. She was English, and rather withered and puckery, but she was full of enthusiasms. She had never recovered from a year she had spent in Germany in her impressionable girlhood; Miss Newton was a Teutophile. She still kept a smattering of German from her year abroad, and our German lesson was the one she particularly put her heart into. But I don't think she could have been a very good teacher. At any rate, Charlotte and I struggled fruitlessly with the thorny black letters of the German alphabet, and the result was a confusion that depressed everybody but Miss Newton. She decided that if we couldn't learn to read German we could learn to talk it, and announced that at supper in the nursery only German would be spoken. At first her enthusiasm made a kind of game of it, and Charlotte and I joined in happily, especially as one of the best features of the game was that Mary Ann was hardly able to say a word: the only German she knew was "Nein," and when she tried to reach for what she wanted she had her hand smacked for bad table manners.

But it was not really much of a game, and we soon got tired of it. After one riotous supper when Charlotte and I tried an interesting variation by talking Bandar-log, which excited Mary Ann so much that she became quite uncontrollable and had to be put to bed early, Miss Newton declared a new rule. Hereafter, anyone who lapsed into English had to learn a German poem for every *verboten* word. This kept Charlotte and me busy for a few nights keeping score on each other, and competing for the easiest and shortest poems to learn, but soon the penalties came so thick and fast that it was obvious we could never work them off. Miss Newton dropped the penalties and fell back on enthusiasm. She kept on talking German at supper, and chided us when we didn't, but then she grew absent-minded herself, and gradually the game was forgotten.

At the height of the German period, however, Miss Newton's zeal even affected our food. With Mother's dubious permission and the grumbling aid of the cook, Miss Newton began to introduce us to some very German dishes. Chocolate soup was a qualified success with Charlotte and me, when we managed to think of it as a thin kind of hot sweet dessert in the wrong place; Mary Ann said it made her feel sick, and wouldn't take more than one spoonful. At cinnamon soup we all rebelled. We made such a row, in fact, that Mother came in, and when she was appealed to, sided with us against Miss Newton, who burst into tears and rushed from the room. That was a memorable evening.

When it came to learning German poems by heart, I had protested more loudly than the others, but privately I had liked some of the verses, especially "Die Lorelei," for their sound; I was hazy about what they actually meant. One morning, when I woke early and had nothing else to do, I found to my amazement and delight that I had made a poem myself. I wasn't sure whether I hadn't dreamed it, for it had just come to me with no effort, complete and beautiful. I knew it was a poem because it was like "Die Lorelei": the sound of it gave me the same queer, shivery feeling, and what the words meant it would have been hard to say. I whispered it to Charlotte as we were getting dressed, and she agreed, with a look of awe, that the poem was beautiful. The minute I was dressed I ran in to tell it to Mother, who was brushing her hair. I was glad that Daddy was shaving in the bathroom; I had the feeling I would rather tell it just to Mother, quickly, before it lost its magic. I said it to her in a hushed voice:

> *"In the depths of the dippling sea*
> *There arose such a clamor to me:*
> *A whale in his belly*
> *That sounded like jelly*
> *To me, to me."*

Mother bent her head over further while I was reciting it, and went on brushing her hair.

"Don't you like it?" I said.

Mother stopped brushing her hair, and put her arms around me.

"Why, Tommy, it's lovely! How did you ever do it?"

How had I done it? I had no idea, but I felt sure that it must have come from some place outside me, and it must have been in a dream. Though I knew I had no control over my dreams, which were often invaded by terror, I took credit for the good ones. There was a book in Daddy's study that might have had something to do with it; that afternoon after my nap I went and looked at it again, to see. It was a wonderful book, I thought it was the most wonderful book in the world, though distinctly on the scary side. I couldn't read the title, but I knew it was *Denizens of the Deep*. It was full of monstrous but thrilling pictures: whales sounding, barracuda prowling through the pale-green water, misshapen creatures of the lower depths glaring through blackness with protuberant, fiery eyes. My favorite picture was of a whale diving straight down, with its square muzzle covered by the writhing phosphorescent mass of a giant squid. That must have been the beginning of my poem, I thought, and it gave me the same feeling exactly. You didn't know whether the whale was going to win or not, you hoped he would because he was more like you than the squid was, but both these enormous creatures, and the terrible downward plunge of their struggle, and its soundlessness, and the absence of any human spectator, were in a different world.

I knew from sleep, from my dreams, that there was another world, and that the walls between it and my waking world were insecure. In dreams anything might happen, and there was no protection, no matter how grown-up, that could save you. There was no bridge, apparently, between that world and this; though you might be in an agony of fear or at the last despairing gasp, there was no way of letting anybody know. The people you might be with in the dream paid no attention, or openly mocked at you, or were so cowardly themselves they were of no use to you. The only escape from this world where anything, even the worst, might happen, was like dying: at the last moment your paroxysm of terror mercifully changed into a swoon—and you found, at first with uneasiness and then with joy, that you were awake. That was all very well if the world you woke to was in daylight, but if you opened your eyes on darkness it was worse than before: the nightmare shapes had merely withdrawn a little, pausing in their dreadful game to watch; unless you could get help quickly they would close in again.

Sometimes I had pleasant or funny dreams, so that I woke up laughing. And once I saw God, or rather, the tremendous dais on which God sat, concealed in blinding light, and from which God himself spoke to me warningly, in reverberating thunder—"TOMMY!"—whereupon I woke and found I had wet the bed. Usually my dreams were alarming. Sometimes I couldn't remember what it was that had frightened me so, but two dreams recurred so often that, although the approaches to them varied, I never failed to recognize their landscape with a sinking heart, before I had gone far.

The first always started out as mundanely as a walk with Miss Newton: I would be trying to find my way through the gloomy corridors of an empty house, dimly lit by an occasional gas jet, or I would be walking through shadowy streets, walled in by silent factories or shuttered city houses. Sometimes I would have friends with me, and as long as we were together I felt apprehensive but not panicky. Then for some inexplicable reason we would lose each other and I would be alone, walking on with apparent aimlessness but in a dreadful mounting excitement, turning corners at random and eventually finding the deserted house I was looking for. Here I knew I must go very softly. I tiptoed up the stairs, turned the corner of a passageway, and came to a shut door. I knew the door was locked, and for a reason. I knew that if I tried to open it or knocked, or called attention to my presence in any way, something dreadful would happen. But by this time I could no longer help myself. In an ecstasy of fear I crouched down at the bottom of the closed door and screamed through the crack. Instantly the door burst open and I was buffeted into senselessness by voices like great winds.

The other dream was even worse, for my part in it was altogether passive, and it was a double dream; it had to start by my dreaming that I was awake. I could never be sure at first whether I was dreaming or not. There I was in bed in the nursery, and there were Charlotte and Mary Ann sound asleep in their beds, and the door into the hall was ajar, with the hall light shining through, and here came Mother through the door—no, it was not Mother. It was those three tall black shapes, like silhouettes of cowled monks or night riders. Now I knew I was caught; I tried to call for help but could make no sound. The three Shapes glided up to my bed, they bowed low over it, pressing me down, smothering me. I was trying terribly to cry out—ah, now I was going to be able to, for the three Shapes swayed upright again, and bowed in unison. At my first gasping scream their outlines began to grow shadowy; they vanished and I knew I was really awake, but in outrage and fear I screamed again and again. That always brought Mother or Daddy hurrying in to see what was the matter. At first it would also wake Charlotte and Mary Ann, but as "Tommy's nightmares" became a recognized institution they slept peacefully through my yells.

Afterwards I was a little ashamed of this screaming, which was mainly a relief to my feelings; but if Mother-and-Daddy had asked me why I did it I would have said I had to. I wanted someone else to suffer for my fear, if he couldn't share it; and my loneliness was too haunted to take back into sleep with me without some reassurance. That I always got; I was patted and tucked in and told to turn over on the other side. And that was usually enough. But if the nightmare was a very bad one, or if, as sometimes happened, I had turned trustingly on my other side and slid straight into the maw of another one, then no reassurances would do. Then the only place in which I could feel safe was Mother-and-Daddy's bed. Cuddled down between these two warm grown-up bodies I was in sanctuary at last; nothing could happen to me there. Once, my heart still thudding from a nightmare, I lay safe between Mother-and-Daddy and saw, with interest but no fear, that the evil shapes had followed me even here. I watched them gather in the dark corners and wondered how far they would dare. I stretched out my leg slowly, slowly toward the bottom of the bed, until I could feel the tucked-in sheet. Instantly Their teeth fastened on my foot. I quickly curled it up under me again. If I had been in my own bed, I knew, the whole pack would have been on me in a twinkling. But not here. I sighed and turned on my other side and fell asleep.

Sitting around the nursery fire after supper, in the half hour before Miss Newton herded us to bed, Charlotte and I would sometimes tell each other ghost stories. Mary Ann was put to bed earlier, and was always sound asleep when Charlotte and I crept into our beds, wishing we had not been so intense or so convincing in our story-telling. I pretended to Charlotte that I was quite immune to ghost stories, and indeed I was to the ones she told, which always started out with a great white shape in the door or at the window which turned out to be Mother or Daddy or Miss Newton. The stories that scared me were the ones I told myself; but the temptation to tell them was too much for me when I saw Charlotte's eyes getting bigger and her mouth like an O, even though I knew that the price of this triumph was that I would be twice as scared as she.

At the height of the *Jungle Book* period, when I was being Bagheera the Black Panther whenever I could remember to be, I discovered a new gambit to this dangerous game. At times I felt so completely a panther that I felt sure I must look like one; but when I went to the mirror to see, it was obvious that I was still much more Tommy than Bagheera. By dint of practice and strong conviction, and with the mirror as referee, I succeeded at last in finding a panther face. One day when Bagheera came upon the plump figure of Mary Ann, who had been allowed by her foolish *amah* to stray outside the compound and was playing with her doll on the very edge of the jungle, the sudden sight of the stalking panther was realistic enough to reduce her to screams of genuine panic. For this feat I narrowly escaped a spanking, and was strictly forbidden to stalk children. Mother pointed out to me that Bagheera never did such a thing, and I had to admit that the book was on her side; but I felt the Law of the Jungle, no matter what the book said, could not be fully stated in terms of Anglo-Saxon decency, and that I hadn't really offended against it by frightening an ignorant little white baby, whose bad luck it had been to tempt my panther nature.

I continued to practice panther faces in the mirror, though now I was careful not to wear the finished article when there was any danger of being caught by a grown-up. And at last I got more than I had bargained for, or was it only as much? I was staring into the mirror, my eyes wide and unblinking, nostrils distended, nose and mouth puckered into a muzzle, when with horrible swiftness the outlines dissolved and nothing was left in the brightness but two glaring eyes, animal-like and threatening. Then the face came back, and it was not my face, nor the face of a little boy, nor the face of Bagheera; it was a face unknown to me, full of terror and strangeness. I shut my eyes, catching my breath, and turned away from the mirror without looking into it again.

Daddy was a special kind of clergyman called a dean, and his church was just across the street from our house. Only it was not a church but a cathedral. I always thought of it as Daddy's cathedral, though Charlotte informed me that it was not Daddy who owned it, but the Bishop. It was a graceless, soot-blackened brownstone Victorian building, whose squat unfinished towers barely topped the gable of the nave, with a grimy rose window between, looking down on broad stone steps leading up to the big door. It seemed to me more than beautiful; it was awesome. Inside it was more so: a lofty flat-vaulted ceiling painted in faded blue and gold with the stars of the firmament, the two gilded cliffs of organ pipes on either side of the chancel, the towering altar, the shadowy tunnel from which the choir mysteriously emerged and into which it mysteriously disappeared when the service was over, chanting the final Amen from somewhere far away, and all the dusky nooks and crannies into which the light from the gas chandeliers could never penetrate. It was always murky inside the Cathedral, the atmosphere had something of the quality of night, but of a night that suggested the eternal darkness of outer space. It was not the possibility of lurking Things in these dark recesses that made me walk softly and reverently hold my breath, but the obvious presence of God himself. If anything, I felt there was too much light in the Cathedral: the altar, blazing with candles, was too undazzlingly clear to be God's throne: besides, I could see there was no proper place for Him to sit. When Daddy marched up into the pulpit to preach, and the choir settled back in their benches with a subdued fluttering of anthem music, and the lights were turned down one by one, I always felt with relief that now the Cathedral was more like God's dwelling.

During the sermon Mother gave us pencils and paper, so we could draw pictures and not disturb the congregation by squirming; but when Daddy was preaching it was hard to keep your undivided attention on what you were drawing, even if it was battles. Daddy had a thin, penetrating voice that carried very clearly, and he pronounced his words with a kind of vindictive distinctness. He never slurred a final *s*, and the effect was often like a startling hiss. Also he had a disturbingly energetic way of beginning again in a much louder voice after his last sentence had died away, by the sound of it, into what might have been the end of the sermon: "And so it is," he would suddenly cry, perhaps taking you so off your guard that you would drop your paper and pencil on the floor, and Mother would frown and whisper not to make so much noise. Or sometimes the silence would go on so long that you would look up to see what Daddy was doing, and he would be leaning out over the edge of the pulpit, looking over your head and smiling in a triumphant way. When you saw him smiling like that, you knew it was not the end of the sermon, only the end of a bit. He had just asked someone a question he couldn't answer, or had answered one himself. I sometimes listened to parts of Daddy's sermons in spite of myself, but I couldn't understand what they were about. I could always tell, however, that Daddy was winning, and that gave me a respectful feeling.

Daddy prided himself on never preaching longer than twenty minutes, but even twenty minutes is a long time to sit quietly, if you are not a grown-up. When I heard the releasing "And now to God the Father, God the Son, and God the Holy Ghost," it was with a sigh of physical relief. When the Bishop preached, he went on so long in his hollow-booming, stunningly soothing voice that

I was usually asleep when he finished, and had to be dragged to my feet.

With the end of the sermon, the choir came to life, the congregation sat up, everyone felt that the worst was over. At this point I always fixed my eyes on Mr. Stapps, the organist (he pronounced it Stops); I could just see his sharp, ferrety profile as he raised his head with a confident air, and catch the flash of his pince-nez in the tilted mirror above his head as he cast his eye along the ranks of the choir. For a tense moment Mr. Stapps held his inquiring pose, then gave a quick nod and sprang tigerishly at the keyboard, and first one bank of organ pipes, and then the other, burst into rippling thunder. I thought Mr. Stapps must be either very strong or a kind of magician to make these huge pipes, so far away from his organ bench, play now on one side of the cathedral, now on the other, sing softly, high, shrill and sweet, and then blow such a trumpet blast that the whole cathedral shook. And he always had one final trick up his sleeve: as the choir marched out, singing the recessional hymn at the top of their lungs, just as the trebles and altos disappeared into that dark tunnel from which they had first emerged, Mr. Stapps's head would give an extra jerk and the great organ fell silent, but its muted tones could still be heard, coming from outside, where the choir was. Sometimes you could hardly hear the organ yourself, but you knew the choir must be able to, for there was Mr. Stapps still rocking back and forth over the keyboard.

Now the service was practically over. If you were as young as Mary Ann you thought it was over, and would begin talking to Mother and be hushed; but Charlotte and I were old enough to know better. Everyone knelt down again, and I listened for the far off sing-song chant, all on one note, that I knew was Daddy saying good-by to the choir. Then the choir, thanking him and saying good-by too, with a hearty Amen. Now at any moment the acolyte would appear in the chancel, carrying his long candle-snuffer. I watched with interest to see if he would get every candle at the first snuff: he hardly ever did. When the last candle was extinguished, the acolyte made his final bow to the altar and went out. At last you could get up and put on your coat. In the cold, watery daylight outside the front door of the Cathedral there would be Daddy, dressed in a long black gown and wearing a funny kind of hat on his head, bowing and smiling and shaking hands with the people as they came out. He would shake hands with us, too, for a joke. Daddy was always in a good humor just after morning service. Then across Seventh Street, holding onto Mother's sleeve and looking out for cabs, up the front steps and then upstairs to get washed for Sunday dinner. I felt relieved and happy, and I knew there would be roast beef and Yorkshire pudding, and perhaps ice cream.

Next door to the Cathedral, and connected with it by the choir tunnel, was the Cathedral House. It was much bigger than our house, but it had none of the Cathedral's awe-inspiring quality. It was just a big city house, dirty and dark, where typewriters clicked and a lot of people bustled through the corridors. The Bishop had a room there called an office, and so did Daddy. Sometimes I went there on a weekday, with Miss Newton or Mother, when they wanted to give Daddy a message. I liked to go, because I knew I would see Miss Whetstone. If she wasn't too busy she would show me how her typewriter worked, or make pictures on it for me. She made wonderful pictures, all by typewriting: birds flying, and a squirrel, and even a big ship with smoke coming out of the funnels. Sometimes the Bishop would come in while I was there. This was rather embarrassing, because he would lean over and put his hand on my head and ask me questions in his hollow voice. The Bishop was not tall but he was very square and solid, and had an old face, a good deal like God's, I thought. He didn't seem to mind whether I answered the questions or not; even if I was trying to, in a minute he would pat me on the head and say, "Well, well. Be a good boy, and a credit to your father," and lumber off. He wasn't nearly so impressive as when he was dressed up in his Bishop's robes with puffy sleeves—Charlotte said they were stuffed with cotton to keep them that shape. But I knew he must be very old, because his brother, a general, had been killed at Little Round Top, which I knew was a battle in the Civil War, a long time ago. I thought of it as a very narrow escape for the Bishop.

Until I started to sing in the choir I never went inside the Cathedral House on Sundays. My entrance into the choir was my first encounter, except for a few cousins, with boys of my own age. It was Mr. Stapps who suggested that I was old enough (I must have been seven or eight) and when Daddy agreed, Mr. Stapps said he would give me a voice test. That turned out to be not so dreadful; Mr. Stapps seemed to want me to pass it, indeed determined that I should, so of course I did. Then he told me I was to come to two choir practices that week, and sing with the choir next Sunday. Furthermore, I would actually be paid ten cents a week—if there were no fines. Mr. Stapps smiled quickly when he mentioned the fines, as if to say that *I* needn't worry about *them*.

It soon appeared, however, that fines were very much something to worry about. At my second choir practice we sang one of my favorite hymns:

> *Glorious things of thee are spoken,*
> *Zion, City of our God.*
> *He, whose word cannot be broken,*
> *Formed thee for His own abode.*
>
> *On the Rock of Ages founded,*
> *What can shake thy sure repose?*
> *With Salvation's walls surrounded,*
> *Thou may'st smile at all thy foes.*

When we came to the third line the little red-haired treble next to me turned his head and sang "He, whose nose cannot be broken . . ." I would have laughed if I had not been so intent on the glorious sound of the hymn and had not felt myself a still-unadmitted mortal among these seraphs. But the boy beyond me sniggered. When we came to the end of the verse Mr. Stapps held up his hand and said quietly, looking at the red-haired boy, "I'm going to fine you for that, Maschke. Now we'll try the offertory." Maschke turned red and muttered something I didn't understand.

Mr. Stapps was strict, but he was nothing compared to Daddy. Next Sunday morning, when the choir was lined up in the passageway leading into the Cathedral, I was in my place among the trebles, fourth from the front, very conscious of my stiff Eton collar and starchy-clean cotta, and hoping I wouldn't trip over my cassock, which was a little too long for me, and wondering whether Mother and Charlotte and Mary Ann would see me, and whether I would be able to sing, my mouth felt so dry. I hardly noticed the muted scuffling in the line ahead of me. Suddenly Daddy strode past me with a swirl of vestments, his hymn book in his left hand caught up to his chest like a shield, seized a boy by the ear—it was Maschke again—and dragged him out of the line. In a low but furious voice Daddy told him to get dressed and go home. Maschke, sniffling and grinding his fist into his eye, dragged off to the choir room. There was absolute silence in the passageway. I was impressed by this thunderbolt action, also horrified. Maschke had not behaved as he should, but what a devastating and ruthless retribution! It was like witnessing the banishment from the human race of someone who had been too human. This was a public aspect of Daddy I had never seen, and it left me with a strange mingling of awe and shame. The next minute we heard the first notes of the organ, and burst into the processional hymn.

I learned that there were others in the choir besides Maschke who feared Daddy but did not love him. These boys were polite to me, because I was the Dean's son, and it was naturally to be supposed that I would tell on them if they weren't. When I was around they took care to lower their voices and nudge one another if they thought there was any danger of my overhearing what they were saying about "him"; but now and then I caught a word or two. As for my reporting what I heard, it never occurred to me; I felt their cautious scorn or resentment not as disloyalty to the Dean but as a personal criticism of Daddy, and that embarrassed me so much that I pretended even to myself to have heard nothing.

Because Cincinnati was the first city I knew, it became for me the type of all cities. I never understood why it was called "The Queen City," and for me that title called up depressing images. I thought of "city" as a place of horrors, an urban desert. "City" meant factories spewing out smoke and stinks, the grimy, endless vistas of warehouses and little shops, the clang and screech of trolley cars, the clatter of horse-drawn beer wagons over cobblestones, the ponderous rush of a fire engine, smoke pouring thick from its shiny funnel, its bell clanging and clanging, and the great white horses galloping heavily. There were oases: the zoo, a hilly garden where a band played and we saw the Ben Greet players acting something called Shakespeare, and the pacing imprisoned animals gave off sharp acrid smells of misery and evil; the Rookwood Pottery, at the top of a hill too steep for a trolley car to climb, so the car was lifted slowly up on a platform called "the *in*-clined plane"; the department stores, whose names still sound magically in my ear—Shillito's, Pogue's, Alms & Doepke, Loring Andrews, Mabley & Carew; Fountain Square, where the water pouring down from the fingertips of the statue's outstretched arms made your own fingers tingle to look at it.

And there were memorable occasions. Once we were taken to see Keller, the Great Magician, who was disappointingly bald and elderly, but who amazed even the grown-ups by his feats of magic, the most startling of which was to make his beautiful assistant disappear from a cabinet. And I remember a concert, where the orchestra played *The Flying Dutchman* and the noise (and what I knew of the story) scared me. My most vivid recollection is of seeing my first moving picture. It came, as I think was usual in those days, at the end of a vaudeville program. I believe it was a farce, but I saw nothing funny in the flickering, jerky figures on the screen, under a constant bombardment of black specks, nor in their increasingly frightful predicament: a wife was entertaining a lover (this was in the comparatively uninhibited early days of the cinema) when her husband unexpectedly came home. The lover darted into the fireplace and crawled up the chimney (at this point we saw the chimney in cross-section, with him in it). The husband lit a fire, and the flames and smoke drove the unfortunate lover further and further up the flue until he was wedged in, choking, and could go neither forward nor back. I don't know how it ended, as by this time I felt so sick that I was taken home.

"Sick in my throat" was my attempt to describe how I felt. It was an all-too-frequent feeling. My sisters and I had the usual children's illnesses—measles, mumps, whooping cough, chicken pox—but what I was famous for was being sick in my throat, particularly in public conveyances. Any form of travel tended to turn my stomach upside down: motorcars, streetcars, trains, boats of all kinds and sizes. Certain smells and sounds still bring back the memory: the ruminative *chunka-chunka-chunka* of a stationary streetcar, and the faintly burnt smell (I always thought of it as used-up electricity) that comes up from under the car recall the sickening lurch and swoop of a sudden curve, the side-to-side swaying of wheels on imperfectly fitted track.

Now that steam locomotives are almost a thing of the past on American passenger trains, and air-conditioning has taken the place of open windows in summer, only bits of those overnight journeys come back to me: the sieve-like mesh of the wire screens that kept out the larger cinders but let in a gritty powder of coal dust, so that in the morning the sheets and blankets of the lower berth were covered with it; the shiny brass spittoons in all the cars, often with cigar butts floating; the mingled smell of stale cigars, coal gas and coffee that turned your appetite for breakfast into an increasingly awful conviction that you were going to throw up, and your numbing disregard of where you happened to be when you suddenly did.

Boats were worse than trains. At first the slight bobbing motion of our launch on Lake Michigan was enjoyable or at least not unpleasant, but the day we started to go all the way to Charlevoix, and the bobbing grew more pronounced and I saw the endlessness of water ahead, my telltale greenish face and my fearsome reputation as a sudden vomiter were enough to turn the expedition back. As I grew older the boats grew bigger—the ferry from St. Ignace to Mackinac, the Great Lakes steamer to Duluth, the 10,000-ton transatlantic liner *Minnewaska*, and when I was eleven, the great *Olympic* herself, at that time the largest ship afloat—but unless the water was like level glass I knew it, brooded on it, and sooner or later threw up.

Why should I have been so much queasier than my sisters? I have no idea. I remember hearing discussions about the inner ear and its relation to the sense of balance, but on dry land, or when I wasn't being whirled along on wheels, my sense of balance was apparently no more precarious than other people's.

Our parents were understandably anxious about our health, and we felt their anxiety and learned to share it. But were we in fact as delicate as we were brought up to believe we were? I doubt it now, though I accepted it then as a matter of course. It seems to me likely, at least, that this was part of a larger insistence on the difference between us and other people. The fact that we were different was never absent from our consciousness. We were ashamed of our timidity and our lack of sturdiness, but we despised the rest of the world for all that, and looked down on everybody who was not like us. And we were sure that nobody *was* like us.

As a well-brought-up child, I was learning during these years to do what was expected of me. It seemed to me that I would never learn it all. So much was expected, and there were so many different authorities to be sorted out. If I had known then, or even suspected, that I would spend the rest of my life trying to unlearn what I was now so painfully learning, I think it would have been too much for me. But my suspicions of the future—and they existed, dimly—were not at all of that kind. I knew, or had an anxious premonition, that there was a job cut out for me (in the words I learned in church: "a state of life to which it hath pleased God to call us") but what that job might be or how I should ever be able to do it well were dark and heavy questions.

At the age of eight, life has no discernible shape, but the child who does not question authority can begin to feel the limits of his life: the limits of what he will be permitted. I was a child who did not question authority, and it never occurred to me then that authorized limits can be extended or denied. Not by a good boy; and I knew that only a good boy becomes a good man. Only if you were a good enough boy to be stamped by the approval of those unimpeachable authorities could you ever be admitted as a man to their own lower ranks. And it had not dawned on me that there was anywhere else to go.

MY FATHER'S GOD

IN MY FATHER'S HOUSE, the day officially began with family prayers. We gathered—the last-comers on hasty tiptoe—in my father's study, and plopped down on our knees at the first convenient chair or sofa. The sofa was more comfortable to lean on. My father immediately began to recite the Our Father, in which we all joined; he went so fast that sometimes the younger children could not keep up with him. Then he read a series of family prayers, in a low rapid voice but without slurring any of the words: he read beautifully and enunciated with great distinctness.

The prayers my father read us every morning were literally crawling with verbal thankfulness, and though I wouldn't have dreamed of taking exception to it, the abjectness of the gratitude depressed me. "We, thy needy creatures, render thee our humble praises, for thy preservation of us from the beginning of our lives to this day, and especially for having delivered us from the dangers of the past night. For these thy mercies, we bless and magnify thy glorious Name; humbly beseeching thee to accept this our morning sacrifice of praise and thanksgiving. . . ." They were also full of petitions with escape clauses: we were asking God, who did everything needful for us, to do a little something more—but not, of course, if He didn't want to or if it made no sense. "Fulfil now, O Lord, the desires and petitions of thy servants, as may be most expedient for them." This kind of prayer seemed to me to cancel itself out, to be really "vain."

The odd thing, to me, was that when my father read the thankful prayers he didn't sound abject, nor anything less than sensibly lawyerlike when he came to the petitions. The general impression he gave was of a man engaged in a solemn early-morning chore; he was keeping his temper under control while he did it—and we knew his temper was especially uncertain before breakfast—because it was a serious matter. It never occurred to me—how could it?—that we were greeting the new day with a song and trying to

30

express our joy in being alive. There was no song, and there was no feeling of joy.

I was more than fifty when I heard—in church, of all places, and during the three-hour service on Good Friday, of all times—that "the sole purpose of creation is to increase joy." I am still shaking my head over that one. It is certainly not the tone of voice of old Mother Church that I remember from my childhood. What struck and held my attention then were the forbidding statements, and the kind of petition urging God to "keep us ever mindful of the time when we shall lie down in the dust." But the more my father prayed and the faster he went, the more my spirits rose; I knew that prayers would soon be over and then we should have breakfast.

Breakfast was the real beginning of the day. It started on the dot of eight, and no one was late for it—or very rarely. I don't remember that any formal punishment was the penalty for lateness, but that was not necessary: the atmosphere into which the latecomer walked was so icy that it was some time before he felt warm again. He was liable to get one quick glaring stare from my father, or, what was even worse, a frozen disregard that held in it the threat of being sent to Coventry for good. If you got to your chair by the last rippling note of the gong, you were safe; but a moment later was a moment too late. By that time my father would have started saying grace.

Of course, if you had been at prayers, and hadn't dawdled on the way into the dining room, there was no possible excuse for your being late. But sometimes, on account of dreamy dressing or a broken shoelace or some other misdemeanor, you missed prayers. An occasional absence from prayers was not considered a crime, but it was a crime to be late for breakfast.

My father said grace before and after each meal, and we stood up for both graces. He would usually warn favored guests about this "double-barreled grace," as he called it, so that when the meal was over they would not be embarrassed by finding themselves strolling toward the door while the rest of the company stood behind their chairs, with their heads bowed. My father usually waited for the hushed silence that showed everyone else was waiting, but when he was in a bad mood he would sometimes start saying grace almost inaudibly, and then one of us might be caught not paying attention, or even whispering.

My mother was always preoccupied at breakfast; she was so anxious about a number of things that she sometimes gave the impression of being rather absent. She had to see that the children were all eating enough, and properly; that my father got his coffee exactly when and as he wanted it (she often failed in this); that the maid was not annoying or about to annoy my father by some clumsiness or lack of attention, or by not getting things from the kitchen fast enough; that breakfast in general went off smoothly, like a well-ordered drill (it often didn't). Whether she spoke soothingly or sharply to one of the maids, it was always in a low voice, and usually with an air of apology; even when she had to play the sergeant major and relay the commanding officer's displeasure to some unfortunate underling, she managed to convey the impression that no real crime had been committed, though a rule might have been infringed or an order not smartly enough carried out.

My father never spoke in a low voice at breakfast. He either barked at one of us or at my mother—usually it was at my mother—or said nothing at all. The silent breakfasts were perhaps the worst. If we talked among ourselves, then it soon became evident that we were deliberately excluding him from the conversation, and his silence became increasingly and unforgivingly hurt. If we all said nothing, following his lead, the atmosphere grew rapidly heavier and darker, piling up and up to an intolerable suspense. Sometimes, on such a morning, if I glanced at my mother, I would see that her eyes were full of tears. But, as she said herself, she cried too easily.

Breakfast, the thing itself, was a feast, though perhaps a not very digestible one. Before the days when orange juice became the American fashion, we began with grapefruit or figs or blueberries, whatever fruit was in season. Sometimes we had bonny clabber—a kind of natural junket formed by milk that had soured in the pan—with sugar and cream and grated nutmeg. There was oatmeal, as well as various patented breakfast cereals. For the children and for weaker-stomached grown-ups there were eggs and bacon. But the main dish, except on Fridays, when we always had fish, was meat: chicken stew, or pork tenderloin (invariably on Sunday mornings in winter) or liver and bacon, or baked ham. Toast of course, but almost always some other kind of hot bread as well: scones, biscuits, popovers, muffins, or buckwheat cakes, waffles, or griddle cakes. These last were eaten first with eggs or meat stew piled on them, and the last rounds with syrup—real maple syrup, not the inferior kind made from corn. The children had milk—in the early days thickly laced with a molasses-y concoction containing cod-liver oil—and the grown-ups coffee, with both hot milk and cream.

As children, we naturally thought everyone had breakfasts like that. It wasn't till I went away to boarding school, where there were sometimes cockroaches in the shredded wheat and second helpings were frowned on, that I realized there was something old-fashioned and peculiar about our family breakfasts. But long before that I had begun to see or think I saw some connection between food and my father's bad temper. I had noticed that his humor was worst before breakfast and was apt to improve as the meal wore on. Might it be that food had the same effect on him that drink had on others? I think it did. It is said of some people that they were born several drinks under par. He must have been born snarling with hunger. It was amazing how quickly food seemed to go to his head and restore him to geniality.

When my father was jovial, as he sometimes became even at breakfast, he made jokes. I seldom saw the point, but laughed rather doubtfully anyhow. One of them, I remember, he always repeated when we had bonny clabber and a guest who had never tasted it before. He would start by challenging the guest to spell bonny clabber, then shake his head violently at all the versions offered. When the victim surrendered, my father would lean across the table towards him and slowly and distinctly enounce: "B-a-u-g-h, baw; n-a-u-g-h, naw; c-l-a-u-g-h, claw; b-e-r, ber." Then he would give a victorious shout of laughter, in which we would all join.

My father laughed a good deal when he was feeling well. Years later, when I was grown up and had begun to wonder whether I had inherited his sense of humor, I read a book called *The Secret of Laughter*, by a man named Ludovici. The author seemed to think that a sense of humor, as generally understood, was always exhibited by what he called "showing teeth," and was really nothing more than a feeling of triumph. He had some very ingenious evidence for this thesis, most of which I have forgotten, but one instance he gave was the laughter of very young children: they show their teeth when they have successfully wobbled across a slippery floor, or when they see someone else fall down. As I read the book, I thought of my father laughing at breakfast, and his triumphant eyes when he laughed.

My mother, whose role it was to keep the peace between him and the servants, between him and the children, followed an un-deviating policy of appeasing him. I am sure she did not always think he was right, or just, or even reasonable. But he was the head of the household, and as such his needs and demands must be deferred to. Besides, she hated scenes. So the scenes were almost invariably staged and produced by my father, a one-man show witnessed by an embarrassed, sullen or agonizingly interested audi-ence. Mother's watchfulness sometimes wavered, or seemed to; she simply had too much to look out for—six of us children and a couple of maids, besides my father. So occasionally she left undone those things which she ought to have done, or didn't get them done quickly enough to suit him. If she had forgotten to ask him soon enough if he would like a second cup of coffee, no matter how penitently she apologized or begged him to pass his cup, he was adamant, saying, thank you, no, it was too late, he had finished his breakfast. The implication was obvious to everybody that she had succeeded, thanks to her careless neglect, in ruining everything.

At such times he would withdraw into haughty distances, read-ing his letters with the air of a man boiling with patience, who should have been at his important business long ago, and whom only the deplorable dawdling of his children and his flustered wife —and his own terrible correctness—still kept at the table. Now and then he would follow up his advantage by a crushing counter-attack. He would say to my mother: "I just want to call your attention to the fact that no one has drunk any water because the water is lukewarm. Can you make some arrangement about it? Yes? *All right!*" Or his first shirred egg had not been hot enough to suit him. "Now, if they're going to bring me another egg . . . I don't want it unless it's *sizzling.*"

The maids, who were generally terrified, frequently enraged him by some ineptness—usually caused or complicated by their fear of him, though it is true that some of them were green girls whom my mother was in process of training. That must have been like trying to teach unbroken ponies an equestrian act in the ring next to the roaring lions and tigers. When one of the maids committed some grievous fault, such as offering him a plate on the wrong side, or failing to bring the next batch of hot bread quickly enough, he never spoke to her directly, though he might give her a quick snarl and shake of the head. It was my mother he always held responsible, and it was she whom he reprimanded if anything went wrong. We found his language lofty, and its barely muted sarcasm terrible; perhaps she did too. "I presumed that you, having access to the kitchen, would know . . ."

Not all the maids were abjectly afraid of him. I remember one sullen Irish girl named Bridie who did not knuckle under. She never said anything, of course, but you could tell by her wooden face and unflustered manner that she found him merely a vexation, perhaps even slightly ludicrous. On unusually stormy mornings she would report to the kitchen: "Ah, he's wicked today; he's wicked today."

My father's breakfast behavior did not improve with age, but we became more accustomed to it as we grew older, and eventually managed a certain amount of conversation among ourselves, heedless of his glowering presence. Sometimes we went too far, not unlike Squirrel Nutkin frisking around Old Brown and teasing him to pounce. Sooner or later he usually pounced. We might be talking about people he didn't know, referring to them by their first names. My father would stand it as long as he could and then interject, in a tone of angry contempt: "Nina *who*? Nina McAlpin! Oh." That would generally knock the bottom out of that conversation.

In this mood, whatever he did or said was intended to be an insult. His challenge was not always, or even usually, taken up as such, but the challenge was there. Since he so seldom drew any direct response, perhaps he had ceased to expect one: his behavior was more an assertion of his superiority over the person he was affronting, whose inferiority, in turn, was intended to be made obvious. And the person was not always addressed directly, or in words—sometimes it was a salt shaker snatched up and thumped down on the table, or a prayer book smacked against the pew, or a general and somewhat veiled animadversion on the ghoulish habits of New York doctors.

To my astonishment (it still seems like a trick that I might have uncovered if I had been looking hard enough) our childhood did not last forever. Most of us grew up and got married and thus left my father's breakfast table. But it still went on just the same, as we discovered when we came home for visits. It went on after my mother died and he was left alone. There were certain mutations, naturally. As an old man my father did not eat so hearty a breakfast as he used to; also he got in the habit of eating it backwards, starting with pork tenderloin, toast and marmalade, and ending with oatmeal. The maids were no longer green: they had turned gray in his service. But breakfast continued to be a silent and oppressive meal. If you seeded its thunderous clouds you did so at your peril. Being my mother's son, I still let well enough alone and held my tongue.

(On a soft, sunny January morning, when I was thirty, my wife and I sat on a balcony overlooking the quiet harbor of Palma de Mallorca. We were having breakfast—*cafe con leche* in big bowls, and *ensaimadas*. It was scandalously late, according to my way of thinking: well after nine o'clock. The children were up and out long ago, off somewhere with their nurse. I was still in pajamas and slippers and dressing gown, and I hadn't shaved. The balcony, though we were in a hotel, was perfectly private, being screened from its neighbors by solid walls. The winter air was as mild as May, and the blue sea as fresh as if it had been made that morn-

36

ing. I felt irresponsible, wicked, and grown up at last. It was lovely.)

My father had been the youngest of a large family. Whether or not he was conscious of having been spoiled as a child I can't say; but from what he used to tell us, I gather that he was spared the rod. When he was very naughty, his mother threatened to "beat him with a broomstraw." I should think that, for a favorite, he was probably a very good child—like me, but doubtless more headstrong, more indomitable. On the rare occasions when he hardened his infant heart against clear and present duty and something drastic had to be done about it, he was led or persuaded to the top of the cellar steps, and invited to "kick Captain Snarley downstairs." He liked doing that, and apparently it restored him to moral health.

Perhaps he was always rather an elderly child; at any rate, another of his reminiscences about his early days seems to show the kind of precocity that is in a hurry to get childhood done with. When he was about five or six his parents took him on a steamer trip from Put-in Bay, on Lake Erie. On the boat little Paul was missed, searched for and discovered on another deck, passing his hat—and getting money in it too—for a recitation he had just delivered.

Though I suppose he must have played some outdoor games at school, he never mentioned them; tennis and croquet were the only ones I ever saw him engage in. When he was a fifth-former at St. Paul's he had a severe attack of pneumonia, which ended his school career and kept him out of freshman year at Princeton. After he got to college he made up for lost time by becoming one of the successful campus intellects: he was editor of the *Nassau Literary Magazine* and the Latin valedictorian of his class, which meant that he stood high in his studies.

The most mysterious part of my father's life, to me, is the period between his adolescence and young manhood. What was he like then? What did he do? Did he ever take too much to drink? Did he ever kiss a girl? What did he think and dream about? I have no notion; I know only the barest outlines of this part of his life and cannot fill them in. I never even wondered about it very much until the evening, some time after his retirement, when he invited an elderly gentleman named Philip Rhinelander to dinner. Mr. Rhinelander, it appeared, had been best man at his wedding. That immediately roused my curiosity about my father as a young man, for what on earth could those two ever have had sufficiently in common to be such friends?

I never saw Mr. Rhinelander before or after that evening, and my memory may play me false in some particulars, but the general impression strongly remains of a red-faced portly man of the world with no apparent intellectual interests and no apparent conversation but ejaculations in praise of the food. We had soft-shell crabs for dinner that night; I remember it because of Mr. Rhinelander's saying, and he said it again and again: "Mm, *mmm*. Soft-shell crabs. I *love* soft-shell crabs." He even tried to say it while he was eating them. This verbal gamut seemed to me too narrow for a man who had been my father's chosen stand-by on such a great day in his life.

He might have asked Irving Johnson to be his best man. My father wasn't married until years after he left the seminary, where the lifelong friendship between him and Johnson had begun; after graduation they had gone together to an Associate Mission at Omaha. Though their work separated them after that, it also brought them together on stated occasions, especially after both of them had become bishops. They corresponded frequently and met whenever they could. As my father didn't like to visit people (and didn't much like Mrs. Johnson) and as Bishop Johnson did a great deal of traveling, he became an accustomed guest in our house.

Bishop Johnson was a square, sturdy man who managed to look rumpled even in his vestments; his ordinary clothes never seemed to fit him very well, and were likely to be streaked with ashes from his pipe or spotted with bits of gravy or egg that hadn't quite reached his mouth. He was a hearty but careless eater. He was supposed to be a very ugly man, though I didn't think so, and he took some jovial satisfaction from his rough-hewn looks. His face was sad in repose: heavily lined, with great pouches under his eyes.

Although he had an enormous mouth, which opened to its fullest extent when he roared with laughter, as he often did, his tongue seemed too big for it.

As friends he and my father were an odd fit, but they were a fit. Bishop Johnson's nature was blunt, warm, gregarious, while my father's was sharp, chilly, aloof. I think my father roused Bishop Johnson from the lethargy that threatened in later years to sink into melancholy, and I know that in his presence my father was more charitable, tolerant and even-tempered.

When Bishop Johnson or some of his other parson-cronies were there, and they started telling stories, sometimes, to my astonishment and delight, I would be swept into a roar of laughter—even when it was my father who had told the joke. He was as expert at telling funny stories as the others, and at these times I forgot my doubts or my dislike of his sense of humor. I can't believe that he was merely parroting these stories; it must have been that his friends brought out in him a kindliness and joviality that were buried under the hard jocosity we were more accustomed to.

Until the day he died Bishop Johnson was my father's closest friend, but his constant companion, the person he depended on and couldn't do without, was my mother. As a child I didn't like the way he treated her, but neither did I like the way he treated anybody else. It wasn't till I was adolescent that I fixed on his behavior to her as the thing I particularly minded. Breakfast was awful, but breakfast wasn't the only time he was hard on her. I suppose she really did a good deal more work than he, and with much less help; I don't remember ever seeing her idle except when he insisted on it, because he wanted her to sit with him "and enjoy the view," or because she knew it would suit him for some other reason. Left to herself, she was continually busy, with more than enough to do. Consequently, when they were going anywhere together, especially if there was a train to catch, she was apt to cut things a little fine, and not be ready when he expected her to be.

My father's feeling about time was like a disease, and the disease became worse as he got older. He must have looked at his watch a hundred times a day. At night he didn't need to look at it: he just pressed a button in the winder and a soft chiming told him the exact hour and minute. I don't think he ever missed a train in his life. He had a missproof system: he aimed to get to the station at least twenty minutes ahead of time, and almost always succeeded. "Almost always," for Mother sometimes whittled down this margin of safety.

When it was "time to go"—by his system—my father would be in the front hall, his hat and coat on; the car would be at the door, and the bags in. My father would frown at the grandfather clock, corroborate its damning evidence by pulling out his watch, and utter his first cry: "Come along, Elsie, it's time to go!" For the next few minutes, until she hurried down the stairs in a fluster of last-minute instructions to the maids, he would prowl back and forth in front of the door, shaking his head, looking at his watch, and calling to her with louder and angrier insistence. We were used to these scenes. We were also used to their frequent sequel: three or four minutes after they had gone and the house had settled down, the car would reappear at the door, and my father's despairing shout or my mother's pleading call would send someone scuttling upstairs to collect the vital handbag, or passport, or jewel case that in her haste she had forgotten. I am perfectly certain that these lapses of hers were, in each and every case, quite accidental; might they not also have been her unconscious protest, the only effective one she could make, against my father's false urgency?

Another notable thing about my mother was the way she kept losing her jewels—not all of them, and only from time to time, but some of the grander pieces. My father invariably gave her jewelry on her birthday, on their wedding anniversary, and at Christmas, each piece more expensive and magnificent than the last. They were all insured, of course, but some of the jewels Mother lost were never recovered. It strikes me now that perhaps the reason she was so prone to lose them was that she really didn't like jewelry.

Mother was capable of showing temper, but if she ever showed it to my father I was never a witness of it. In the forty-odd years of their marriage they must have had their quarrels, but in their world and in those days, when divorce was considered an indulgence contemptuously granted only to the "fast set" and the dirty linen of all decent people was washed in the privacy of the home, open bickering would have been as outrageous and exceptionable as it is now common and condoned. My father's tyranny was noisy and seemed to dominate everything, but it was erratic and temporary, like a thunderstorm, or, at the worst, a cold spell; in the midst of these ups and downs it was my mother who made the weather we lived in, counted on, and hoped for. He could make life miserable, and often did; she made it all right again, or at least better than he had left it. Whatever scenes took place between them—and there must have been some—were never staged where we could witness them.

They had a long and settled life together. But how really settled were they, I wonder? And how truly and lastingly did they love each other? Such questions, that would once have seemed to me almost blasphemous, I couldn't help silently asking, as I grew up and watched them. I was never sure of the answers, but I became increasingly sure that they were awkward questions. My mother might have said, I think, that they were not the right questions; in any case, her life was concerned with answering, not asking. If I had ever asked her, for instance, whether she liked playing cards with my father, I am pretty sure she would have said that of course she did. He loved to play cards, and as he grew older would often spend several hours of his day that way; he preferred two-handed games, and his favorite was Russian Bank. My mother would play this with him for long sessions, and sometimes even suggest herself that they have a game. But did she really like it? I don't know, of course, but I suspect that she didn't.

My father was unusual among clergymen in the fact that he was rich (though "rich" was a dangerous word never used in my family; "comfortably off" or "well-to-do" were the favored expressions). For many years I thought he had become rich by marrying my mother, and that unpleasant supposition pretty well canceled out the information, supplied by her, that he had never taken a penny of salary. But after her death, when her estate was being settled, I was happy to learn that he had been "independently wealthy" (another favored phrase) before he married, and had never received any money or stock from my mother or from her family. He had inherited something between $75,000 and $100,000 from his parents, and he very probably got some useful tips from his father-in-law; at any rate, he invested in Procter & Gamble preferred when it was first put on the market. This turned out to have been a shrewd move, for as the company prospered the stock split again and again, like a fecund amoeba. Encouraged by his success, he bought more stock, mostly Procter & Gamble. In 1913 the brand-new income tax began to put a brake on his and how many others' profits, but by that time he had amassed enough to feel secure.

My father was by nature orderly, but not particularly neat— lesser forms of orderliness, he tended to feel, were up to my mother and his secretary. He had a notebook in which he kept a kind of financial diary; dates and amounts of payments due, stock transactions, loans and gifts, and so on. I don't think he had a particularly good head for figures, but by constant reference to this notebook, which he sometimes carried in his pocket and sometimes kept in a drawer of his desk, he was able to survey his financial landscape with a clear eye.

My own head for figures has always been deplorable. I was severely frightened by arithmetic—among other things—at an impressionable age, and never really recovered from the shock. This early timidity was further deepened by my first year in college, when I was most unwillingly confronted with conic sections, trigonometry and calculus; that dreadful experience (repeated in my second year, as I had hopelessly failed every one of them) left me a mathematical imbecile. The rule at Princeton in those days was: if your mathematics in school has not taken you beyond plane geometry, you must pay for it by taking trigonometry, etc. in freshman year. This rule seemed to me merely punitive, and still does; it has long since been dropped.

When I went to college my father put me on a full allowance, and at first he insisted that I show him a monthly statement of every penny I spent. I managed to make these statements balance by lumping all the expenditures I couldn't account for under

"Miscellaneous," and this item was usually by far the largest. The invariable result was a bad quarter of an hour with my father, who naturally refused to accept this vague statement as satisfactory. But I had nothing else to offer. It was not the statement, I knew, so much as I myself that was unsatisfactory; this was not a mathematical but a moral examination. Finally I hit on a desperate solution. If it was the moral-mathematical truth he was after, I would give it to him, and with bells on. On my next monthly statement no "Miscellaneous" appeared. Instead, the largest item of expenditure was headed "Liquor." My father accepted the statement without comment, and never asked me for another.

My father looked and sounded his best, a rather splendid best, in church. There, reading the Psalms or the Lessons, or celebrating Holy Communion at the altar, or pronouncing the benediction, his voice was vibrant and assured, and needed no microphone to carry it clearly to the farthest recesses of the nave. He was not a great preacher. His sermons had the virtues of brevity and clarity; they were meant, I think, to be persuasive, but sounded more like a one-sided argument in which his silent opponent could never answer back.

His vestments were tailor-made and fitted him beautifully, and when he was in full pontifical regalia, with cope, mitre, pectoral cross and pastoral staff, he looked every inch a bishop. My sharpest memories of him in church, however, are of the early days in Cincinnati and of his last years, after his retirement. As a child I don't think I actually confused my father with God, but I felt that, in church at least, the two were fairly close, and I knew they had a lot in common. If I had been able to put my feeling into words, I would have said that both God and my father were unrelentingly strict, of an uncertain temper, and had to be approached with care. I knew—that is, I had been taught to believe—that both God and my father loved me, and in much the same awe-inspiring and peremptory way. It was a demanding love, not comforting like Mother's.

In church, when my father was speaking in God's name ("in

the name of the Father, and of the Son, and of the Holy Ghost")
or doing something very solemn for God, like absolving us of our
sins, or pronouncing a blessing on us, it was impossible not to feel
that he was God's deputy. And if we feared God, as we certainly
did, how could we avoid a feeling of awe in the presence of his
deputy? We made a distinction between my father at breakfast or
in his study and my father in church or at prayers, but I don't think
we were aware of anything incongruous in the difference.

We were pious little children, in the sense that we obediently
attended whatever services we were taken to, learned our Cate-
chism, saved pennies for our mite-boxes in Lent, and went to Sunday school; that much, after all, was required of us. But I was ambitious to do more than was required; at the age of seven I wished
to be a zealot. One Ash Wednesday morning I dawdled so purposefully that the others went to breakfast without me; I then stole
down the back stairs to the cellar, looking for sackcloth and ashes.
I hoped to find something like an old gunny sack, but could discover nothing in the cellar remotely suitable. I covered my head
with ashes from the furnace, however, rubbing them in so they
would stay put. When I slipped into my seat at the breakfast table,
for once my lateness was barely noticed or reprimanded; and nobody commented on the interesting condition of my hair. What
was the use, then, of sackcloth and ashes? Finally I whispered to
Charlotte, asking her if she didn't see something different about
my hair. No, nothing. I urged her to feel it; she did, made an
exclamation of disgust, and the attention I had sought at last came
my way. I was removed in disgrace to have my hair washed.

My zeal at this period took another and I think equally ques-
tionable form. I started voluntary churchgoing, to a series of weekday Lenten services. These were conducted by my father in a bare
little chapel in the Cathedral, and must have been in the late afternoon, for I remember the glare of gaslight reflected from a whitewashed wall. My father must have been preaching—or "giving an
address"—no doubt on the meaning of Lent, and the obligation on
us to behave in a special Lenten way. But I wasn't paying attention
or even trying to understand the big words; my zeal had exhausted
itself in getting me here, and I just sat, staring fixedly and unthink-

ing at Daddy's animated face, with a halo of gaslight blotting out the wall behind him.

As I stared, in an unblinking daze, the halo seemed to spread and grow blindingly bright; Daddy's face disappeared into the blinding brightness. It seemed to me that this light, out of which I could hear Daddy's voice coming, must be God himself. Then the voice must surely be God's voice. As this thought slipped into my mind the light shrank and changed, and Daddy's face reappeared against it, clearer than ever; but now his face was changing too, sharpening and horribly altering its shape—it was the face of the devil! At this point—perhaps I was nearly asleep—I came to with a start, and everything slipped back into its normal appearance. But the memory of this waking nightmare stayed with me. If I drew any meaning from it, it was as a premonition of hell, of which this visual blasphemy of mine had been a warning.

By the time my father retired he had been Bishop of New Jersey for nearly twenty-three years, and his eldest children were approaching middle age. He had added a private chapel to his house in Princeton, and he preferred to conduct his own services there rather than go to the local church as a member of the congregation. When he did, occasionally, go there, he could not be expected to feel or behave like a mere layman or even a clergyman emeritus; once a bishop, always a bishop, retired or not. The church was God's house but he was more at home in it than the other tenants, and had more rights there.

Robed and in the chancel, he had been accustomed to give a laggard congregation short shrift: at Morning Prayer, for instance, when he was reading the Psalms for the day, he would announce the psalm and start reading the first verse before the slower hands had found the right page in the prayer book. Everyone hurried to catch up, like an anxious, stupid flock with an impatient sheep dog snapping at their heels. Before they had finished reading their verse my father would cut in with the next one. When he was in the congregation, however, the shoe was very much on the other foot. Now his technique was not to cut in but to drag, and woe betide the unfortunate clergyman who tried to interrupt him; my father, though now he deliberately slowed the tempo, read the responses in the same incisive, clear and carrying tones, and nine times out of ten the poor man in the chancel, after one or two futile attempts to keep in step with the rest of the congregation, simply gave up and waited each time for my father to finish.

Why did my father do this? Was it because old age was slowing him down and he couldn't read any faster? The evidence would hardly support that theory. No, it was not a question of age but of place: his place was not in the nave but in the chancel, and he couldn't help showing that he felt it. He had another way of emphasizing the same point: when he stood up he would stand half in the pew, half in the aisle, to dissociate himself further from the laity.

My father didn't much like children. I think he would have agreed with the friend of mine who held that "children are savages and crave authority." He supplied the authority, though I can't remember craving it, and it often came down on us unexpectedly, like a dead-letter law that may be suddenly and whimsically enforced. And the punishments he inflicted on us did not so much fit the crime as blot it out. Long before I read Pope's line, "Who breaks a butterfly upon a wheel?" I knew the answer to it. It is the punishments I remember, of course, not the crimes—though perhaps my misdemeanors were so grave that memory cannot bear to dig them up. What had I done, for example, that hot summer morning in North Carolina when I was eight or nine? We were walking to church, I remember, either to the little board chapel at Bat Cave or to the chapel at "the Sisters," which was farther. Whatever it was I did, my father suddenly sentenced me to go home in disgrace.

After nearly fifty years I can still feel a faint reflection of that awful Sunday morning as I plodded sobbing along the endless, baking, silent mountain road: a sense of abandonment, of terror at losing my way, a wilder terror of rattlesnakes, shame at my disgrace, bitterness at its injustice.

In his younger days my father played a good deal of tennis. Lawn tennis in the 1880s was a recent invention, and according to my father his brother Mortimer was the first to introduce it to Ohio. My father was never a very good player, but he was a fearsome opponent and an even more fearsome partner. I remember many a family game with him on our clay court in Glendale, and later in Princeton. For a heavy-set man he was pretty active. He had a wicked chop, both in his serve and his ground strokes; I don't remember his volley, but in those days people didn't try to get to the net the way they do now. Like many better players, he loved to win and hated to lose; I can't remember any family tennis in which he did lose. Occasionally he would play singles with me, and always beat me. I finally beat him when I was sixteen. That was a terrible day; he tried hard to be a good sport about it, but made it out to be such a final victory that I felt miserably that I had dethroned him. As I remember it, he never played me again, and gave up tennis soon after.

Family tennis with my father was not so much a game as an exercise in keeping the rules, and it was not much fun. He was a stickler for the rules, and always right about them. He was even more of a stickler for his own unwritten rules, which had to do with etiquette, behavior on the court. That was what made it so awful to be his partner. If a ball was hit down the center of the court and you took it and he thought it should have been his, that was "poaching." If you left it for him, on the other hand, and he thought it should have been yours, that was plain stupidity.

When he was serving, he always cried "Play!" in a threatening tone just before he served, and his opponents were apt to find this unnerving. Between serves he changed his position on the base line and waited for his partner to supply him with the right number of tennis balls—one if he needed one, two if he needed two. If you gave him two when he needed only one, he would hurl it back at you or toss it angrily away, and shout "Play!" Getting the balls to him acceptably was a tricky business. The safest way would have been to hand them to him on your racket, but he didn't like that. So you were supposed to bounce them at him, one at a time, in such a way that they came neatly to his waiting hand on the

47

first bounce. If you aimed badly, or misjudged the throw, he simply let the ball go past him, and stood waiting till you had retrieved the ball and done it over again, right.

My father always got quite hot, in two senses of the word, when he played tennis. His face would turn a mottled purple; his cries of "Play!" or "Oconomowoc!" or "Gitchee Goomee!" were the vindictive yells of a warrior on the warpath. No quarter was expected, none was given. It may be from those days that I began to evolve a theory about tennis: a game that may not always bring out the worst in everybody but does cast a hard, unsparing light on the player's character.

With a carving knife in his hand instead of a racket, my father showed a more reassuring and attractive side of himself. His expertness as a carver was a source of pride to all of us and of obvious satisfaction to himself. He enjoyed carving, and it was a pleasure to watch him. Standing up, as he always did unless the patient was flat out, like a steak or a cross section of halibut, he would give a quick and apparently careless glance at the fowl or joint the maid had put before him, and set to. He always knew exactly what to do, and the first cut was like the sure incision of an experienced surgeon. Guinea hen, turkey, duck, roast beef, porterhouse, rump steak, red snapper, their anatomy was as familiar to him as ABC, and the knife in his hand was like an extension of his fingers. As with a lecturing surgeon, the quick movements of the knife were sometimes accompanied by a running comment on what he was doing.

If he had a fault as a carver, it was in the singleness of purpose that kept him hewing to his line, let the dish-gravy spatter where it might. This occasional slight spattering, however, was—and I think rightly—not held against him in a house that deeply believed in gravy and felt that it should not be confined to gravy boats but first appear in the platter. These spots on the tablecloth were written off mainly as the exuberance of a master craftsman, but also partly, perhaps, in the comfortable assurance that there was plenty here and more in the kitchen.

On special feast days like Thanksgiving we had two turkeys and two carvers, my father at his end of the table and my mother at hers. She was much less obviously expert than he, but quite competent. The reason for having two turkeys was that one had oyster stuffing, the other chestnut, and everybody was allowed a choice. These Thanksgiving dinners were enormous affairs, and went on for a couple of hours. Until we were quite grown up, the drink was ginger ale, from those Cantrell & Cochrane bottles with round bottoms. By the time the fruit and nuts-and-raisins were brought on, none of us could do more than nibble. Then my father was at his most expansive and most genial and would tell familiar stories and sometimes a joke we had never heard before. He often told us about "old Mr. Procter," his father-in-law's father, who could carve a duck while holding it in the air. We were sure that he could have done it too, if he wanted.

My father liked to travel, expecially when he was traveling for pleasure. As a young man he had been to Europe and Palestine, and had spent a year at Oxford. A good many of the journeys he took later, however, were business trips, or moves from one job to another. He moved his family three times: to Glendale, to Minnesota, and finally to New Jersey. And he once took us all to England for a year. Travel was supposedly simpler then, in the sense of being less cluttered up with visas and customs and all the frontier nuisances we have now. Were there even any passports? I'm sure none of us children had one, at any rate. And traveler's-checks hadn't yet been invented. You carried a letter of credit, an impressive document that folded into a red morocco wallet, and when you wanted money you brought your letter of credit to Brown, Shipley & Co., 123, Pall Mall, and they subtracted the amount they gave you from the total of your credit.

Travel was also slower, of course, and solider. Everybody took trunks with them when they went abroad, "steamer trunks" for the cabin, where they would fit under the berths, and bigger ones that went in the hold. When a family the size of ours went abroad, the number of trunks, suitcases, carry-alls and odd pieces of luggage mounted up. There were ten in our party: my father and mother and six children, the youngest an infant in arms, a governess and a nurse. I'll never forget my father putting on one of his scenes at an English railway station, a little country junction where we had to change trains.

I suppose it must have been the usual confusion: porters officiously seizing bags or demanding to know who belonged to which, children ambling aimlessly about or jigging up and down out of boredom. My father leaped into this chaos and stilled it by a terrible series of shouts. He was red in the face and very angry. He made everyone stand still. He made all of us, including the porters, put down everything we were carrying. Then he counted us, in a loud, indignant voice. Then he counted every piece of luggage (there were twenty-six pieces of hand luggage—*and* trunks) and checked the total against a list he had in his hand; this had to be done several times before it came out right. Though it made a lasting impression on me, my father's anger and excitement seemed at the time unaccountable or at least disproportionate. Years later, when I was traveling with my own smaller family and with much less luggage, I realized at last why he had been so exercised. When you're in charge of an amorphous body of people and suitcases moving from point to point, you've simply got to keep counting them.

After he retired he traveled more than ever, and of course my mother went along: to the Caribbean, to Hawaii, and finally around the world. Perhaps that last one surfeited even his appetite for itineraries. Anyhow, he never repeated it nor attempted a journey of anything like its size again; but he kept his interest in timetables.

As soon as I was old enough to like traveling myself, I never wanted to travel with my father: his ways, I felt, were not my ways, but I always had to conform to his. In the summer of 1920 we went abroad together but separately—that is, we crossed the Atlantic on the same one-class ship, but he was with fellow bishops going to London for the Lambeth Conference, and I was with a varying pack of my contemporaries, undergraduates who were off to Europe for a good time. On the ship my father and I saw very little of each other, and as soon as we landed went our different ways, but we were to meet later and spend four days looking at English cathedrals. We did. At the time, they seemed like four of the longest days in my life.

I was nineteen, and in a state of secret rebellion against him, silently disagreeing with everything he said, silently disapproving of everything he did and stood for. Whenever we took a train we went first class, which shamed and embarrassed me; I thought we should go third, as all nice people did as a matter of course. "The noble experiment" of prohibition had the United States in its grip —that was one of the principal reasons undergraduates wanted to go to Europe—and my father considered it his duty, as a good citizen and a high official of the Church, to obey his country's laws whether he was outside the country or not: he wouldn't take so much as a glass of beer, and drank Apollinaris with his meals. We never discussed the matter, we never discussed anything, but I too took a stand, and except for breakfast ordered wine or beer with every meal.

We could hardly have been together for four days without exchanging a word; we must have asked for the salt or ventured some comment on the cathedrals we saw or the hotels we put up with; but apart from these unregarded clichés the silence between us was complete. For my part, I found it a constant strain, like struggling vainly to escape from under a too-great pile of heavy blankets. I was seething with unspoken thoughts, resentments and adolescent impulses, and felt that I would have given anything to unburden myself, even to my father—or perhaps especially to my father—but if he was aware of my state of mind he did nothing about it. I don't think he could have been aware, for when I later complained to my mother about our speechless journey she was surprised, and said that my father had told her how much he had enjoyed it, and "what a lovely time" we had had together.

In the early days of motor cars, when they were uncertain quantities, prone to all sorts of breakdowns, my father went driving mainly for pleasure, as most car owners did then. He even learned to drive himself, after his fashion, but he never really got the hang of it, and after the accelerator pedal replaced the hand throttle he gave it up. It was high time. He had an alarming habit of racing the engine before he let in the clutch, and the roar of the motor, which he knew was preparing to leap (he always let the clutch in too suddenly), excited him; if he had to back or turn a corner he gripped the wheel in both hands, turned red in the face and shouted—whether warnings or demands for help could not be heard above the roaring of the motor.

When my father was made a bishop he found that the most convenient way of getting around his diocese was by car. He visited every parish at least once a year, and by the time he retired he must have become heartily sick of the New Jersey roads. Walter, the chauffeur who had been with us since Ohio days, was younger than my father, but he too dated from the pre-automobile era, and I don't think driving a car came naturally to him either. But it was his job and he mastered it, though his driving always had an individual flavor. His foot was particularly heavy on the brake, which he usually applied suddenly. If a passenger on the back seat wasn't prepared for this, he was likely to be catapulted forward; but my parents were both rather heavy, and they were also accustomed to slipping an arm through the padded loop that hung down at each side of the back seat, so that when Walter jumped on the brake they merely bowed slightly. They were used to his driving and saw nothing unusual in it.

My mother, as I say, hated scenes, and was quite incapable of making one; on those infrequent occasions when she nerved herself to it, the "scene" was so mild that often Mother was the only one aware of it. My father, on the contrary, liked to make a row.

These scenes were most likely to take place in restaurants or hotel dining rooms, when his temper and appetite were both at a fine edge. The particular outrage that set him off might be one of a number of things: the table to which we had been ushered was too sunny, or too dark; there was an abominable draught, or too little air; the waiter was surly or the waiter was too slow; the soup was cold, or the meat uneatable. Pepper was a regular *casus belli*. If he found white pepper on the table, as he usually did, he would demand black, and if it were not instantly produced would send the headwaiter to the chef to fetch some, "as no good cook would think of using white." Whatever it might be that set him off, he always got away to a fast start, and in a moment the whole restaurant knew that something terrible had happened. If the headwaiter did not come scurrying to answer my father's shouted summons, he was quite capable of leaping to his feet and semaphoring with his napkin. But the headwaiter usually did come immediately, and his attitude was almost always one of agonized anxiety to do whatever it was my father wanted to have done, to restore peace and quiet at any price.

When he was in a good mood, or after one of these storms had passed, my father could establish almost jovial relations with the same sort of man who at other times exploded his wrath: he would have genial passages with train conductors, waiters, doormen and especially policemen. With policemen he was apt to be particularly affable, when he was being affable; and their attitude to him was one of smiling deference. He enjoyed being given special treatment by the police, and part of his enjoyment lay in the belief that he was fooling them. Like other public underlings, they often took him for a Roman Catholic priest. This misunderstanding helped him out of many a traffic jam and transformed many a cop's brutal stare and bullying harangue into a tolerant smile, a wink, and an "O.K., Father." It also worked well with customs inspectors, who "expedited" him over the heads of nondescript citizens.

I found it embarrassing to witness these semi-deceptions, though I couldn't have said exactly why; they were not really my father's doing; at least, he never began it. The scenes he fomented himself were a different matter.

His social behavior on public occasions did not actually constitute a scene, in my sense of the word, but it was something like it, and at those times I was torn between embarrassment and grudging admiration. Once a year, in the spring, my father gave his clerical garden party. It was an ordeal that demanded the utmost from the entire household, and preparations for it began at least a week ahead. The clergy of the whole diocese were invited, with their wives and families; the earliest arrivals came immediately after breakfast, and most of them stayed on till dusk. Some played tennis, or croquet, or clock golf; the majority sat or wandered under the trees, or in the walled garden. Everyone chatted incessantly. Lunch—tons of creamed chicken, peas, potato chips, salad, store rolls, ice cream and cake, and gallons of iced tea and iced coffee—was served from big trestle tables on the lawn; I think Mother managed to give tea as well to the large minority that stayed on for it.

Several hundred collapsible chairs were rented from the local undertaker and scattered in groups under the trees. The chairs were small and easily upset, and the clergy—especially their wives —tended to topheaviness. There was one garden party at which so many guests tipped over that Mother had to go and hide behind a tree to laugh properly. The weather could usually be counted on at that time of the year, but when it did rain it made everything twice as hard: the guests seethed and teemed humidly in the packed house, the stairs were cluttered with sitters, and my sisters had to organize impromptu indoor games and then coax people into taking part.

My father played his role of host with evident zest. He liked being the center of things, and shone more brightly when he was. Clergymen on an outing are generally jovial and frolicsome to an almost ludicrous degree; they seem to enjoy kicking up their heels as if they were little lambs at play. My father's jocosity was as loud as his guests', his quips no funnier and his puns more outrageous, but—though I often wished his behavior were a little less flamboyant—he never seemed really ridiculous, as many of them did.

One protracted scene my father put on left me in such a rage that as soon as I got home again I sat down and wrote the whole thing down, just as it occurred, to get it off my chest. I showed what I had written to my wife, and was surprised and taken aback when she burst into laughter.

My mother was returning alone from England, where she had been to visit one of my sisters, who was studying at Oxford. It had been arranged that my father and I were to meet her. Her ship, the *Europa*, was to dock in the evening, so my father and I met at a hotel restaurant in New York and had dinner together before going to the dock. Here are some excerpts from my account:

My father showed our dock pass to the man at the barrier, who waved us on and then called out, "Wait a minute, wait a minute. Whattaya got in there?" I hadn't noticed till then that my father was carrying a small cardboard box, done up in paper ribbon. My father bent over like a conspirator and said, "These are gardenias. Do you want to see them?" The man waved us on again, and my father laughed. "What do you suppose he thought they *were*?" He was still in a very good mood.

There was quite a crowd out on the end of the pier. The ship was lying at an acute angle to the slip, with her bow just inside and her stern pointing upriver; there seemed to be some trouble about the tide. The crowd around us was quiet, the ship was still too far away for them to start shouting. My father began making remarks in a loud voice, dropping his r's. He sounded self-satisfied, but I knew it was because he was excited. Still, I wished he wouldn't. Then he turned to a young policeman standing next to him, and was soon having a friendly chat. I only caught bits of it, but my father's tone of voice and accent were normal again.

We went back inside the pier and stood near the barrier by the first-class gangway. As the *Europa* slid in, I saw Mother standing alone on an upper deck, looking for us in the crowd. I reached over and tapped my father on the shoulder. "There she is, see? On the upper deck." She saw us and I waved, and she waved back, but not as if she were certain who it was.

"Are you sure?" said my father.

"Yes, I'm sure. Look, she's waving."

"I can't tell. These old eyes—" But he took his hat off. Mother waved hard then, and blew her nose. Then she walked quickly off out of sight. When I saw her coming down the gangway, I told my father. As soon as he had kissed her he fell back into his administrative role, shouting, "Gangway, gangway! Come on, you're blocking up the way!" When we got out of the crowd and were walking over to the letter under which Mother's luggage would be collected, she said, "Didn't you see me? I waved." He said, "These old eyes—"

When my father and I had come up in the elevator from the street, he hadn't taken off his hat, though there was a woman in the car. This time, going down with Mother, he took his hat off. So did everybody else, I noticed.

There was a hitch about getting the bags into the car. First of all we lost the porter, and when I finally found him up an alley, where he said he had been waiting for me for half an hour, there was further difficulty about stowing the bags. Only two big ones would fit on the luggage rack behind the car, and it was a problem where to put the others. A small crowd of roustabouts and porters collected, giving advice, wanting to know who was going to pay them, and when. Walter was struggling with the bags on the luggage rack; there was a good deal of confusion. I just stood on the curb and let the situation come to a head. My father, who had seated himself in the car beside Mother, cried, "I'll handle this!" and clambered angrily out. To every porter he saw with a bag he said hotly, "Put it down!" and if one of them was so foolish as to offer a suggestion, he cried, "Never mind!"

But by this time Walter also had lost his temper—he was suffering from a bad cold, and had just got out of bed that day—and said peremptorily, "Bishop, let me handle this!" My father said huffily, "All right, all right," and told me to get into the car. There was a further mix-up about where we were all to sit; the three of us couldn't possibly sit on the back seat, but my father, who was still out of the car, kept crying to me to sit down. Mother, trying vainly to make herself heard, explained to him that the back seat would not hold us all, and for *him* please to get in; I saying nothing but standing angrily doubled up under the roof waiting for the facts of the case to dawn on my father so that he would get in and sit down so that I could sit down myself. When he finally understood what the trouble was he said to me, "Then why didn't you let me get in first?" I snapped back at him, "Because you told me to get in!"

All the way down the West Side Drive and through the Holland Tunnel and over the Skyway and past Newark Airport, Mother had to humor us both back into good temper. At first my father's conversation was confined to hurling accusatory questions at my mother: "Did you get my cablegram at Bremen? You didn't? Oh, you did! Well, did you get my cable at Southampton?" And so on.

By the time we got home—Walter was angry too, and drove faster than he usually did, so we made good time—my father had recovered his temper; I'm sure it was with no irony that he said, as he left me at my door, "You've been a great help."

My father was an orderly man, as I have said, and liked to plan: furthermore, he liked to see his plans carried out. Did he have a plan for his final years? I think we all hoped so, and were dismayed to find, as we gradually did, that it was not a long-term plan. Apparently all he wanted to do after he retired was to set his affairs in order, do some last traveling with my mother, and then wait for the end, which he felt would not be long in coming.

It must have been a far greater shock to him than to any of the rest of us when Mother, who had never complained of anything wrong with her except a nagging arthritis, was operated on—"successfully," of course—for "traces of cancer" and then, a little more than a year later, quietly and quickly (for cancer) died of it. This dreadful emergency brought out the best in my father: he met the occasion well. Why could I not meet it with him? My sisters did. One of them, whom I always thought temperamentally the most like him, and certainly the one who understood him the most sympathetically, seemed to lead him to greater heights. She was a widow with three little girls, the youngest of whom, Veronica, had tragically drowned in infancy, six years before. Members of the family who had died, especially those who died young, were enshrined in our private hagiography and always mentioned by name in family prayers. For a long time my sister Harriet, who had died at eighteen, many years before, had been the principal family saint; now she had been joined and almost overshadowed by little Veronica.

We were all present at my mother's deathbed. As everyone knows who has been there, it is a long wait, even for those who are only watching. Sometimes there are false alarms. If Mother had been able to tell us, I am quite sure she would have said, "Now,"

57

or "Not yet"; for she hated to give people trouble, even if it was only keeping them waiting. But for once she was too busy with her own affairs to bother about us.

I don't remember what time of day or night it was. Someone had summoned us; the end was thought to be only minutes away. We knelt around her bed while my father, in a clear and unshaken voice, read the prayers for the dying. When he had finished, we could see that Mother was still breathing. It had been a false alarm. But it was only a matter of a few days, and the next alarm was not false. She died on the anniversary of little Veronica's death. At the very end my father bent over her and called in a loud voice, almost a shout: "Veronica is waiting at the gate!" She gave no sign that she had heard or understood.

This action of my father's shocked and angered me. All during my mother's last illness, I had become increasingly critical of him; the more he rose to the occasion, the more I said to myself: "Count me out of it." I didn't try to explain my feelings to myself, and perhaps I should have. One reason I didn't was the remembrance of my mother's constantly repeated warning that I must not "impute motives." I felt that she was probably right; I did impute motives to people, and seldom very good ones; I was sometimes ashamed of it but I didn't seem to be able to help it. And how could I be so sure (Mother used to say) that the motives I imputed were the true ones? I couldn't be sure, of course, only sometimes—well, I just couldn't believe that people always knew what they were doing, or could be trusted to tell the truth about it if they did know. Mother's death reduced us to sobbing children; my father took it dry-eyed. Was he suffering agonies of grief in private? He gave no sign of it.

He rose to the greatest heights at her funeral, which he conducted himself. The church was packed. My father had never been more self-possessed. His voice had never had a clearer ring. It was a beautiful service, everyone agreed, and very moving. My rector in New York, who had made a special trip to be there, was so impressed by my father that he wrote to me in a letter next day: "Ecce magnus sacerdos!" ("Behold, a great priest!") I could see that it was a tremendous performance. It left me cold as a stone.

After Mother's death and funeral, at one of several family conclaves held in my father's absence, we agreed that he could not be expected to go on behaving so splendidly; after the strain he had been under there would probably be a natural let-down, an inevitable reaction. And there was. His normal bad temper reasserted itself, his behavior became crotchety and cantankerous; he reduced many of his household to wounded silence or angry tears. He was obviously disgruntled and miserable himself. Something had to be done about him. It was agreed that my sister Peggy, who was a widow, and who also had the happiest touch of any of us with my father, should keep house for him. This assignment turned out to be only partly possible, for there were times when he preferred to be alone and times when only a dog could have stood him; but during the seven years before he died she was either with him or on call.

His greatest problem was to fill his empty days. His solution, which my sisters in varying degrees found pathetic, seemed to me tragic or dreadful: he developed a routine for killing time. His day began, after a usually restless night, with eight o'clock breakfast, during which he read his morning's mail. After breakfast, he said prayers, and then, if he was feeling well, he conferred with Dolly, the cook, about lunch and dinner. Then he went to his study and for an hour or so answered his letters. Generally he wrote them out himself, in his large, beautifully flowing hand—his writing got bigger but not perceptibly shakier with age; his flourishing signature must have been nearly two inches high—but from time to time he had a secretary come in to type his letters. Whether from carelessness or fear of him, the secretary was prone to make mistakes in typing or spelling, which my father always corrected in ink.

When his letters were done he would settle down to the morning's pastime: reading, or cards, or backgammon. If there was anyone to play with him, it was cards or backgammon; if worst came to worst, it was reading. He almost never read the newspaper—the one he subscribed to, because of its Republican politics, was the

New York *Herald Tribune*—occasionally he read a story in the *Saturday Evening Post;* but mostly he read detective stories. In mid-morning he took a glass of sherry and a biscuit. At 12:30 exactly he was brought a rum old-fashioned. (When I was having lunch with him I was given an old-fashioned made with bourbon, and was sometimes offered a second. He never took more than one himself.) At ten minutes to one he turned on the radio to listen to Elmer Davis' comments on the news. These comments were usually sardonic or gloomy, or sounded so. My father listened with pursed lips, in silence; when Mr. Davis intimated that things were even worse than usual my father would slowly shake his head, in mute agreement. At one o'clock, on the dot, the gong rang for lunch.

Immediately after lunch my father went upstairs for his nap, and did not reappear until about four. At five, the hour when my mother had always served tea, he had a bourbon highball instead. The two hours before dinner were spent in playing backgammon or cards, or reading. I was one of the people he had catalogued as a backgammon player, and when I was visiting him we never played anything else, though at times I got heartily sick of it and would have welcomed a change to Russian Bank. A backgammon session with my father went on for hours, only temporarily interrupted by meals, and might even last for several days, like a cricket match. He always kept careful score, which mounted continuously for as long as the session lasted. This in itself annoyed me—why couldn't he forget the long morning's struggle, and start with a clean slate after his nap? But I think the continuity gave him a sense of accomplishment—though his behavior while we were playing annoyed me much more.

He commented on every throw of the dice, like a crap-shooter; unlike a crap-shooter, he didn't urge the dice to do better but implored some invisible and sympathetic onlooker to observe how badly they had done. These remarks were really directed at me, and the burden of them was always the same: some people have all the luck; what can you do against someone who throws nothing but doubles, etc., etc. When his dice turned up a two and a one he would say bitterly, "Deuce ace; *heavy shot!*" If I threw doubles twice in a row he would cry to the invisible observer: "Look at that!" If he threw doubles three times running, he (and by inference, his friend the observer) merely noted with quiet satisfaction that there was some justice after all. If this running commentary had not been so invariable and so continuous I might have found it less exasperating; as it was, the more my father yelped and frisked the more my teeth set in a silent growl. We never played for money but we acted as if we were, and would challenge each other to double and redouble as if a thousand dollars were at stake. When it was a "double game" my father would lay his pocketknife alongside the board; for a redouble he opened one blade, for a second redouble two blades. It was a question which of us was the worse sport; I suppose I was, because I tried not to show it. The fact was, we both hated to lose.

Shortly after dinner, except on the rare occasions when he had guests, my father went upstairs—but not to bed; he never went to bed until well after midnight. He undressed and got into his nightshirt, dressing gown and slippers, and settled himself for the long evening in an armchair in his bedroom beside a table on which there were a reading lamp, pipes and tobacco, detective stories and crossword puzzles. There he sat, reading, smoking and solving puzzles, for the next four or five hours. Some time after midnight, sometimes as late as one or two in the morning, he would go down to the kitchen to get himself what he called a "midnight snack."

There were never fewer than three servants in his house, and it would have been a simpler arrangement to have a maid bring him a plate of sandwiches and a thermos bottle of soup or coffee before she went to bed, but my father would have none of that; he insisted on his "right to raid my own icebox"; and no doubt it was one of his few remaining pleasures to prowl down through the sleeping house and see what surprises he could find for himself in the kitchen.

In his house in Princeton, where he spent about half the year, he could take a short cut to the kitchen by using the elevator he had had put in when my mother's arthritis had made it difficult for her to climb the stairs. One October night on his way down to the kitchen, he got into the elevator and pressed the button; the car whirred slowly downwards—and stuck between floors. He saw what had happened: he had not quite closed the doors on the floor above, or they had come apart again; but they were now over his head, just out of his reach.

When he realized this, and had tried without success everything he could think of to make the elevator move up or down, he began to shout, hoping that one of the servants would hear him. But it was half past one in the morning, the servants were asleep in the back of the house, and nobody heard him. So he settled himself as best he could to wait. The elevator was very small, just big enough for two people; I suppose he must have been able to cramp himself into some kind of sitting position. But he was an old man, over eighty; it was a chilly autumn night, and all he had on was a nightshirt, a flimsy dressing gown and slippers. He was immured in the elevator for at least six hours; when I heard about it (not from him) I thought it a wonder he had not come down with pneumonia. Around seven-thirty, when he knew the servants would be up and about, he began to shout again—and soon one of the maids heard him. Instead of retiring to bed with hot-water bottles, however, he got dressed, came downstairs, and ate a more than usually hearty breakfast. He suffered no apparent ill effects, and was quite pleased with the sensation he had made.

As a young man my father had been, if not brilliant, at any rate outstanding among his contemporaries at college, at the seminary, and in the Church. He was made a dean at an early age and refused several elections to a bishopric before he finally accepted. He had had a successful career.

In his earlier life he must have had fairly strong intellectual interests. His shift from the Presbyterian to the Anglican faith, in his seminary days, had been an affair of the mind; his mind rejected the blinkered dogmas of Calvinism but found an invigorating and welcome illumination in the theology of the Nicene Creed. He was not a scholar but he must have been a better than average student, and at one point in his career he had taught several courses at a seminary (Pastoral Theology was one of them) while carrying on his duties as a dean. I remember something of what he must have been like as a teacher, for he used to explain to us as children some of the knottier puzzles in the Church's teaching. His explanations required diagrams, neatly drawn in pencil, which he lettered with big misty words starting with capital letters.

I remember his patient–impatient eagerness, his smile that said, "Now, wait till you see this!" the quick, neat penciled line completing the triangle, or the square, or the circle—and there was another puzzle solved: the Trinity, or the Incarnation, or the Atonement. At the time it was breathtaking, overpowering, *ingenious*. The trouble was, I could never remember afterwards how it was done, only the sense of having witnessed a remarkable piece of sleight-of-hand. What did religion mean to my father—theology? And what did theology mean to him—a crossword puzzle? It couldn't have been as crude as that. No doubt he was a better teacher of seminarians than of his own children, or no doubt some of my sisters understood his explanations better than I did; but in baffled anger I told myself that if that was religion it had nothing to do with me—and, as far as I could see, very little to do with my father either.

As my mother would have said, how could I be so sure? And of course I couldn't be. As time went on I became less and less sure —even of the deep disagreement between me and all official explanations, including my father's. I was never altogether able to reconcile the idea of my father (or any bishop) with the idea of Christianity; but what did I really know of either? Nevertheless, though as my father's son I couldn't hope to take a fair view of him, it did seem to me that as an old man he should be less apathetic, if not happier, than he was. Even if he hadn't been really religious, even if his interest in the Church had been only the concern of a professional with his profession, what had happened to it and to him that all he cared about now was reading detective stories, playing cards, and solving crossword puzzles?

This, as I say, was not altogether fair to him; he still celebrated Holy Communion every Sunday and on special days, in his own chapel; he said his prayers every day; he would still talk Church politics with old cronies, and he took a fitful interest in plans for the cathedral in Trenton that he had begun to build when he was an active bishop—though here his interest narrowed more and more to the "Cæsarea Chapel," which was to be in effect a memorial to himself.

Before my mother died he had embarrassed us often by his placid but insistent references to his own approaching death. After my mother had upset his plans by dying first, it took him a long time to readjust himself to his planless future, and the heart had gone out of his planning. He no longer hinted, at least in the same way, that he was ready to die, and we could see that he wasn't, but also we couldn't help seeing how little pleasure he got from being alive. How could anyone, let alone a man of my father's intelligence, take pleasure in a life of such appallingly trivial routine? I was sure that a great part of his wretchedness must come from this never-ending, hopelessly boring flight from boredom. He had put his mind to bed like an unwilling invalid, and it no longer had strength enough to get up, though it was miserably unready to die.

He would not read anything that cost him any effort. Perhaps he could be persuaded to write something. An apologia for his life? No, he felt that would be altogether beyond him; in any case, his life was over and done with; it would have to speak for itself. But we nagged him, wheedled and encouraged him. As an editor, I assured him that it need not be such an onerous task; he wouldn't have to do it all at once, just bit by bit, a little at a time—and gradually there it would be. And eventually he did in fact bring himself to "write something," which turned out to be, in a way, the story of his life. He wrote it in the form of letters, which he addressed to his various grandchildren, and illustrated with family photographs. When it was finally done, I don't think he even tried to get it published, but had it privately printed at a Trenton shop, and sent copies to everyone in the family and to some friends. The book was so well received that he wrote another, also in the form of letters. But this second attempt completely exhausted his interest in writing, and after that even his letters to us became shorter and more perfunctory.

Perhaps his religion gave him more comfort than I knew. Does an aged and lonely man evolve his own mysticism? Or do religious beliefs, eroded by a long life, tend to become rounded and gentler, so that they seem to blend with the foothills of agnosticism? I think my father's case was something like that. On matters of religious belief he certainly grew more tolerant—I sometimes thought, more indifferent—with age.

My sister Peggy, the one who lived with my father during his last years, was an ardent follower of Gurdjieff, and she must have had something to do with the softening of my father's creed. I remember being astonished to discover that he accepted her official line—that you could be a practicing Gurdjieffite and a believing Christian at the same time—though the line seemed to me as suspect as Communism's attempts to make a united front with parties it intended to swallow. He continued to repeat his belief in "the Resurrection of the body: And the Life everlasting," but in expectation of death he turned for comfort and enlightenment not so much to the Church as to a Hindu sage, Krishnamurti. He included Krishnamurti's metaphor about dying in his second book of letters:

> *I am standing upon the seashore. A ship at my side spreads her white sails to the morning breeze and starts for the blue ocean. She is an object of beauty and strength, and I stand and watch her until at length she hangs like a speck of white cloud just where the sea and sky come to mingle with each other.*
>
> *Then someone at my side says: "There! She's gone!" Gone where? Gone from my sight, that is all. She is just as large in mast and hull and spar as she was when she left my side, and she is just as able to bear her load of living freight to her destined port.*
>
> *Her diminished size is in me, not in Her. And just at the moment when someone at my side says:*

"There! She is gone!" there are Other eyes watching her coming, and Other voices ready to take up the glad shout: "There She comes!"

And that is dying.

My father's patron saint, St. Paul, had put it better, I felt, if not so simply. The passage, like all the great words of the Church, must have been much more familiar to my father than to me: "For this corruptible must put on incorruption, and this mortal must put on immortality. So when this corruptible shall have put on incorruption, and this mortal shall have put on immortality, then shall be brought to pass the saying that is written, Death is swallowed up in victory. O death, where is thy sting? O grave, where is thy victory?" Perhaps such words, that he had repeated all his life, had become too familiar; perhaps, like many simple Catholics, he found more comfort in looking at a cheaply pretty image than in contemplating the crucifix.

My father had been spoiled all his life—"humored" is the word we apply to the continued spoiling of grown-ups—and so he inevitably became a domestic tyrant, a bully. Why didn't my mother stand up to him more? I never knew, I don't know now. It must have been only partly her hatred of scenes; it must have been partly that she forgave him. I hated scenes as much as she did, but I couldn't forgive him. Nevertheless, I learned slowly that what he really wanted was, in one way or another, to be stood up to— at least by certain people, at least up to a point. By the time I knew that I could stand up to him, however, I no longer needed that defense against him—and by that time he had begun to admire me for qualities I didn't possess; so that was another problem.

Perhaps my mother's way with him was the best after all. They certainly understood each other better than we could understand them, and differently.

Shortly before her death, when she was at the hospital in Baltimore, and we had all gathered there, there was a scene I still remember with shame for myself, with wonder about those two. The doctors had just brought in their unanimous verdict: death. My father and the rest of us were together on a porch; as soon as anyone could speak, the question was voiced: shall she be told? My sisters and I were insistent that she should be, and that my father must do it. He demurred, mildly, saying: "But I think she knows." Nevertheless we insisted, almost angrily, making a further condition that we should be in the room when he spoke to her, so as to be sure (we didn't trust those Victorian circumlocutions) that he told her straight. My father, with surprising meekness, gave way, and we all followed him in to my mother's room. He took her hand, and said, "Dearest Elsie—"

That was as far as she would let him get. She gave him such a smile, and said, "Oh, Paul: I *know*."

She had her own ways, much criticized, of dealing with him; and now I cannot say for certain that they were not the right ways. But after her death Captain Snarley came back with a vengeance, and he could no longer be kicked down the cellar stairs; on the contrary, he took command of the whole house. Once things got so bad that my two sisters who were staying with him then simply took their children and left the house—and kept away for the rest of the day. When they finally came back in the late afternoon, my father was sitting by himself in front of the fire, and his mood had changed. He didn't apologize, but he looked up with a shy smile, and said, "Your mother has been with me."

She was not a constant presence in his last years, but I think she was also with him when he died. He was in Florida, alone at the time with his staff of three faithful servants. His final illness was brief but long enough for several of his daughters to get there before the end. I was thousands of miles away, in the English countryside, and the first word I got was that he had died peacefully and in good spirits. I flew to New York that night and reached Princeton the day before the funeral.

We were all gathered in his house, and had just finished making plans for the ceremony next day, when someone discovered in his study a letter from him, setting out in minute detail the order of service he wanted. The agreed program was hastily countermanded. His letter had overlooked nothing; at the end he gave careful directions for his burial in the family lot, next to Mother— and added an exhortation to us to be sure that the graveyard sexton carried out his instructions to the letter, warning us that these fellows were often cantankerous and overbearing, and that we were to be careful not to let him get away with it in this case.

My father had a longer life than most of us have, perhaps longer than he wanted. He must have had times of happiness, but to me his black moods, when he was making himself and everyone around him wretched, were more visible.

He too must have seen and felt much more than he could comprehend; he too was confused and divided, far more than he would admit; he too said more, and less, than he really knew. As long as he seemed to be in charge of my life I disliked him and often thought him hateful. Even so, when my fear of the future was stronger than my fear of him and at last I went to him for help, I found mercy, and a helplessness like my own. Then I could acknowledge that I was indeed his son.

Toward the end of his life, on at least three occasions when he thought he was saying goodbye to me for the last time, I saw a look on his face that went to my heart: a look of sadness, loneliness and longing.

MY MOTHER TOLD ME

HOW CAN A SON DESCRIBE HIS MOTHER? Where is he to begin, and how can he pretend that he ever knew her as she once knew him? At her first sight of him, this tiny red squalling creature whom she has carried inside her and at last brought forth, she learns him by heart. What she feels about him is too deep for words. When he is older they will talk to each other, after a fashion; but now, in his infancy, they have their only mutually contented conversations, breast to mouth.

Is that when he first sees her? He stares up at her, unblinking, sucking away: and she gazes down at him, her unappeasable yearning matched, for the moment, by his complete need of her. If she thinks at all, she thinks, "He must be seeing me now." And perhaps he is. But he won't remember.

It's a question whether he ever really sees her at all—at any rate, not until much later, when, looking back, he can catch a wavering image like the watery reflection of a person. For in his early years she is not so much a person as a presence—sometimes a dreadful absence. He is not aware that she is young, for she is ageless; or that she is pretty, for she is simply mother-size and mother-shape; or that she has a life of her own, for she is the sky and horizon and weather of his life.

One of the earliest things I remember about my mother is that she was always dressed in black. She was "in mourning" for somebody who had died, and the periods of mourning went on so long that there was always fresh cause, so that she never emerged from them. That, at any rate, was what I remember being told. I never suspected that her mourning went on so long because there was something penitential about it; that it was a kind of intercession for her dead father. I was forty-five when I first learned that her father had shot himself.

It had been a well-kept family secret, though apparently my sisters had known it for years, and they were surprised that I didn't. My mother had never told me. She held strong views on suicide: she believed it was a sin to take one's own life. On the other hand, she loved her father and doubtless felt that in his case there were compelling excuses. And yet she couldn't condone his act or altogether explain it to herself, and must have regarded it as a disgrace in which she shared. Knowing my mother, I think I can say further, a disgrace for which she felt partly to blame. If she had been a better daughter to him . . . I can almost hear her thinking it.

The secret of my grandfather's suicide could not have been so well kept today. But in those early days of the century the Procters and their connections were powerful enough to keep the news quiet. My grandfather had been president of the Procter & Gamble Company, as his father had been before him and as his son was after him; he was one of Cincinnati's first citizens. He was also the beloved head of his family and a devoted, perhaps a doting, husband. My grandmother, who was born in Ireland, was a gay, lively woman overflowing with the zest of life. I could just remember her as a laughing, encouraging presence, all rustly black silk and hugs; while he remains in my mind as a silent, benign old gentleman with silky side whiskers and a broad expanse of waistcoat looped across by a massive gold watch chain; he would stoop and pat your head and then very deliberately fumble in one of his waistcoat pockets and produce a small silver box from which he would invite you to help yourself to a delicious hard caramel.

I always think of him as being with my grandmother, and after her death he must have had little heart for children and caramels. He fell into deeper and deeper melancholy, and one black day shot himself. That was the reason I first remember my mother in what seemed to me permanent mourning. Why did she never tell me the reason? Perhaps she meant to, some time, when I was "old enough to understand." Perhaps she came to the conclusion that I would never be old enough, or that she was incapable of explaining—perhaps, again, because she herself did not altogether understand, and could not explain to herself just what she was ashamed of, or why she was ashamed. This refusal to judge, together with her fear that judgment was called for, might at least partly account for her anxious warnings to me not to "impute motives." What motives she herself must have been tempted to impute, in this and other cases, and then rejected as unworthy or incredible, I can only conjecture.

I never considered my mother an evasive person, but she was notoriously indirect. She had had a gentle upbringing, at the end of the euphemistic nineteenth century, but that doesn't altogether explain her delicacy and shyness; her three sisters had been equally sheltered but were all heartier and less apparently defenseless than she, and beside her some of them seemed almost coarse. As a girl she was slim and must have appeared tall. I grew up to her height when I was about fifteen, so I suppose she was five feet six or seven inches. Her face was a long oval, the features proportioned more to beauty than to prettiness; her coloring was dark: brown hair that was almost black, and a delicate ivory skin. Her hazel eyes were not unusually large, but it was their questioning sadness (when they brightened to gaiety she looked "pretty") that made her face beautiful. Her only brother, Cooper, was the one who most resembled her, both in looks and in temperament, though his man's world had hammered his thin skin into a tougher covering; he had the kind of strong quietness that never has to raise its voice. In my mother's case the armor was inside—what there was of it. It never seemed to protect her very effectively. She was unable to keep her feelings from her face, and she could never hide it when she had been hit; the corners of her mouth would quiver down and her eyes would fill with tears. She hated this giveaway weakness in herself, but she was unable to control it.

She was equally unable to conceal her feelings of sympathy and liking—or their opposites—though her subsequent attempts to deny the obvious led her into some of her most notable indirections, and roused us to hoots of laughter. "Why, I don't know what you children are talking about!" she would protest, flushing faintly. "I thought Mr. Mumchance was a very nice man—and he's doing a wonderful work among all those poor people. Of course, his *manner* is unfortunate, but you can't blame him for that." The fact was that people she thought she ought to have liked she sometimes didn't, and people she ought not to have liked she sometimes did; and, much to her chagrin, you could always tell.

When she tackled someone or something head on, as she frequently forced herself to do, there were characteristic signs that she had nerved herself to do it: her color was unusually high, her smile was falsely brave, and she had a certain way of clearing her throat. I remember once, when her children were all grown up and married, and several of us were having tea with her around the living room fire, she gave this unmistakable throat-clearing signal, and began: "As I was coming out of Lane Bryant's today—" but that was as far as we let her get. We all knew that Lane Bryant's was a shop that specialized in maternity clothes. "Mother!" I said, "do you mean that Peggy's going to have a baby?" Yes, that was exactly what she meant, and she would have told us, but she had to start in her own way.

How many times must she have steeled herself to "have a little talk" with my father and how she must have dreaded it, every time. I know about the "little talks" she had with me. My heart sank whenever she proposed one, but I think she minded them more that I did. The clearing of the throat, the anxious smile, the "Tom, dear, when can we have a little talk?"—how I hated the invariable, timid invitation that I knew would have to be accepted. These conversations were sometimes about money, sometimes about sex, but increasingly, as I got older, they tended to be on the sore subject of religion. With my adolescence had come the usual reaction against orthodoxy, embittered in my case by a reaction against my father's God—or what I took to be his God. In our talks, my mother would hopefully advance the theory that I would soon be all right again, that I was just "going through a phase" (by which she meant that I was having religious measles, but would certainly recover). Most of our talks ended with my mother in tears and myself in cold, exasperated hostility. The suffering she must have undergone on such occasions—and from experience must have known she would undergo—never made her give up nor kept her from coming back for more. If it's not too Irish a way to put it: my mother was a brave person with no courage.

When we think of people we have known a long time, we are apt to remember them as we last saw them; it is only with an effort, a squint of memory, as it were, that we can peer through that up-to-date likeness to find an earlier one behind it. Photographs are not much help; we laugh at their evidence, though we can't altogether deny it. I have seen a photograph of my mother as a little girl, almost a baby, chubby, ringleted and pouting; I could see a faint resemblance, but the picture seemed to have no bearing whatever on the woman I knew as Mother. The photograph of her that was my favorite showed her in a high-collared black dress, a proud and sensitive young woman (if I almost thought "widow" does

72

that mean that I wanted to kill my father? Perhaps it does). But of the old woman with a sad and beautiful face, which is the likeness of her that is clearest in my memory, there are few photographs—for the good reason that it was almost always my mother who took the family pictures; no one else would bother.

When we were small children she was so much part of our background that I cannot separate her from it. She became a rescuing presence when you called desperately for help; when some vague discomfort brought you half-awake, you felt her hovering over you and there was another blanket being tucked around you and now you were warm and fell cozily asleep. Though we had nurses and governesses to look after us, Mother was never far away, except on rare and long-remembered occasions such as the winter when she went to Florida with my father and the baby, and we were sent to stay with "the other Matthewses." We took our revenge by coming down with measles, one after the other. Except for such dreadful desertions—and perhaps there were no others; I can't recall any—Mother was always there, physically close, and available in spite of the flimsy authority of governess or nurse. No doubt she was too available, and perhaps she interfered too much. Nothing could break her of her habit, which she continued to the end of her life, of making a round of the house in the middle of the night to make sure that everyone had enough covers; or if a storm came up to close any necessary shutters or windows against the wind or rain.

Was it she who got up at 3 or 4 A.M. to investigate the suspicious noises that might have meant a burglar? In my family all strange noises at night were put down to burglars or other night prowlers, and were to be investigated. The duty of investigating devolved, as a point of honor, on the head of the household. I later met a retired burglar, Jack Black, who strongly advised against any such action, which he called both foolhardy and unnecessary: he said it was much wiser to stay in bed and (using Canon Welles's technique) simply call out, "Is that you, Jack?"—whereupon the already skittish burglar (if he's there) will almost certainly take to his heels; if on the other hand you go after him, he may very likely get so frightened he will shoot you. This sounded like good sense to me; nevertheless, in my family all night noises had to be looked into.

The nurses and governesses we had when we were little were the outward and visible sign of my mother's anxious protectiveness; they were a kind of first line of defense against the threatening world outside. But her concern about us was so unremitting that she was always patrolling the defenses, and she was not content with inspecting the sentries; she would often relieve them and take over herself. Was she a more anxious and more protective mother than most? She wouldn't have considered herself so, but I think she was. Even at the time, I couldn't help noticing some differences between my life and the lives of other boys.

The most noticeable thing was school. All the other boys in Glendale, including my cousins (except the little Clevelands), went to the public school; but I had a governess until I was ten. Then we went to England for a year, and I was allowed to go to a private school there; that must have been considered safe. Safe from what? I suppose I was given solemn, or perhaps they were hurried, explanations of the dangers that lurked in the public school; but the only translation I find in my memory is that the schoolyard was full of little hoodlums. And I was not to run the risk of associating with hoodlums of any size, because I was delicately different.

Small boys generally trust their mothers, and if my mother told me, in words and worry, that I was delicate and different, I believed her. But I sometimes wished I weren't quite so much of either. There was the unforgettable but puzzling affair of the Wild West show, for instance, when I was nine. I had seen the advance posters, I had pleaded to go, Mother had promised to take me. When the great afternoon came she drove me there herself in a buggy. The show tent was pitched in a field on the outskirts of Glendale; as we neared it I could hear (or did my disappointed imagination make that up?) the exciting sounds of a circus band. But where were the crowds? No one was there but a gang of half-grown boys sitting on the fence. Mother stopped the horse and spoke to them—or did they call out to us first? All I remember clearly is Mother's heightened color, and the jeering sound of their voices. Mother turned the horse and we drove home. She said we had made a mistake, it was the wrong day, there wasn't to be a Wild West show after all. I was bitterly disappointed, and I also felt hoodwinked; I never believed that Mother had told me the whole truth about why we missed the Wild West show.

Another sign of my difference was the clothes Mother got for me. They were not as extreme as Little Lord Fauntleroy's velveteen smocks and lace ruffles, but when I was dressed up on Sunday in an Eton jacket and broad stiff collar I knew that no other little boy in Glendale would be seen dead in such an outfit, and I protested. Nevertheless, I had to wear it. Except for a few catcalls from the other side of the street, I escaped paying the expected penalty for this fancy dress, for most of the time I had it on I was in the protective convoy of grown-ups.

A few years later, however, when I was going to a day school in Cincinnati, I was not so lucky. For boys of my age at that school the iron fashion decreed knickerbockers and long black stockings. One morning, for some reason, there were no clean black stockings in the house. Mother saw no reason why I shouldn't wear a pair of my sister's. I tried to tell her that it was quite impossible; they were the wrong color, they were tan. She couldn't understand, she thought I was exaggerating. Off I went to school in tan stockings, to face the music. And, sure enough, the music had to be faced. I was the laughingstock of the school; even some of the big boys came to look. I felt, as was afterwards said in another connection, it was a day that would live in infamy.

This cavalier attitude of my mother's towards the dictates of children's fashion didn't come, I am sure, merely from a conscious wish to set us off from the rest of the world. She simply didn't bother to keep up with the fashions; and I think my sisters suffered more shame on this account than I did. It was only occasionally, when I moved into the new environment of a different school, that I realized there was anything queer about my clothes or equipment—as when, arriving in the middle of winter as a new boy at St. Paul's, I discovered that I was the only boy among 475 without a pair of hockey skates; in my ignorance (and my parents') I had brought an old-fashioned pair of rocker skates that clamped on to my shoes and were tightened with a key. Yes, ignorance of the prevailing styles would explain part of my mother's indifference to these childish problems—which nevertheless were excruciatingly painful to the child—but still there was something lordly in her ignorance, something that seemed to take it for granted that she and we were in fact different from the rest of the world, and could afford to ignore the world's opinion.

And yet I said that it was my father who taught us to despise; that my mother taught us to be ashamed. These are deep waters, and I can only splash about in them, disregarding my mother's warning and imputing motives right and left. I think she tried to feel superior, in my father's sense, out of loyalty to him or in emulation of him, but she couldn't really do it. She certainly recognized a difference between her and the great majority of people, who had not had such rich parents nor such a protected life; and she disliked and feared the covetous and predatory world outside her sheltered home. At the same time the consciousness of her good fortune brought her a troubling sense of embarrassment amounting very nearly to guilt. This came out clearly in her talks with me about money (at the time her false air of brave cheerfulness and her obviously secondhand reasoning merely made me uneasy; I knew she was not being herself); the key word in these talks was "stewardship." It appeared that money was in fact not a possession but a trust, and the "owner" of money simply its trustee. Therefore, if you had money to spare, it was up to you to use your extra money in various charitable ways—not, in the main, by shoring up rickety individuals but by making careful contributions to solidly worthy institutions.

This still seems to me an impeccably businesslike, cold and worldly-wise point of view, but absolutely unlike Mother; when she gave me this counsel, it was as if she were parroting a lesson. I have heard my father praised as "a good businessman"—which I didn't regard as an unmixed compliment; I felt that a clergyman should be dedicated rather than efficient, and I half-exonerated him by suspecting that he wasn't as businesslike as he seemed. I never heard it said of my mother that she was shrewd about money. I don't think she "knew the value of money," in the sense that those who have had to earn it know its value. I think money to her wasn't a thing to be acquired and spent but a kind of bothersome heirloom to be looked after, kept in good shape and eventually handed on.

In her private moral ledgers she was never sure where to enter the money she had inherited from her father: on the credit or the debit side. (The money would have been a problem in itself, quite apart from his suicide; but I think the manner of his death must have made the problem more complicated.) She thought she had been presented with a method of balancing the books, and she pretended that it satisfied her. But she was never any good at pretending. I saw at last that the "stewardship" my mother preached and practiced was really an attempt to appease her sense of guilt.

My mother was fiercely and anxiously protective of all her six children; as her only son I felt the weight of a special protectiveness. In her anxiety to keep me from being corrupted or hurt she could prevent me, at least for a while, from going to school with a lot of rough little boys, but she couldn't hope to isolate me completely from my own kind. She could, however, to some extent screen my playmates, and worry over the effectiveness of the screening. She did both. After one trial, little Freddy Zimmerman was not welcome to "come over and play"; little James Bell Benedict was—though he was rather reluctant to come, and usually had to be sent by his mother.

My nearest neighbor and most frequent playmate was not-so-little Teddy Townsend, and my mother was dubious about him, though for the wrong reason. He was the only child of a widowed mother, and both of them were big-boned, rather flabby people, physically affectionate and emotionally uncertain. Teddy was large for his age, clumsy and not outstandingly good at games, but his weight and bigness gave him a kind of authority.

Mother liked us to play organized games, though even then her ever-anxious eye scanned the lurking possibilities of ugliness and harm. At least she knew at those times what we were up to. On ordinary days she could not always be certain. Boys being boys,

77

we might be playing Indians or one-ol'-cat—or we might be doing something worse. At that age, when our games broke down or petered out, nothing worse happened than talk, and much the same sort of talk—I later discovered to my disappointment—that older people indulge in: boasting or making fun of someone. These verbal scuffles sometimes ended in physical scuffles which we called fights. One day, whatever the reason or for no reason at all, I lost my temper and my head and attacked Teddy Townsend. This was foolish, and must have appeared so, for he was half again as big as I was. At first he was surprised and embarrassed, and simply held me off with his longer reach; when I continued to flail at him in ineffectual frenzy he hit me a couple of times in the face, not very hard, and seized me in a bearhug that kept me helpless, weeping with rage.

When he finally let me go I stumbled into the house, still weeping, in an agony of shame. I knew he had been much easier on me than I deserved; all I wanted to do was kill him. Mother was of course horror-struck at my "condition," which was far less physical hurt than ruffled ego, and she leaped eagerly at my snuffled report that "Teddy had hurt my back." I'm not sure that she didn't send for the doctor. If she did, I am sure the doctor found nothing wrong with me, but kept a straight face and tactfully played up to my mother's indignant concern. I was forbidden to play with Teddy, and the ban lasted for several weeks. This painful episode renewed in me the knowledge that I was delicate and different. It also gave me my first hint (which I knew I must keep secret) that I was a coward.

The reminders of my difference from other boys continued. In my school in England, where I was the only American among fourteen little Britishers, they were hardly necessary; but even there I remember one. For the first two terms I was a day-boy, but I ate my lunch at the school. The food was Edwardian: heavy, badly cooked and plentiful. Each boy had a hunk of dry bread at his place, but no butter. As an occasional treat there was treacle tart. At these times, because my mother had given orders that I was not to have pastry, I was given a little roll of butter and two Huntley & Palmer biscuits.

A few years later, when we moved to Minnesota and I entered Shattuck School, a government-approved military academy, as the youngest boy there, I had to be a boarder—although my family lived in the town, just across the river—because the school would take no day-boys. Unless guard duty prevented it, however, I went home every Sunday for lunch. That was not enough for Mother. Every night, between tattoo and taps, I had to go to the guardroom, where the only telephone was, and call her up to say good night. My being so young must have saved me a good deal at Shattuck, which was not a tender-hearted place.

In my first year there I was given another proof of my mother's far-darting care. A play was coming to town, a rare event in that theaterless region, and a rumor ran round the school that we were to be marched down to attend it, the whole battalion of us. The play was "Within the Law," and weeks beforehand the plot, the stars, the comments of the Broadway reviewers were all common knowledge in the school. When I heard it was "a problem play" (I think it had something to do with divorce and perhaps also adultery) my heart leaped and sank in the same motion. If my parents heard about it, I knew I should never be allowed to go. I didn't once mention the subject during my Sunday visits home, and as the great day neared and neither my mother nor my father had said anything about it either, my hopes began to rise in spite of reason and experience.

The day came; the battalion fell in at a special assembly. Number four in the rear rank of the last squad in B Company, I stood rigid at attention, holding my breath. The cadet captains reported "all present or accounted for"; the cadet major filled out his chest to roar the order that would set the battalion marching—no, at this last minute out ran a messenger to my company commander, who frowned, bent his head, about-faced and barked: "Private Matthews, fall out!" The battalion marched off to the sinful excitement of "Within the Law," and I spent those two hours in the guardhouse.

My next school, St. Paul's, was too far away from home for a nightly telephone call; but I think there was a rule, as in many schools, that we had to write to our parents once a week. That was not good enough for Mother; she wanted me to write every day. And she sent me off with a quantity of penny postcards, which she had addressed herself. I must have used some of them, but I remember bringing the leftovers back at the end of term, which goes to show that I had at least begun to resist. Mother never gave up the struggle, however; years later, when I was at Oxford, I was summoned one day by the august warden of my college, who showed me, with a mixture of annoyance and bewilderment, a cable from my mother, inquiring whether I was all right. She had had no letter from me for two weeks, and had thus set about getting one.

I suppose my mother, consciously or not, wanted me to feel dependent on her; and I did. In fact, I came to count too much on her protective understanding, and there were times when I considered myself cruelly disappointed. One of the most vivid is also the most ludicrous. My tenth birthday came while we were on our way to England, on one of the earliest days of the voyage. Two of my sisters, who were in on the secret, had told me that Mother was going to give me the most wonderful present I could possibly imagine. So I imagined it, to the last detail, and made up my mind exactly what it must be: a toy diver that went up and down in a round tank of water when you pressed or released the bulb that regulated the air in his diving suit. I suppose I must have seen one in a shop window somewhere.

The day came, but not the diver. My present from Mother was a pair of gold cuff links with my initials on them. Though the sea was calm, I became violently seasick, and stayed sick for seven days. Between my retchings Mother read to me a supposedly humorous story, to cheer me up: *The Casting Away of Mrs. Lecks and Mrs. Aleshine*, by Frank Stockton. It was bad enough, I thought, when Mrs. Lecks and Mrs. Aleshine slid down the Alps on mattresses; but when they found themselves alone in a leaky lifeboat on the huge Pacific, and tried to use the oars like the brooms they were accustomed to, my gorge rose again, and I asked Mother to stop. I never afterwards went back to that book, and never again liked her to read to me.

In any case, as soon as I could read I preferred reading to myself. We were always being given books, and I think we read them all at least once. Soon I began exploring the shelves of my father's library. Many of the books there were forbidding; some, I discovered to my surprise, were forbidden. Censorship became an early fact in our lives. Was Mother the censor? She must have been, for in that field my father was more easygoing or more venturesome, and I can't think he would have bothered much about what we read. We couldn't read any "grown-up" book without first getting permission from one of my parents—and the same thing applied to stories in grown-up magazines. (This censorship had a curious result in the case of one of my younger sisters. After she grew up she spent several years in pre-Hitler Germany, fell in love with the country, and regarded the outbreak of war in 1939 as a calamity. She subscribed to the most isolationist paper available, the New York *Daily News*, and read it carefully, cutting out every reference to the war and every picture bearing on the war, before letting her small daughters look at the paper.)

I suppose we all complied with this censorship outwardly, but I broke the rules surreptitiously whenever there was some book I very much wanted to read, or look at. I had discovered a collection of engravings from the pictures of a nineteenth-century French painter, Gérôme; some of them showed delightfully naked women—a Turkish harem, Phryne before her judges. I hadn't actually been forbidden to look at them but I felt sure I would be, if I asked. It was a nervous business, stealing into the library when no one was around, sliding out the tall white folios and untying the ribbons that bound three sides of them. I don't remember ever being caught at this furtive game, but I didn't dare indulge in it often.

There was one forbidden book that so fascinated me I couldn't stay away from it. It was called *Russian Fairy Tales;* it was as grim inside as its gloomy Victorian cover, all about headless horsemen galloping through the night, and Babajagas riding the storms, not on a broom but seated in a mortar. These stories were frightening enough in the daytime, and remembered fragments of them haunted my nights. For some reason this book was on the prohibited index, and part of the thrill I got from reading it was the knowledge that I was committing a deliberate crime. I used to hide with it in a closet, leaving the door open a crack so there was just light enough to read by; and these guilty and gloomy surroundings added to the excitement and fear roused in me by the book.

This censorship seemed to get more severe as we approached the dangerous age of adolescence—or perhaps we simply noticed it more, by contrast to the customs in other households. I remember particularly a popular song that Mother censored. It was a song about the Model T Ford, which in those days was getting millions of dollars' worth of free advertising in the form of jokes and vaudeville acts. This song, with a refrain, "The little old Ford rattles right along," had a line in it that went, "A left-hand drive and a right-hand squeeze." Mother rewrote the line: "A left-hand drive and a good sea-breeze."

Even at the age of thirteen, as I then was, I knew there was something wrong—though I couldn't have said what—in my mother's attitude. Vulgarity made her ashamed, but there was something under the vulgarity that she feared. My own shame, complicated by a vague awareness of hers, was further deepened by the secret knowledge that I could sing the tune and all the words of "Three Whores of Canada," and knew most of "The Bastard King of England." (Mother had been right to be dubious about Teddy Townsend.)

When we were little, my mother used to sing to us herself. We never got enough of her singing, and used to beg her for the same songs over and over. Her voice was a low alto, rather husky and with a tremble in it, more suited to mournful love songs and ballads than to the lively ditties she had learned in her girlhood. We liked them all, indiscriminately, as she seemed to: "A Frog He Would A-Wooing Go," "Won't You Come Home, Bill Bailey?" "Clementine," "The Animal's Fair," and one about the adventures of an ostrich, with a chorus that went:

> *I'm a sim-ple lit-tle os-trich, but-*
> *I—know—it—all!*

My favorites, for the tune, were "De Year ob Jubilo" (which Mother had altered to "Year ob Jubilee," perhaps from some obscure feeling that "white folks" should laugh "ho-ho," and "darkies" should laugh "hee-hee") and one we called "Cla' de Kitchen," which I loved for the tune and words and the jiggy quick-time of the chorus. It went like this:

> *A bullfrog dressed in soldier's clothes*
> *Went out one day to shoot some crows;*
> *De crows smelt powder an' dey flew away;*
> *De bullfrog mighty mad dat day—*
> *So cla' de kitchen, young folks, old folks,*
> *Cla' de kitchen, young folks, old folks,*
> *Ol' Virginny neber t'ar.*

> *Ah wish Ah was back in ol' Kaintuck,*
> *Fo' since Ah'm here Ah've had no luck:*
> *De gals so proud dey won't eat mush,*
> *An' when you go to kiss 'em, dey say "Oh, hush!"*
> *So cla' de kitchen, young folks, etc.*

A few of Mother's songs, it seems to me now, hardly jibed with her strictures against lyrical vulgarity—but the songs of our own youth are immune to criticism. Even so, some of the lines, for Mother, were pretty brazen. I remember one verse that used to make us squeal with laughter:

> *Monkey married the baboon's sister;*
> *First he hugged her, then he kissed her,*
> *Kissed so hard he raised a blister.*
> *She set up a yell!*

Mother entertained the nursery in other ways. Her most famous story was "The Crooked-Mouth Family," which seemed to me not in the least funny but a profound fairy tale of breath-catching suspense that never lost its excitement with repetition. How would that candle ever get blown out in such a family, every one of

whom blew crookedly but in a different way? And Mother became each one of them in turn, lifting or dropping her voice and
never forgetting which way to droop or fold her lip; when they
were all at their wits' end and slating each other for the general failure, her quick changing of parts was really masterly. And
what a relief, what an ending both happy and true, when the one
normal member of the family came quietly downstairs and
straightforwardly blew out the candle!

We never tired of this performance, but perhaps Mother did, or
perhaps it was her shyness that, as the years went on, required an
increasing amount of persuasion to get her to repeat it. She had
another accomplishment, for which she was also famous in the
family, that she was even charier of displaying: her "stage laugh."
But on very special occasions, at a family party when she was a
little carried away by the general festivity and was so suddenly
appealed to that she had no time to take refuge in shyness, she
might, with no preliminary but that inevitable clearing of the
throat, burst into her "stage laugh." It was a startling, even a blood-
curdling series of sounds, beginning with a rapid low ululation
like a war whoop and soaring into a harsh cockatoo scream, the
rise and fall twice repeated. Mother's face, as these frightful sounds
were heard, wore a look of wild desperation struggling with zany
triumph. A moment of stricken silence followed, while Mother
blushed from her exertions and embarrassment and smiled shyly
to show that it was all over, thank goodness; then we shouted with
delight to have her safe back again and with relief at having survived ourselves. Nobody really wanted to hear Mother laugh like
that very often.

Everyone, I like to suppose, has a natural inclination toward the
beautiful, in preference to the ugly, and everyone, I suppose, thinks
he knows which is which. But perfect taste, that is also untutored,
must be as rare as perfect pitch. In the Middle West of my childhood almost no one suspected that taste either has to be formed or
else unconsciously conforms; everyone took it for granted that,
with a few eccentric and amusing exceptions, those who could

afford to buy what they liked knew what they wanted and what they were getting.

To that shrewd materialist community, price was a pretty good indication of real worth. Uncle Cooper knew that a Frederic Remington bronze cowboy or an oil painting ("The Defense of the Water Hole") was good because it came high. Of course he had to like it too. Oriental rugs were appreciated at their full value; Aubusson carpets weren't. And all notable family purchases, from a new house to an old picture, were a matter of concern to the whole family. They came to look, criticize, discuss, and pass judgment. Sometimes the verdict was favorable, sometimes not; in either case they spoke their minds freely. In all cases they could be reasonably certain that the newly acquired object of art would be within the limits of their common canon of taste. They did not regard those limits as narrow or superficial; why should they? The things they bought were solid and expensive. All the houses inhabited by my family and their connections were richly, heavily and hideously furnished.

My mother's house (in this sense it was more hers than my father's) was no exception. Most of the furniture, of course, had been handed down to her and dated from the middle or later days of the nineteenth century. These great masses of black walnut and mahogany seemed to me as inevitable and became as invisible as the house itself, and perhaps she saw them the same way. It is the small "modern" touches which she herself must have contributed that most stand out in my memory: the Wallace Nutting colored photographs of country scenes, the bulbous bowls and vases, with fired-in streaks of color and misty pictorial designs, from the Rookwood Pottery. Even well-brought-up children cannot escape impressions. My impression of our house—of every house we lived in—was one of heaviness and gloom.

And yet there were bright spots in this domestic darkness, havens of cheerfulness lighting up the surrounding shadows. Even there the brightness was more felt at certain seasons and times of day and when my mother was there too; a corner of her bedroom (my father's room also, but this corner, where she sat and sewed and looked out at her favorite tree, was peculiarly hers), and the living room at teatime in the winter, with the lamps lit, the curtains drawn, and a log fire winking between the glistening brass andirons. Were these little oases all she could contrive against the engulfing desert, the dreary, expensive ugliness favored by the family taste—her own and my father's included? No, for she had her garden.

My father became Bishop of New Jersey in 1915, and moved his family to Princeton the following year. Mother never had to move again: she lived there for the last thirty years of her life. The house was the largest and ugliest of all our houses. It had been built, at some time in the nineties of the last century, in three sections: the front of rough pinkish stone, the third floor capped by a cupola; the middle section of brick painted brown; and the back (kitchen, pantry and servants' rooms) of wood. The tall living room windows had semicircular lunettes of stained glass over them, and there was a stained-glass window set into the middle of the living room chimney.

The house aroused the latent architect in my father, and a few years later he had it completely remodeled. In order to make sure of getting a professional architect who would do what he wanted, he employed his nephew, my cousin Stanley Matthews. Stanley's tastes were just as definite and even worse than my father's, and between the two of them they produced a house that was more of a piece but hardly less ugly than the original: they chopped off the cupola, changed the entrance from the front to the side, covered up the stained-glass windows in the living room (inserting stained-glass medallions and leaded panes in the library instead), added a chapel, a number of gables and fake half-timbering, and swathed the whole thing in stucco.

When we first moved in, the house had been standing empty for several years, and the grounds too were in a sad state of neglect. But the grounds were the best thing about the place: eleven acres of ragged lawn, scattered shrubbery, and big trees—elms, chestnuts, firs and copper beeches; there were also the ruinous remains of a grape arbor, beside a tennis court overgrown with weeds. Mother looked at this chaos with the eye of a creator, and went happily to work.

We never realized how much she planned to do until it was done, or so nearly done that even we could see what was happening, as she had seen it all along in her mind's eye. But I remember the first thing she did, and how hopeless it looked to me. At the back of the house there was a tangled thicket of rhododendron—in the North Carolina mountains the appropriate name for it is a "rhododendron hell"—and in its midst the tottering ruin of an ancient privy and a scattered cache of rusty tin cans. Out of this noisome eyesore Mother set to work to create her first garden. It was referred to in the family, ambiguously, as "the shady garden."

Before the shady garden was finished to Mother's satisfaction she had embarked on much more ambitious projects. I can't remember now the order in which she tackled them, but I saw the results. She never succeeded in getting grass to grow properly under all the trees—though she stymied the worst offender by planting a huge circular bed of lilies of the valley around its trunk—but gradually most of the ragged field on three sides of the house was turned into a presentable lawn. At the back of the place, next to the old barn that had been converted into a garage and gardener's house, a kitchen garden grew and grew until the fruit and vegetables that came from it (the celery, asparagus and lima beans, especially) were better than any to be had from the fanciest grocer's. Where the kitchen garden stopped, cold frames and a greenhouse, supplying more than enough flowers for the house the year round, took over.

Mother did a great deal of work outdoors herself, weeding and planting; she was not content with merely supervising. When she was expanding a garden or laying out a new one she got extra men to help Frank, the gardener, and his assistant, Eddie, and later she took on an old German to do odd jobs like cutting the grass and raking leaves. But as her gardens grew, her outdoor staff had more and more work to handle. After the shady garden was finished, she planted rows of flower beds between it and the tennis court; then she made a small sunken garden on a terrace next to the side porch; and finally a much larger walled garden, with a summer house, fish pool, and banks of flowers along all the walls. Meantime there were the kitchen garden and the greenhouse to be looked after, not to mention the lawns, border shrubbery, weeding and driveway edges.

The trees were also a great concern to her. A deadly elm blight was spreading through the eastern states, and all the elms in Princeton were doomed, but Mother fought for the life of every one of hers: by surgical operations, filling cavities, artificial feeding, even by supporting guy wires. When, in spite of everything, she lost a tree, she immediately planted another, as large as possible, to take its place. These experiments in transplanting grew more and more daring: they reached their culmination when she was finishing her walled garden.

On a small fenced lot adjoining the back entrance to our property stood the borough water tower, a landmark that could be seen for miles around: a cylindrical iron tank, capped by a conical roof, rearing a hundred feet in the air on girder stilts. On summer afternoons, when we were sitting in the arbor by the tennis court, the water tower looming above the treetops was the most noticeable thing on the horizon.

From the roofed terrace at one end of the walled garden where she had planned to sit and pour tea and talk to her children and friends, the whole cloistered view of lawn and flower beds and fish pool was intruded on, utterly spoiled, ruined by this monstrous water tower. It was like being stared at, in your own garden, by a hobo leaning over the fence, a gigantic hobo who wouldn't go away. I don't know whether she actually tried to get the Borough Council to move the water tower, but I wouldn't be surprised if she had. Anyhow, when she realized that the thing was immovably there, she determined to plant it out.

She was told by the experts that this was quite impossible; no tree of sufficient size could ever be successfully transplanted. Nevertheless she went ahead, and after tremendous labors and heaven knows what expense a tree that must have been 40 or 50 feet high was trucked and manhandled into place to blot out the eyesore. Furthermore, the tree survived. And it very nearly—not quite—did the trick: at the leafy height of summer, if you didn't know the water tower was there, it was hardly noticeable; and in winter, when the bare branches couldn't hide it, nobody was likely to be sitting in the walled garden, anyway.

This culminating effort of my mother's seems to me to indicate the whole direction of her life. Princeton, when we first went there, was a small, sheltered town, hardly more than a village, and its inhabitants could be as private as they liked. We were protected from our neighbors by the size of our place; Mother entertained little (on her own account I think it would have been never) and went out rarely; I think she really wanted to see nobody but her own family, and the walled garden was for herself and them. She didn't want anybody or anything from outside looking over the wall, either.

Except for her own family, who were in a specially favored position, and who in any case had been getting to know her all their lives, I remember only two women whom Mother regarded as real friends. Typically, they were not close neighbors; one lived fifty miles from Princeton, the other twelve hundred miles away, in Minnesota. Mrs. Phelps, the nearer, was a transplanted New Englander, a handsome, downright, chairwoman type; in her kindly, active presence I always felt like a committee that was about to vote Aye as soon as she put the question. She and Mother must have had something in common. Was it a mutual understanding of the sadness of life? My mother's face, "in repose," was beautiful but sad. I never saw Mrs. Phelps in repose, but no doubt my mother did.

The other friend was of longer standing, and I think more intimate. Mrs. Theopold had lived, all her married life, in a small town in Minnesota. When we moved there—for good, as we thought, though we stayed only a year—she and Mother took to each other immediately. It was easy to see what they saw in one another: Mrs. Theopold was gentle, feminine, funny, with an underlying melancholy. We called her "Aunt Emily."

After we left Minnesota the friendship continued, and Mrs. Theopold often came for a visit; between times, she and Mother corresponded regularly. I know Mother loved her and felt very close to her. And yet . . .

The other day I discovered, tucked away in a book on my shelves, an unfinished letter my mother had written to her dearest friend. Both of them had been dead for many years, but I felt like an eavesdropper. Nevertheless, I wanted to read the letter, and I did.

It was written in pencil, on small pages torn from a scratch pad; Mother was on the train from New York to Princeton. It was a hot July day in 1929. The one audible note of affection (but if you knew Mother, it was very audible) was the beginning: "Dearest Anne . . ." She never lightly called anyone "dearest," especially in writing. The letter itself was, apparently, a completely factual report on the doings of various members of the family:

Peggy has closed down the nursery school for the year and is about to have her tonsils out; Mary Ann has gone to Wilmington for the weekend to stay with her future husband's family; except for her discouragingly stubborn skin trouble she seems very well; she and Mother have been shopping for her trousseau (all purchases listed); last week Mother had taken two grandsons to Mantoloking for the day, "but it was too cold and windy to go in bathing. The March storms almost ruined the beach there—it is now very steep and unsafe, and some of the cottages were undermined. The Jersey shore is the limit anyway—I don't see why anybody goes there who can afford to go elsewhere"; she has had a telegram from Ben from Cincinnati: he expected to take his mother "and an inevitable boy" to Washington and Asbury Park, and she hopes he will come over by himself on Sunday; she was very glad to get Anne's letter last week, and will answer it "after I get home, as I haven't it with me."

Mother's letters had to be read between the lines, or as if they had been written in invisible ink. This one might have been posted on a bulletin board with no fear of its secret messages being deciphered. But Aunt Emily knew what Mother was writing about, for she knew Mother. This letter was not the flat catalogue of shopping chores and family plans it seemed; in her own indirect terms, it was a statement to her dearest friend of Mother's hopes and fears about the remedyless round of life. What *is* it Peggy wants? Is Mary Ann really all right, and will she be happy in her marriage? Oh, why can't we live in a place we love, or at least in some better place than this? Why isn't Ben more interested in girls? I miss you and wish you were with me.

This letter to a friend is a fair sample of the kind of letters Mother wrote. They could always be counted on to tell you what was happening in the family circle. They were written in a hurry, at odd moments, in her overcrowded day, and she would have thought it affected to try to write them well. When she "answered" a letter, she commented on every statement her correspondent had made ("What a shame . . . How nice . . . I'm so sorry"), made sure that she had replied to all questions, and then scribbled her own statements and questions—to which she in turn expected answers.

Her letters to me were generally full of questions, and even when they weren't, the next one would often chide me: "You didn't *answer* my letter!" When I tried to tell her that I considered it no treat to have my own letters returned to me in this piecemeal fashion, she would say that she knew her letters were dull but that I would just have to put up with them. She was right: they were dull, and elicited an answering dullness from me. Mother was not one of those people who talked like poor Poll but wrote like an angel; she was all of a piece, and the same repressions governed both her talk and her writing.

I don't think I have ever found a four-leaf clover in my life, but I have been with Mother, one Sunday morning in England, coming home from church, when she picked more than a hundred from a few square yards of greensward. When it came to four-leaf clovers, there was something almost magical about her eye; and it was as if she felt their presence before she even began to look, for I never remember her searching for one without finding it—and several more into the bargain. Those were the days when she used to walk with us in the country, when we were little. We called them "mushroom walks," because what we were really after were mushrooms.

In the open fields around Glendale we hunted for puffballs:

round white funguses sometimes as big as small footballs; when they were overripe they dried up, and if you pressed them or kicked them they gave out little puffs of smoky-looking stuff. The good ones were dense and earth-smelling, and we carried them home in a basket. A big one, sliced and fried, was enough to feed the whole family for a meal. In Michigan we went with Mother in the woods to look for other kinds: our favorites were shaggy-manes, tall mushrooms with long conical caps and peeling skin that curled up at the edges. We knew from Mother that some mushrooms were poisonous, and we were constantly hoping to find "the deadly Amanita." Mother knew hundreds of different kinds, and brought back the new ones to look up in her mushroom book.

Was she happy in those days, and were these meandering searches a sign of it? Or was it restlessness that drove her out to the woods and fields, and resignation that brought her back to cultivate a garden? Was she happy as a mother? Perhaps she was, when we were little; I don't see how she could have been, later. She never wanted to let go of any of us, and so, when we grew up, the complications of our lives increased her worries. She was sensitive, and she must have been constantly wounded by the sulkiness and self-regarding—Matthews traits, not Procter—in her children.

Was she happy as a wife? I think she loved my father, and she had been brought up to believe that a wife must also honor and obey her husband. Believing as she did, she must have found in her long married life inexhaustible food for thought and less and less that she could honorably say. In later years, when we had one of our "little talks," I would try to turn the conversation from the particular to the general, and get Mother to admit things about life that she wouldn't admit; each of us thought the other's statements maddeningly unsatisfactory. She certainly knew much more than I did about what she was not saying, but I was always sure there were things she wouldn't say, while she invariably and vigorously denied it. I remember once, in prohibition days, a barkeep in a speakeasy saying earnestly to one of the regulars: "If he wouldn't have to ask me so many goddam questions, I wouldn't have to tell him so many goddam lies."

One of the great Matthews virtues, in which a large part of the rest of the world was generally found lacking, was a sense of humor. Curiously enough, my mother seemed to be exempt from this judgment, not because she was "famous for her sense of humor"—she wasn't—but because it just didn't seem to apply to her. She laughed when something struck her as funny, but many of my father's jokes only made her smile, and the teeth-baring yells of triumph with which the Matthewses hailed their own wit did not carry her along with them. I loved to hear Mother laugh, but I didn't often hear her laugh on cue, and wholeheartedly, at something a Matthews said.

I used to think the Procters had crinkly faces from laughing so much, and being so ready to; they didn't have to wait for a formal joke; people—and mainly their own family—were what amused them. When the Procter aunts ("the Glendale aunts," we called them) got together, they were so full of anecdotes and have-you-heards and let-me-tell-yous that the sound was sometimes like an aviary of screaming parrots. When the one who momentarily had the floor reached the point where she had to laugh herself, she cut the cackle in half—a single explosive "Ho!" instead of "Ho-ho!"—so she wouldn't be interrupted.

They were half Irish, so they liked to poke fun at the human condition; though in all material things they were conservative to their last share of stock, they were also fleetingly disloyal to the notion of civilization, which they couldn't help getting glimpses of, at odd moments, as a pompous sham: a lot of forked radishes like themselves all dressed up in grand clothes and grand sentiments.

The impudence of the Procter laughter knew no bounds; it even lapped at the base of the marmoreal Matthewses. A story went the Procter rounds that old Mrs. Miller had said: "I dreamed I saw God; he was wearing Father Matthews' hat, and he told me not to eat meat. And when I did, after that, it came up on me."

Of such rather coarse and admittedly pointless stuff the sense of humor (but it was never called that, it was never referred to) of my mother's family was made. She herself was incapable of anything remotely resembling coarseness in speech or thought but she did sometimes (as in the words of songs) quote surprisingly vigorous expressions. She used to say she was too Irish to object to strong language, but she did draw the line at blasphemy—"taking God's name in vain."

In the course of her life, my mother naturally had a good deal to do with a good many different doctors. Until she was old she was the embodiment of health herself, but my father was not, and my sisters and I went through the whole gamut of children's diseases, though Charlotte was the only one who had diphtheria; that was one you could be inoculated against, even fifty years ago. After Charlotte came down with it, we were waked in the middle of the night (so we wouldn't yell so long) and stabbed in the bottom.

In my childhood, when Mother seemed to be on the doctors' side, it never occurred to me that she had her doubts about them. As I grew older I became aware that she made distinctions among doctors, largely on the strength or weakness of their characters, the likeableness or unlikeableness of their personalities. Wherever we moved we always had a family doctor, and he was always a man we liked. Mother must have liked him in the first place. I don't remember her ever making a sweeping statement about the medical profession—she was not given to making sweeping statements—and I doubt if she ever even told herself what she really thought about it. She might have warmly denied that she was skeptical of all doctors to start with, and had grown more and more skeptical with experience. But her actions showed that she was. She would get whatever medicine the doctor prescribed, and put it, often unopened, in the medicine closet in the hall. Once a year this closet was cleaned out, and dozens of bottles of medicine, never touched, were thrown in the garbage can.

Whatever faith she had had in medicine must have been nearly destroyed when one of my sisters died, at eighteen, of blood poisoning. If they had had penicillin in those days, or perhaps one of the other "wonder drugs," her life could have been saved; as it was, the doctors could do nothing. Mother never said it, but I am sure she thought they should have been able to do something. She would have been reconciled to the fact of an older person dying like that; but not a young one, and not one of her own children. She continued to have the doctor in whenever one of us was sick; in fact, she had him in oftener than before, because her anxiety was greater. She was anxious not only about us but about what the doctor could not do.

Until she was approaching old age, Mother herself hardly had a day's illness. Her invariable and unfailing good health were to us a part of the natural order of things. So that when she began, apologetically, to suffer from arthritis, we were uneasy but not, I think, as sympathetic as we might have been; we were almost equally alarmed and annoyed. Mother seemed to share our feeling that she had no right to be ill; she seldom referred to her condition, and when she did, it was with the kind of half-humorous vexation in which she would have confessed that she had stubbed her toe, out of hurry or carelessness. No one paid much attention to Mother's arthritis.

But it got worse. She must have been in pain a good deal of the time. She went to various doctors about it and tried all the various things they told her to try—heat treatments, medicine, the whole bag of tricks. Nothing did any good. One of them told her that the best thing she could do was to go to Arizona; but that would have meant leaving my father, for weeks or months, so she never considered it. She had to give up gardening, her favorite occupation. My father put in the elevator so that she wouldn't have to climb the stairs.

The first time I began to take Mother's arthritis seriously was when I heard she was going to Canada to see Dr. Locke. He was having a great vogue at the time on account of his treatment of neuralgia, rheumatism and other ailments, which supposedly had marvelous results. He practiced in some little town in Canada, where patients flocked to him from hundreds of miles away. He was not at all the kind of doctor Mother had ever been to before. I don't know whether my father tried to dissuade her; none of the rest of us did, but we were a little shocked. At the same time, we admired Mother's initiative. And we sympathized with her gesture of disgust or defiance toward orthodox medicine.

She insisted on going to Canada alone. When she got to the little town where Dr. Locke had his clinic, she took a room in a boarding house (this was also very unlike Mother, but either there was no hotel or she couldn't get a room in one). Every day she went to Dr. Locke's clinic, a large, bare, barnlike building, for treatment. All the patients, she said, sat in a row along the wall, waiting for the doctor. Before he appeared, a nurse came briskly along, telling all the patients to take off their right shoes, and collecting a dollar bill from each. Dr. Locke's treatment was very businesslike: he worked his way down the row, without even looking at the patients, giving each foot a quick twist. After that, Mother went back to her boarding house till next day. She stayed a full week, or perhaps ten days. Then she came home and told us about it. Was she any better, we wanted to know. Well, not appreciably, said Mother; but she thought it had done her good. Shortly after she returned, Macy's department store in New York brought out a "Dr. Locke Shoe" ($5.98 a pair) which was supposed to accomplish the same result as his daily foot-twisting.

Some time passed after the Dr. Locke episode before Mother tried anything else. One day I heard at the *Time* office about an experiment in medical research in which the circulation of the blood in a patient's body had been artificially extended into an arrangement of glass tubes, where the blood was irradiated by ultraviolet rays. This horrifying process—at least, it seemed horrifying to me—had not brought the results hoped for, whatever they were, but as an accidental by-product it did seem to help the patient's arthritis. I told Mother what I had heard, thinking only that she might investigate further. A week or so later she casually told me that she had gone and had the same experiment performed on herself. No results, of any kind.

For a long time after this there was no news about Mother's arthritis. Now and then, when I thought she was looking badly, I would bring up the subject of Tucson, but to no purpose; she would say that she was better, or no worse, and that a journey to Arizona was out of the question. Anyhow, though we didn't know it, she had found a new doctor.

She finally broke the news one Sunday at dinner. She cleared her throat in that particular way which meant that she had a difficult announcement to make. What she was about to tell us, she said, might sound a little strange, and she begged us to keep it to ourselves; it really concerned no one but herself, and the only reason she was telling us now was that she was afraid the news might somehow get back to her sisters in Ohio, and she was sure their attitude would not be sympathetic or understanding. The fact was, said Mother, that she had found a new treatment for her arthritis: she was being stung by bees.

It was a well-known fact, said Mother defensively, that bee venom is good for rheumatism and such complaints, and it further appeared that bee venom is most effectively administered by the sting of a live bee. How long had this been going on? Well, for a little over a year now. And had there been any improvement? She couldn't honestly say there had been *as yet*, but she still hoped that the cumulative effect of a few more months of daily treatment, especially now that she had worked up to thirty stings a day . . . What? Yes, said Mother proudly, thirty. It was not so bad, really; after a while, you almost got used to it. She had evolved a regular technique. She would go out to the walled garden, where she could be undisturbed and unobserved, carrying a saucer of honey, a jar of cyanide and a small pair of tweezers. While a bee was gorging himself on honey Mother would pick him up with the tweezers and put him against her knee, which he would immediately sting. Then she dipped him into the cyanide jar to put him out of his misery. (How does a bee really feel after he stings something? How can anyone know? Anyhow, Mother believed in mercy killing, where bees were concerned.)

I don't think Mother continued the bee-sting treatment very long after this announcement. It must have been a great load off her mind, telling us, and perhaps that made it easier for her to decide that she had followed the regime long enough. Needless to say, the bee stings did not cure her arthritis, though as usual it was impossible to make out from Mother's vague and kindly comments whether the latest experiment had helped or hindered. And this time she was less critical after the fact, if not less frank, than ever. We all understood why. For this time no doctor had been concerned: the bee champion had been her own daughter, Peggy, herself an avowed heretic where doctors were concerned, and who thought there was more applicable wisdom in old wives' tales than in medical journals.

One of Mother's most often-repeated threats—she didn't make many—was that when she got to be a grandmother she was going to wear a lace cap and smoke a pipe. I didn't much like the sound of this, when I first heard her say it; the prospect of Mother getting old was disagreeable in itself, and this professed desire to take to a pipe was a disquieting indication of the unknown amount of repressed Irishness in her. But when she did become a grandmother, and the lace cap, vastly becoming, duly appeared, I was almost disappointed that the pipe didn't follow suit. I used to remind her of her threat, and for a while she kept up the pretense that she just hadn't got around to buying the pipe yet.

She was to be an old lady for years and years; that was the idea. Our idea, anyhow. And I know it was my father's, for it was at about this time that he began to make his embarrassing announcements about legacies, by implication including Mother as the largest legacy of all. Whatever Mother really thought or guessed about her future, she played up to him as she always did. I don't mean that she had intimations of death, and yet I can't think that it was a great surprise to her when she learned that she was going to die.

We were all used to her arthritis, whether she was or not; but that turned out to be a side issue after all. It had been a useful cover-up for what she must have suspected was something worse. When we learned that she "had to have an operation," and the dreadful word "cancer" was breathed, I think for the first time in our lives Mother came into focus as a person in her own right. I know that it was then I first noticed how really brave she was. I couldn't help contrasting her behavior, on the eve of her operation, with the way my father had acted a few years before, under similar circumstances. I had been very much moved at the time by his display of bravery; he obviously considered that he was facing death, and indeed mentioned the prospect in prayers that he himself conducted in his hospital room, the night before the operation. But Mother was cheerful and deprecated any display of emotion; she didn't want a fuss.

The operation was a success, we were told. For some reason I was delegated by my father to have a further conversation with the surgeon, just to make sure. This surgeon was a fine-looking man whose quiet certainty inspired the same trust you would feel in a veteran sea captain; you knew he had weathered all the storms, and that when he was on the bridge everything was being done that could be done. Nevertheless, as we talked, as I kept trying to get him to answer my persistent question ("Will there be a recurrence? Could there be?") and his not-quite-satisfactory replies grew more impatient and finally angry, I realized that I had encountered for the first time the doctor who lies from principle—out of pity, perhaps, for the layman who can't bear the whole truth or be trusted with it. I had forced him further than he wanted to go; in his determination not to tell me everything, he refused to admit that there was anything more to tell, and this answered my question. Though he did his best to deny it, I knew that Mother was still in danger, perhaps doomed. Then, as she made an apparently complete recovery, I found it easier to put the surgeon's ambiguous answers out of my mind; perhaps we all did.

Nevertheless, not many months later, when my father's noncommittal telegram arrived, saying that they were going to Johns Hopkins hospital for an examination, I knew it was a summons and what the summons meant, though I didn't want to believe it. We all got to Baltimore as soon as we could. The hospital Mother was in was a famous one, but I was no longer awed by a hospital's reputation, having had enough experience of them to be more angrily skeptical of their red tape and superinefficiency than Mother ever was about doctors. At one point we were in an anteroom with Mother and a crowd of other patients, in wheel chairs or sitting on benches, in one of those interminable waits for an examination that had been scheduled, postponed and re-scheduled;

we had now been waiting some forty minutes. It was like what I imagined Ellis Island might be, if half the crowded immigrants were also ill.

In a few days the X-rays had rejected the final appeal and confirmed the verdict: death, in a few weeks. As usual, my father rose to the occasion; as usual, my mother didn't have to.

She hadn't looked well, we now realized, for some time; but for the next week or so she was like her old self. It was as if there was a great load off her mind, and she no longer had to pretend. She was quite unaffectedly cheerful and calm; there was nothing whatever, now, she had to worry about. It was late summer and the trees and flowers were looking their best. For most of the days, at first, Mother lay on her chaise longue by the window, in her prettiest dress and her grandmother's lace cap, and looked at her favorite tree. This tree (was it an elm? I can't even remember that) had one great branch with a V-like dip in it that Mother thought particularly beautiful. In a picture she wouldn't have liked it or seen its relevance, but she loved it where it was.

In these first days, when she was able to be out of bed and on her chaise longue, her eighteen grandchildren all came to say goodbye to her in turn. If she was in pain she never admitted it, but she grew obviously weaker, and after a few days had to take to her bed. It was only a matter of four weeks from the time she came back from the hospital till she died, and since than I have watched a longer struggle, but Mother's dying seemed the lengthiest and most difficult ordeal I had ever witnessed or could imagine. As it drew toward its end we took turns sitting in her room through the night, to relieve the nurses. As I watched her gaunt profile, the mask of Tragedy, with silently shouting mouth, against the night light, and listened to her hoarse breathing and her spells of sharp, dry coughing (so different from the well-known self-conscious clearing of her throat) I saw that dying is hard labor.

A fantasy that still haunts me formed in my mind. We—my father, my sisters and I, all of us except Mother—were in a transcontinental train, air-conditioned and luxuriously comfortable. As we met in the dining car for breakfast, after our good night's sleep, we looked out through the closed windows at the desert landscape, baking, dusty, waterless; and there, plodding along beside the track, as she had been all night and as she must through all the days and nights to come, was Mother, with no food, no drink, no arm to help her. She was too exhausted even to look at us, but she was condemned to stagger on, night and day, with no rest, until she died. On board the train our life went on, under a strain that we knew was increasing but that we also knew was temporary. Every day for us was a new exercise in patience—with Mother, for taking so long to die; with one another, for forcing us all to such mutual forbearance. And, as in all such confined situations, the patience and forbearance were in daily danger of cracking. Every day brought us the renewal of a mental and moral struggle to behave at least decently, if we could not act always in love. We could only ease our pent-up irritations in a low key and in oblique directions: in bitter skepticism about the art of medicine, in indignation against the hard professionalism of certain nurses. But mostly we had to swallow our feelings, and they stayed inside us like a lump of ugly pain. I had read, with no conviction, about the political maneuvering and conniving that used to surround the deathbed of a monarch; now, in our own house, I saw and joined in those politics.

Outside in the desert Mother was undergoing a simpler, more continuous and infinitely harder experience: dying.

Up to the last few days of flickering consciousness she was able to keep in touch with us, though her touch grew daily feebler. I still have some notes from those days:

"Aug. 8—She said to Dad tonight: 'I'm glad you're nearly eighty.'

"He said: 'So am I.'

"She said she had no feelings one way or the other about what hymns should be sung at her funeral, or the form of service. She said Mrs. Phillips had once told her that she and her husband Alex (who laughed so much that he was known as 'Ha-ha' Phillips) had once decided that they should discuss the kind of funeral they wanted, and had violently disagreed over the hymns; they finally had to stop because Mrs. Phillips was 'boo-hooing' so. Mrs. Phillips had told her all this shaking with laughter.

"Later that day she said how blessed she was in 'this kind of an ending'—without having lived so long that her mind failed her, and with her children all about her. She said she was sure she would know about us after she died; that (with a twinkle in her eye) 'she would keep an eye on us.' She looked forward not only to seeing much greater distances through space and time, but she was curious to know whether a theory of hers would prove to be right (and she thought it would): that she would be able to see *into* things—see how a tree's life goes on inside it, for instance.

"Aug. 15—They put her in an oxygen tent today, and she said from inside: 'This is a queer arrangement.' My father leaned towards her and said, 'I see you through a glass darkly, darling.' Hours later she woke from a nap and said to him: 'I see you quite clearly now.' "

(The oxygen tent brought out all her old distrust of doctors. She suspected, in spite of solemn assurances to the contrary, that its purpose was to prolong her life—which she considered unfair, and she was not going to be made a party to it. The doctor and my father finally persuaded her to try it, but the trial lasted only a day: she made them take it away again, saying that she felt too cut off from us.)

"Aug. 16—She opened her eyes and said drowsily to me: 'I dreamed you were Secretary of State.' The way she said it made it sound like a criticism.

"Aug. 19—Early this morning (about 6:30) Mother woke and said with surprising loudness and clearness: 'Can't talk. Can't breathe. Can't move.' She said it twice. The nurse asked her if she'd like a hypodermic. Mother muttered something, and then said, 'Try anything.' "

It must have been a day or so after that when she wrote her last note to me: "Tom darling—Please make Daddy go to bed at once —he is *dead* tired—has had a long hard day without one bit of rest. It will be lovely to see you—your loving Mother."

By "seeing me" she meant our final private meeting, which was to take place the next day: the last "little talk" we ever had. Like her grandchildren, all her children came in turn to say their farewells.

My last interview with Mother was a failure; at least, I thought so at the time. Now I am not so sure. To make certain that I said what I meant to, I had written it down. I sat by Mother's bed and read it to her. I was so moved by my own words that as I read them my voice choked, and I wept. Mother listened dry-eyed, with a smile. I think she patted my hand. If I had not known her so well (could I say, now, that I knew her at all?) I would have said that she was a little bored.

A few days later she died; and then suddenly all the things she had not said, all her life long, filled the emptiness and silence like a fanfare. Then that died away too, in the hushed bustle of preparations for the funeral, whose details she hadn't wanted to bother about, but which was efficiently arranged and managed by my father.

During her long dying we had watched her, every day and part of every night, seeing with anxious and helpless anguish how difficult it is to die even when you are willing, even when you are being a "good patient" about dying; that although you may have resigned yourself to death, your body will not resign and goes on refusing, every inch and every moment of the way, with a silent, implacable will of its own, yielding only little by little and more slowly than you would think humanly possible; that it is the hardest physical labor you will ever be called on to perform, and that you have to do it with no rest or let-up to the very end, alone, against an increasing deathly weakness which you must somehow fight until the weakness grows so overpowering that at last it can be fought no longer and at the end helps you to get there, where you have been struggling all this time to go.

We had also seen that when you are dying you become so preoccupied with what you are doing that you have no more strength or caring left to spend on anything else, including the people whom you used to love but whom you are now forgetting; that it does not matter to you now that they are watching you or that they feel a terrible anxiety about you in this suffering labor. They see your deathly weakness, and they cannot distinguish it from suffering; perhaps there is no distinction. You are the one who knows, and you cannot tell them. Their anxiety about you is not only that you may be suffering—in spite of the doctor's reassurance that you are "feeling no pain"; how can the doctor or anyone else but the dying person know what dying feels like?—they are anxious that you should die well.

Bona mors, a good death: meaning one that the onlookers can applaud. If you behave well, to the very end, it will be less painful for them. They want you to reassure them, by dying well, that even dying is not out of character. They see, though they shudder and reject the evidence, that you are giving them a preview of their own end, and they want you to set them a good example, one they can understand and admire and hope to imitate. But how can we tell how "badly" or how "well" a dying person is really acting? Why should we believe that they control their vanishing, their increasingly invisible, behavior? And which of us is in the position to judge?

My mother made a good death. If it were possible to impute motives to the dying, I would say that she did it on our account, so as not to give us more anxiety than she could help.

FINER CLAY, NICER SHAPES

I MUST HAVE BEEN ABOUT SEVEN when my parents decided—mainly, I think, on account of us children—to leave the city and move to Glendale, the little village fifteen miles north of Cincinnati that was largely inhabited and dominated by the Procters and Matthewses and their relations. My Grandfather Matthews had been one of the signers of the village charter, one of my uncles by marriage was rector of the church, and another the apparently permanent mayor. Most of the big houses belonged to members of my family, and the biggest, The Oaks, was my Grandfather Procter's. Glendale was a pretty place, and still is, with hilly, curving, tree-shaded streets, and a tiny shopping center on the depot square; in my day there was a livery stable, Igler's drugstore, a dry goods and notions store, a barber shop, and one or two others. The village has not changed very much in the past fifty years; it was a preserve then and it is a preserve now.

In those days it was connected with Cincinnati by a little branch railroad, the C. H. & D. (Cincinnati, Hamilton and Dayton), which before the days of the automobile carried my various uncles and cousins to their offices in town. Uncle Mortimer, my father's older brother, and the theoretical head of the family, was one of these daily commuters. He was a handsome man, even handsomer than my father: he had a proud, aquiline look and a quick, impetuous way of speaking. He described himself to us as "your favorite uncle."

I don't think we quite accepted this description or altogether believed in the jovial nature it implied, but I think on the whole we liked him. We didn't like his children, though we knew they were very close relations, closer than ordinary cousins; they were "double first cousins." Uncle Mortimer and my father were brothers and Aunt Marianna and Mother were sisters.

"The other Matthewses" lived at Opekasit, a big, dark-shingled house set off by itself on the edge of Glendale. With its dairy farm, the place had perhaps a hundred acres. Across the road from Opekasit, near the entrance to the driveway, was a small red-brick house of mid-nineteenth-century style, known as "the Eliza House." It had been one of the "stations" on the "underground railway"; runaway slaves from across the Ohio were passed from station to station all the way to the Canadian border. It was called "the Eliza House" because Eliza, the fugitive slave in *Uncle Tom's Cabin*, was supposed to have been hidden there after she had escaped Simon Legree's bloodhounds by crossing over the frozen river. This mixture of fact and fiction first made the Civil War real to me.

The site of Opekasit itself was an Indian burial ground, and in the front hall Uncle Mortimer had put an Indian picture-writing (or, more likely, a replica) which he liked to translate to visitors. According to him, "Opekasit" meant "looking westward."

Besides being a lawyer, Uncle Mortimer owned a model dairy farm which produced "certified" milk and no profits. He laughed a lot and made jokes, but we didn't think he was very funny. In the family, however, he had a reputation as a wit, and one of his witticisms was so much appreciated and so often repeated that it was still current by the time I was old enough to take it in: "The Matthewses may be finer clay but the Procters have nicer shapes."

The Matthewses did in fact consider themselves a cut above the Procters, partly because they thought themselves better bred— their Welsh-English descent being, in their eyes, superior to the Irish-English line of the Procters—but principally for two other snobbish reasons: they had been Americans for nine generations to the Procters' three; and no Matthews, so they said, had ever been "in trade." The Procters, on the other hand, had grown rich by the somehow shameful process of making soap, and also tallow candles to begin with. Even in Matthews eyes, however, they had now become respectable, since the Procter & Gamble Company was nearly a hundred years old, and had developed far beyond its humble beginnings. Uncle Cooper was very decidedly "in trade," but he was the grandson of the founder of the company and the third successive Procter to be its President. As he was a reserved, quiet man and had no children to boast about him, I never realized his true position in the family until he was dead.

The Matthewses, being much less shy and quiet, seemed to me far more important people as well as "finer clay," and I never admitted to myself till years later that I liked the Procters better and always had.

The fiercest upholders of Matthews superiority were not my father and my Uncle Mortimer, who as men, and successful professional men, could afford to be self-deprecating on occasion, but their sisters. The most formidable, Eva, was not simply a nun but a Mother Superior. There was always some confusion in our minds about whether we should call her "Aunt Eva" or "Mother Eva."

I think we solved it by calling her "Mother" to her face and "Aunt" behind her back. Mother Eva was regarded by her Matthews sisters as a saint. Her sisterhood, the Order of the Transfiguration, which she had founded herself, carried on various good works, the principal one a girls' orphanage, Bethany Home, and Mother Eva was supposed to be a great hand with children. Maybe she was, but we feared and hated her.

I didn't know what "martinet" meant, and I never saw Mother Eva meting out discipline the way I had seen my father among the choirboys or with Miss Whetstone, but my instinct told me that Mother Eva was more of a martinet than Daddy. And, though they soon learn to sing small and off-key themselves, children have an infallible ear for false notes; whenever Mother Eva came among us, she was accompanied by false notes.

On family occasions, when she was there, Mother Eva was less the Mother Superior but she never seemed to lose her position of authority: there was perhaps not much difference between being Mother Superior and being the Matthews sister superior. At these gatherings she laughed a good deal, and her way of laughing was very like my father's: with bared teeth and glaring eyes, a cry of challenge or of triumph. When she was really amused, which she sometimes was, her eyes screwed shut and her cheeks bunched. She too was famous, in the family, for her quickness of wit and her sense of humor. She was keen on theology, as my father was, and loved to argue about it. Both of them had come a long way from Calvinistic belief and the Presbyterian form of worship; in fact, they considered themselves more Catholic than Protestant. In the church politics of that time and place, my father was regarded as High Church, a position that queered his chances of succeeding Bishop Vincent, who was Low Church and wanted to keep his diocese that way; but his highness was as nothing compared to Mother Eva's. The services in the chapel at Bethany Home were smoky-sweet with incense and tinkly with sanctus bells.

The foreground of my childhood was dominated by the Matthewses and by the knowledge that I was inescapably one of them.

The possibility of escape never occurred to me, nor even the notion that I was caught; but if I could have put it in such terms I would have said that I was a conscript, not a volunteer, and that the prospect of my lifelong enlistment was discouraging. Though already I had learned to look down on the looser standards and lower aims of the Procter clan, I secretly envied their happier and luckier ways. They were not so strictly brought up and they seemed to have more fun. I knew they were unable to be more like us but I wondered why we couldn't be more like them.

These first faint stirrings of doubt did not rise quite to the level of consciousness. Besides, I was too young to know what doubt is for; and doubts about anything (except ourselves) were not encouraged by our parents. Nothing was clear to me, beyond my present duty of being a good little Matthews, and life was further complicated by the perplexing fact that the Matthewses themselves sometimes had fun too. One of these times was an annual party which seemed to me definitely a Matthews occasion, for they bossed it if they didn't own it: the Fourth of July.

My Uncle Mortimer, the eldest Matthews, was the host. Late in the afternoon everyone gathered at Opekasit for a picnic supper and an evening of fireworks. The party seemed to me an enormous crowd; I suppose there may have been thirty or forty people, of all ages. I think we had supper outdoors, but what we ate I can't remember, only that it was a feast, so we must have ended with ice cream and cake. And there was fruit punch and ginger ale; that was before the days of Coca-Cola, and Moxie was frowned on. The fireworks began as soon as dusk fell. The smaller children were given sparklers, and the older ones Roman candles; then the grown-ups took over. First it was pinwheels, nailed to various trees, and red fire; then balloons, and finally the rockets, great arcs of sighing fire that tore the night sky apart.

It's the balloons I remember as the most exciting—perhaps because it was still light enough to watch the preparations and because, if you were a boy, you were allowed to help, and perhaps because their launching was so precarious. The balloons were made of paper, and came folded together in long pleats. I think the big ones were five or six feet tall; at their open bottoms they carried a compact pad of wood shavings soaked in paraffin. They were launched from the stone parapet flanking the steps leading out to the lawn. One man would stand on the parapet, holding the top of the balloon, while his helpers pulled apart the flimsy paper sides. When the launching committee judged that the balloon was sufficiently hollow, the excelsior pad was set alight, and as the hot air began to fill it, those who held the balloon plucked out its folds until it was fully inflated and tugging to go. Then they released it, and slowly, amazingly, the illuminated paper bag rose and went sliding off with the breeze, dwindling into the darkening sky, sweeping out over the valley, shrinking to a dot, becoming a star. Quite often, however, it barely got off the ground before it burst into flames.

Though I remember the Fourth of July as the great family event, the peak of the year, and always connected it with Opekasit, nobody had to tell me that my Uncle Mortimer's was not the principal house in Glendale. It was evident which house that was: my Grandfather Procter's, The Oaks. When I think of a grand house, I still think of The Oaks. Grampa Procter had built it, seventy years or so before I was born; some time around the turn of the century it had burned to the ground and he rebuilt it just as it had been.

Perhaps it was not as grand as Jefferson's Monticello or Washington's Mount Vernon, but it had some of the same features and gave me some of the same feeling of classic simplicity. The Oaks was built of brick, painted white—and like them it had a row of two-story columns along its front. These columns rose from a broad porch that ran along the whole front and the west side of the house, and supported an extension of the roof. The house faced a sweep of flat lawn, bordered by tall oak trees. The front door was in the middle of this pillared portico, but when you arrived at the house you never went in that way; the entrance to The Oaks was at the side, under a porte-cochère, whose smaller pillars matched the ones in front. A flight of steps led up to a vestibule and into a conservatory, green with ferns and steamy with damp heat.

Name and Address

Inside The Oaks, my memories refuse to join. I couldn't draw a plan of the house, or even trace a sure line from one remembered spot to another. In some narrow hallway—was it upstairs or down?—hung a steel engraving of Grace Darling, the lighthouse keeper's daughter, valiantly rowing out through solid lumps of towering waves to rescue the crew of a wrecked vessel. She was only halfway there, but I could tell by her muscular style of rowing and the confident expression on her face that she would get every man jack of them. And on the newel post of the stairs stood the image of a turbaned Negro boy holding a fringed lamp. These two objects I remember with great distinctness: they must have been my favorite things to look at in The Oaks.

For the rest, the atmosphere of the house comes back to me as a faintly remembered smell: of furniture polish, floor wax, sachet (that must have been Gramma's room) and in the kitchen, which I loved and where I went often, a medley of odors in which I can only discern brown soap, tea and something like stew. On account of my grandmother, I suppose, all the servants at The Oaks were Irish. Two mainstays, who must have come originally as girls fresh out of Ireland, were still there the last time I visited the old house: Biddy McGuigan and Mary Jane. By then they were both ninety or better. They announced that they were not as spry as they had been, but they cackled with delight at seeing me, imperfectly disguised as a grown-up man.

And I remember well the feeling of spacious peace and security the house gave me: the sense of being under the eaves, especially in my grandmother's room, which was like being in a lofty nest. All the rooms had high ceilings, in the old-fashioned style; but her room must have felt just the right size to a child: not big enough to get lost in and full of warm presences, and with the windows looking out under the shelter of the porch roof. The library, with its black leather furniture and towering shelves of books, was too dark, and both the music room and the drawing room too large, foreign and formal for me. But I loved the upstairs, particularly Gramma's room, and the kitchen, and the broad porch.

Children have their sanctuaries no less than grown-ups, though they may not be aware of them as such. In Glendale, when we were little, our sanctuary was Cousin Ellen-and-Patty's house. There we always felt secure and free; as secure as we felt at home, and much freer. Cousin Ellen-and-Patty were cousins of my mother. They were old maid sisters, but the jolliest couple we knew. We always spoke of them as Cousin Ellen-and-Patty because it took too long to put in the second "cousin" and because Cousin Ellen was the elder. They were inseparable companions; it would have been impossible to think of one without the other. But they were very different to look at.

Cousin Ellen was dark, with a rather puckered expression as if she were biting off a thread. When she laughed, her face completely gave up, with the same Irish surrender to helpless wildness that Cousin Patty showed; you saw their likeness when they laughed. And when she was trying not to laugh Cousin Ellen could often not control her small dark brown twinkly eyes.

Cousin Patty was light, and her face was looser and easier than Cousin Ellen's. We thought she was pretty. Cousin Ellen would occasionally reprimand us, in the absent-minded way in which she might have spoken to kittens, sharply but hopelessly, and over in a minute. It was impossible to imagine Cousin Patty scolding anybody for anything.

Everything about their house was a delight to us. It was a small, dark-shingled frame house with a low privet hedge and a few bushes in front, and a cement walk leading in from the street. There were dozens of houses very like it in Glendale, but it seemed magically special to us. Even the cellar door, as it was called in our part of the country (the two slanting wooden flaps covering the outside steps down to the basement), which was exactly like every cellar door we had ever seen, was more fun to slide down than any other.

As you came up the walk to the front door of Cousin Ellen-and-Patty's house, as you set foot on the first of the two low steps that led to the porch (so went a family saying) you had better start talking then and there, and loudly, if you wanted to get a word in; because the next moment, the instant you opened the front door, you would be engulfed in cries of welcome, screams of laughter, cascading questions, comments and explanations, and swept away in the torrent. As children we didn't feel swept away but caught up in it and swirled along into accustomed delights that never lost their freshness; we liked the kind of noise Cousin Ellen-and-Patty made. It was a loud, cheerful, warming noise, like being in a nest with two large mother birds.

There were plenty of things to do in that little house. If you wanted, you could make a beeline for the spinning wheel that stood in a corner of the living room. In an ordinary house we would not have been allowed to touch it, for we knew it was very old and consequently valuable—had it come over from Ireland with Cousin Ellen-and-Patty's mother? In this house we could pedal it to our hearts' content, until our legs gave out. We enjoyed these vacations from home as only strictly-brought-up children could: the general relaxation from table manners, from being seen but not heard, the temporary amnesty from constant grown-up corrections. No doubt about it, Cousin Ellen-and-Patty spoiled us, and we liked that. But I think we liked even more the sense of being enjoyed and laughed at, the feeling of being loved.

We knew that there was some sort of grown-up ordinance against "eating between meals," but in this house the ordinance was a dead letter. Cousin Ellen-and-Patty took it for granted that children were always hungry and frequently needed at least a glass of milk and some oatmeal crackers. When there were fresh cookies or a cake, or blueberries were in season, we got them too.

Next door to their house, and in our minds almost a part of it, was Auntie Kent's. Auntie Kent was a stronger brew of tea than her nieces. We paid frequent calls on her, usually shooed over there by Cousin Ellen or Patty, and we didn't have to be told to be on our better behavior. There was something about Auntie Kent that said it for her. Not that she was awesome or that we were afraid of her; she was a lively old lady, and very entertaining; but in her presence we felt boundaries. Though she must have been in her seventies, her thick eyebrows and hair, low over her forehead in a widow's peak, were still almost jet black. She wore a lace cap and lace mantle. She looked rather like Cousin Ellen, but she had Cousin Patty's zest. Her house was neater and quieter than Cousin Ellen-and-Patty's, but Auntie Kent was quite capable of uproar. It was a controlled uproar, however, managed by herself, like a "spontaneous demonstration" at a political convention.

And in fact it was political. Auntie Kent was a Bryanite, and so were we when we were in her house. She marshaled us like doubtful delegates. She would gather us around the piano and teach us Bryan songs; they were more like lively hymns, and when Auntie Kent sang them you could feel her wild Irish fervor. If Auntie Kent had been a man, I am sure she would have enjoyed brawls. In her quieter moods she would read to us, and that was always pure entertainment, with no overtones of political zeal—Palmer Cox's Brownie books, or the adventures of a sea urchin.

For a brief period Charlotte and I were sent to Cousin Patty to learn our lessons. Perhaps it was a despairing interregnum between hopeless governesses. At any rate, it didn't last long. Cousin Patty was much too jolly and too easily thrown off the subject to succeed in teaching us anything. The attempt was a failure; or rather, from our point of view, a pleasant success that happily came to nothing. The failed experiment led to something even pleasanter: overnight visits to Cousin Ellen-and-Patty's house. On these delectable occasions we went two by two, as happily expectant as the fairy-tale animals into a child's Noah's Ark.

Even if we had had to sleep together we would have enjoyed the change from our own private cots at home. But, at least when we were very little, we didn't sleep together: one of us slept with Cousin Ellen and the other with Cousin Patty. In that household it was comparatively easy to postpone bedtime, or the final act of getting into bed, by various dodges; and with luck we would still be drowsily conscious when the gas light, turned down on our account, was put out altogether, and we felt the bed sink a little under the warm weight of a great female body. I preferred Cousin Patty to Cousin Ellen as a bed mate, though I was not sure why. Perhaps because she was prettier and slightly younger, perhaps because I thought she smelt nicer. Cousin Ellen in bed smelt faintly of pepper. I couldn't put a name to the smell I connected with

Cousin Patty. It was sweeter, more inviting, less spinstery. I think it was good-hearted femaleness.

Billy Burchenal, my second cousin, was my first real friend. He had a broad, flat face, the eyes wide apart (which I had been taught to believe, and still partly do, is a sign of good temper; my own are close together) and a flattened nose, which must have been broken when he was little and not set properly; it gave him the look of an old boxer. He was younger than I by some months, but already beginning gawkily to grow into the huge, big-boned frame that would dwarf his older brother and make even his father seem frail beside him. In those days he was still a little boy, near enough to my own size.

His life seemed to me catastrophic compared to my own: physical violence, with Billy as the target, was an everyday occurrence. If it wasn't his brother Chuck who beat him up for some crime of presumption, such as laying hands on Chuck's private property or trespassing on an area which was sacred to Chuck and his pals, it was his father who whaled him ruthlessly for not doing what he had been told, or for being "fresh," or for "being mean" to his younger sister (a dangerously expert tattletale), or for any one of a dozen reasons. Billy was amazingly absorbent of punishment. His yells of pain were as genuine as his tears, but as soon over. If the beating had been worse than usual, Billy might whimper out some threats from a safe distance, but these feelings faded away faster than the sting of his hurts, and soon he was back again in the purged, happier-than-ever present.

I liked Billy because he was happy, no matter what hit him. Billy himself didn't draw sharp distinctions between one person and another or care much who his playmates were; everybody liked him, so, within limits, he liked everybody.

When air rifles, which we called BB guns, came into our lives, it's a wonder none of us had an eye put out. The guns were not very powerful, luckily, and I suppose their lethal range was well under fifty yards; but even so . . . We soon got tired of shooting at targets, which we had been emphatically told were the only things we were allowed to shoot at. Lead soldiers were all right for a while, but even when they were protected by trenches a direct hit would knock their heads off, and there were no possible replacements till Christmas. We tried shooting at sparrows ("chippies," we called them, and pretended we needed them for soup) but when we accidentally hit one and only hurt it so badly it had to be finished off by smashing it with a rock, we felt sick.

Hens were a different matter. Billy explained that a BB pellet couldn't really *hurt* a hen, as its feathers were so tough; so for a while, whenever the devil entered us, we took pot shots at roving hens—trying to think of them, I suppose, as buffalo on the Great Plains. And once we staged Custer's Last Stand, with ourselves as the ruthless Sioux and an unguarded chicken run as the Little Big Horn. I can still remember the squawking, dusty panic of the bewildered hens, flapping and hurling themselves around their wire enclosure, and the *whump* of the pellets hitting them. (But no casualties; Billy was right.) We should have been rounded up, disarmed and confined to the reservation for that one, but we weren't caught; our criminal course still had a little way to run.

The streets of Glendale were lighted in those days by gas lamps, large, fragile, tempting targets shaped like old-fashioned policemen's beehive helmets upside down. At first we tried long shots from safe cover; when that resulted in misses or in merely cracking the glass we grew bolder, and from shorter range smashed several to smithereens. That caused grown-up talk which we overheard, and when we saw the marshal himself prowling around the town, in his broad-brimmed black hat, swinging the truncheon which we knew for a fact was tipped with a tiny needle point one touch of which was certain and instant death, we stopped shooting at street lamps.

One day I was up in Billy's room, on the third floor of the Burchenal house. The side window overlooked the house next door, about fifty yards away. This neighboring house belonged to Cousin Mary Johnston, an elderly spinster with bushy eyebrows who looked forbidding but wasn't. We both liked her and had nothing whatever against her. That was neither here nor there. We saw, as if for the first time, and perhaps simultaneously, Cousin

Mary's side windows. They were asking for it. By standing well back in the room, where we couldn't be seen, we had a clear, dipping field of fire against the whole side of Cousin Mary's house.

Did we each have our gun, or did we take turns with Billy's? At this point my memory begins to fail. But I remember to this day the little coughing pop of the gun, the streaking pellet catching the light in the sun, and the heartening tinkle of breaking glass. Something told us we had to work fast. After the second direct hit there were unmistakable signs from next door that the house was springing to life: purposeful voices called to each other, groping hands appeared at the windows, pulling the shutters closed. And here my memory calls a complete halt. It stands to reason that we were caught and punished severely. I suppose we were beaten. Our guns must have been confiscated, and somehow we must have been made to pay for the damage. We certainly must have had to tell Cousin Mary that we were very, very sorry. Perhaps the sequel was so awful that I refuse to remember it. Whatever did happen, the fact is that this inexcusable episode, which has left an appetizing taste in my mouth, ends in a blank.

Sometimes Billy and I were overnight visitors at Cousin Ellen-and-Patty's and were put to sleep in the same bed. By the time we got there—certainly at a much later hour than we could have managed at home—Billy was sleepy and would have dropped off the minute his head touched the pillow, if I had let him; but I wouldn't let him. I had discovered something which I didn't understand but which excited me to wakefulness and a determination to keep Billy awake too: I had discovered that Billy was more important to me than I was to him, but that I could make up stories he liked to listen to, even when he was sleepy. My whole effort was to hold his attention and keep him awake, like Scheherezade in the Arabian Nights; and, like her, I adopted the trick of telling a story to-be-continued. I had to, for Billy invariably fell asleep before the end. But I knew that he liked to listen, because the next time he would ask me to go on, or at least agree to my suggestion that I should.

I got so interested myself in this story-telling that I decided to write it down, so as to preserve it for—who knows?—a wider and more wide-awake audience than Billy. The eventual result was a story, which I imagined to be a novel, in some eighteen brief chapters, relating the adventures of a Spanish gentleman-brigand called Don Rodriguez. It was written in the most flowery language I was capable of—much fancier talk than I ever tried on Billy. I don't think he ever read the written version, or would have liked it much if he had.

It disappointed me too, in one way; I knew my novel was not as convincing as the enchanted stories I read to myself, like *The Black Arrow* or *Quentin Durward*, though I couldn't have said exactly how or why; but in another way I felt lifted up and carried forward on the wave of an enormous discovery. My yearning for Billy's friendship was not diminished, but it was matched and overmatched by this newfound magic, whose first taste brought a longing for more and more. I felt hungrily that there was some better relationship with words, if I could achieve it, than I could ever find with any person I knew. I didn't think such thoughts, in such terms; but I felt their presence.

When I went out to Glendale for Uncle Cooper's funeral, in 1934, I hadn't been back for fifteen years. I knew I was going to a family reunion; I didn't know it was to be the last one. I knew it was not to be a happy occasion, and yet I looked forward to it. And family loyalty demanded it. Family loyalty is perhaps not the right name for something deep in the blood that at such times calls us home.

When I woke in the morning and looked out of the Pullman window, the country had changed overnight. But had it really changed much? The same rolling farmland, steep little hills patched with woods, and now and then a muddy creek (could that be the Little Miami?) with a dusty white road meandering along beside it. It was like looking back fifteen years, and finding it all there. When the train rumbled through a small town, past a grade crossing beside one of those old yellow-brick stations (no, "depots") with the name on it painted in dingy 1870 lettering, I was so pleased I wanted to call out to the other people in the car, "See that? Isn't that wonderful?"

But what was so wonderful about this countryside, what was so special about these little roads that laced it together? They're just dusty, narrow, ordinary country roads; there must be hundreds of thousands, perhaps millions, like them, all over the world. No, these are the roads of my childhood; there are none like them anywhere on earth. This casual, unextraordinary landscape is really unique; it is not simply home but home long-lost, a place I can revisit but to which I can never go back. This is the land where I was born.

My brother-in-law Hal was at the station to meet me. Hal's hair was beginning to turn gray and he had put on some weight since his last trip east; otherwise he was just the same. His nervous, quiet manner made you feel he was being patient with you, and that his patience might not last forever. He was wearing a black tie, and I was glad I'd remembered to put mine on. When he asked me if I'd had my breakfast, which of course he did right away, his eyes filled with tears. It embarrassed me, there in the bright early May morning sunlight, as much as it must have embarrassed him. I knew he was ashamed of this affliction, which was simply a reflex, something to do with his tear glands, but in this case I knew it was more than that. Hal had been very fond of Uncle Cooper—"devoted" was the family word. It wasn't just that they were connected by marriage and that Uncle Cooper had been president of the company and Hal's boss. Hal had never said much to me about Uncle Cooper, but I knew he considered him a "great man," and the quotation marks were mine. I wondered if Uncle Cooper really was a great man.

We had to drive about fifteen miles from the station to Glendale, and the way Hal went took us through one factory district after another. These rows of factories and dingy workers' houses carried me back too, but not in a pleasant way. The acrid smell of —could it be soap?—was suffocating. I remembered wondering how anybody could get used to working there. I still wondered. Now we were on the Carthage pike, and everything I saw kept coming back to me with a rush. As we got nearer and nearer Glendale I couldn't help telling Hal when I saw houses and roads I remembered; and he would say, "Yes, that's So-and-so," or "No, I never heard of them." I forgot that he hadn't been a boy here too; there was nothing for him to get excited about.

We turned in at a driveway and Hal said, "Here we are." I knew the house well. It was the old Mitchell place; I had come here often to play Indians with the Mitchell boys. There had been a big asparagus bed down by the barn that had gone to seed and made a wonderful forest for ambushes. Now one of the Mitchell boys was dead and the other, I had heard, was a lawyer and wore eye-glasses on a ribbon. I asked Hal if the asparagus bed was still there and he said yes, it had been in bad shape but was coming along all right now. We stopped by the brick steps leading up to the front door, and I was surprised to see that the house looked just as big as it used to. As we went up the steps my sister Charlotte came out to meet us. She kissed me and said how *well* I was looking, and acted horrified at the news that I had had my breakfast on the train. She said I *must* come into the dining room and eat something, just to be sociable. She was in deep mourning, and though she didn't look as if she had been crying all night, the way Hal did, there was something absent-minded about her.

Mother met me in the hall. Tears came into her eyes as she kissed me, but she didn't break down as I was afraid she was going to. Uncle Cooper had been her only brother, and of the four sisters I think she was his favorite. She looked younger, almost girlish— and then I saw why. She had been constantly in mourning when we were children, and now she was dressed again the way I first remembered her.

They had been waiting breakfast for me, all but the children, who had had to get off to school. Charlotte explained that "of course" the public school and all the stores were to be closed to-morrow, the day of the funeral, out of respect for Uncle Cooper, but today everything was to go on as usual. And tomorrow the trains on the old C. H. & D., which carried only freight now, were to slow down to ten miles an hour as they came through Glendale.

As we settled back to the remains of breakfast, Charlotte talked a great deal, as she always did, energetically and cheerfully, about who was here and how well they all looked, and how wonderful

Aunt Jean—Uncle Cooper's wife—was being. Nobody else said much, but we all approved of the hearty atmosphere Charlotte was obviously determined to create. It was rather a strain but evidently the right thing to do. The only one who couldn't enter in, even passively, was poor Hal. His eyes kept betraying him all the time, and he had to blow his nose. Finally he made some excuse and left the room. Charlotte explained to Mother and me, though we both knew it, about Hal's affliction and how he couldn't help it— "though of course he feels this *terribly*. He and Uncle Cooper were *devoted* to each other."

After breakfast Charlotte suggested that I ought to go up to Woodlands and see Aunt Jean; she was really expecting me. I knew I should have suggested going myself. Hal had to make some arrangements in the village, so Charlotte drove Mother and me to Woodlands. I had hoped to find Aunt Jean alone, or almost alone, but from what Charlotte said, she wouldn't be: there had been a kind of continuous reception going on there for the last forty-eight hours. As we were turning in the drive, she told me that just after Uncle Cooper had died, when Aunt Jean was bringing "him" home, she had the chauffeur turn and drive through The Oaks, his father's place and the house where he had been born, "because she thought he would like it."

Woodlands had always seemed to me a very impressive house, almost palatial, but now it looked modest indeed to have been the home of such a rich and powerful man as Uncle Cooper. The little patch of woods at the entrance from which the place took its name stood on either side of a tiny glen that had once seemed to me an enormous ravine; I saw now that I could almost jump across it. The driveway crossed this "ravine" on a stone bridge, hardly bigger than a culvert, and then curved grandly up a hill, past the swimming pool (once it had been a cement tennis court; Charlotte and I had played there as children), swung round the house and deposited you under a porte-cochère of rough stone and dark shingles, like the house itself. From the screen porch on the left, I remembered, your arrival was always challenged by the excited clamor of dogs—Uncle Cooper's pointers and setters.

Today, no dogs. The cheerful-faced maid who came to the door greeted me by name, though I couldn't remember hers, and said Mrs. Procter was expecting us; she was in her sewing room. In this upstairs sitting room, bright with sunlight and chintz, and looking out on great oaks and a fall of lawn, Aunt Jean sat, in a little circle of sisters-in-law and cousins, most of whom were in fact sewing; the room was rippling with talk, muted to a little below normal. They all looked up with bright faces, and Aunt Jean came over to embrace us—a quick hug and the characteristic kiss of the "Glendale aunt": cheek lightly brushing cheek, mouth slightly pursed or half-smiling, and from the larynx a just-audible humming sound. With her hands on my shoulders she drew back her head and looked at me; behind her always insecurely wobbling pince-nez her eyes showed a quick shine of unshed tears. Then she smiled her undefeatable smile and said how glad she was I had come.

In the flurry of embraces that followed, some were less steady than hers; Cousin Ellen scowled with emotion, Aunt Marianna's mouth quivered; both produced handkerchiefs and blew their noses. While we were still standing, Aunt Jean asked me if I wouldn't like to see my Uncle Cooper. This was what I had most dreaded, but there was no way out. Aunt Jean led us through the open door into the next room. There on the bed, handsome, still, cold, very dead but oddly recognizable, lay my Uncle Cooper. It was the first dead body I had ever seen. One glance was enough, and more than enough, to last me for a long time; I felt it would take me years to digest the memory. But Aunt Jean's case was different from mine. She wanted us to sit down beside him "for a few minutes."

We drew up chairs and sat down. We looked at the body on the bed that was holding its breath with no effort, its eyes closed, its skin, taut over the high cheekbones and sharp-bridged nose, waxy and dry. Aunt Jean talked about him—almost, but not quite, as if he were really there. She told me how he had said to her, just the other day, that he wished he could have known me better; she thought, herself, that we were very much alike in some ways, and everyone had always remarked on our striking resemblance. Her voice was just as unaffected as it always was, just as matter-of-fact and cheerful. You would have thought that this dreadful object on the bed—handsomely arranged and handsome in itself, but dreadful more than handsome—was a familiar and beloved person, or at least an acceptable stand-in for the person. And so it was, so it must have been for her, who had been with him every inch of the way that had finally brought him here. But it wasn't that way for us. We watched him, lying unnaturally, absolutely still, with tethered and horrified intentness; hearing Aunt Jean's lively voice, her cheerfully accepting words, but quite unable to join her in naturalness. It became too much for me; I felt my eyes swimming and a sob rising in my throat. I followed Hal's example, and got up and left the room.

The house had begun to fill up. I nodded to several dimly-remembered faces. The arriving women were all purposeful, clutching something wanted or bringing the needed answer or supplying in themselves the summoned necessity, heading straight for the pantry or the conservatory or Aunt Jean. The men, on the other hand, were aimless and uneasy, and tended to drift outside, where they felt less guilty about smoking. I joined a group near the front door; Cousin Franklin Leach, in a low voice because of the Sunday-like atmosphere, was telling a funny story. Normally, the sudden point would have brought guffawing yells of laughter, but today, though one man doubled up as if he had been hit in the belly and smacked his hand on his thigh, he smacked it softly; another clapped his hand over his mouth, shooting up his eyebrows and staring wildly at me; all our laughter was as muted as if we had been wearing silencers.

In the sun room, a porchlike place with windows on three sides and lined with ferns and potted plants, a group of older men was sitting. They were of an age when they could sit in silence, but today they felt that speech was required of them; slowly, pompously, repetitiously, the inadequate clichés were voiced. Did I imagine it, or did I hear also an undertone of dismay? Is this all? Can no one find anything better to say than this? Why, then, when they come to say it about *us*, it may not even be as good as this! Certainly no better; but this is not good enough.

I went outside again, and found my cousin Bill Burchenal. He said, "Let's get out of here and go to my house." It felt like playing hooky but it was a relief to get away from that tiptoeing, breath-holding, low-voiced, waiting-for-what air. In Bill's study, with drinks in our hands, we could speak out, and in a normal voice. Bill's normal voice was like a threatening bull's. "Cousin Olivia is the best of those sisters," he announced. (I wondered if he'd forgotten that my mother was one of them.) "One minute the tears will be stream-ing down her face, and the next she'll be shaking with laughter at something someone has said. It's the Irish in her." I tried to talk about Uncle Cooper, but there was little I could find to say, except that I had hardly known him. Bill, it appeared, felt that he had not known him much better. "To think I might have seen a lot more of him," he said. "A really great man living just up the street."

That night the younger men of the family, in pairs, took turns sitting up with the body. He (I still couldn't think of Uncle Cooper as "it") had been put in his coffin and carried down into his study. My turn was from three in the morning till seven, and my partner was my cousin Stanley Matthews. We didn't talk much, but one thing Stanley said surprised me: "Uncle Cooper was a fine man but he stood for the wrong things." What did he mean by that? I thought at the time that he was referring to Uncle Cooper's political views, which were Republican—and Stanley was a "Christian Socialist"; but I think now that he meant something else as well: that Uncle Cooper had no right to be such a good man, such a successful man—and also a Procter; his example somehow belittled the Matthews virtues and the Matthews performance. Also I didn't think Uncle Cooper should be discussed in *that* room. I said stiffly, feeling like an admonishing undertaker: "Uncle Cooper was a man; he has come to a man's end—defeat and death." There was no meeting of minds between Stanley and me, then or ever.

Next day, from nine in the morning till noon, the workers from Ivorydale, more than two thousand of them, came to pay their last respects. Since the C. H. & D. no longer carried passengers, they came by car, choking Glendale's little roads with the abnormal traffic. All morning they plodded up the drive to Woodlands, filing into the house and shuffling slowly through the library, past the open coffin. Some brought their children. The old people, who mainly had a German look about them, were the most visibly affected. One old man, his eyes brimming, boasted, "I taught him how to boil soap." Another, tiptoeing out of the library, turned in the doorway and blew a kiss at the dead man.

Before the funeral at the church that afternoon there was a family service at the house, around the still-open coffin. Aunt Jean, my mother, and Uncle Cooper's other sisters, in heavy black, knelt close about its head; the rest of us stood, jammed together in the hushed, stifling air, choking with the scent of flowers. Now, at the end, we felt most like a family. And the sense of family was strong in us as we walked in procession, the older ones first, through the silent crowds outside the church and up the aisle through the waiting congregation to our empty pews at the front. As the choir and clergy marched slowly in ("The strife is o'er, the battle done") I expected to see my father in the place of honor at the rear, but the last man was old Bishop Vincent, much gaunter and more shrunken than I remembered him, and looking almost impossibly old. He was too feeble to conduct the service, but it was he who pronounced the benediction and then, coming shakily down from the altar to stand by the coffin, in his old man's hollow-booming voice gave Uncle Cooper his quittance: "Depart, O Christian soul . . ."

On the hot, slow ride in to Spring Grove Cemetery the tension of the ceremony began to relax, but we still felt committed to ceremoniousness, so that for a while nobody talked, nobody liked to be the first to light a cigarette. All of a sudden we were too tired to keep it up any longer: smoking and conversation burst out like a sigh of relief. When we got to the cemetery we braced ourselves again, in deference to Aunt Jean and to what must be her feelings in this final scene. But it was a lengthy walk from the place where we got out of our cars, through the rolling masses of heavy, expensive, ugly monuments, most of them with German names, to the little hillock, almost like an Indian mound, surmounted by a granite obelisk marked PROCTER; and our procession straggled.

The actual burial of the dead, "the committing of his body to the ground," according to the rites of the Church, always seems to me terribly—or is it mercifully?—quick: the few prayers, the ritual handful of crumbled earth rattling on the coffin lid, the final blessing. The smoothness of the undertaker's art, which is supposed to divert attention from the necessary stage business, in fact does just the opposite. That mounded rug of imitation grass concealing the heap of fresh earth only succeeds in calling attention to the thing it tries to hide; that tubular framework supporting the coffin on broad webbed straps which magically begin to unwind when one of the undertakers crouches deferentially forward and turns a releasing catch—all this is very smooth and artful, but it can continue only up to a point, and now that point has been reached.

The last lines having been spoken, the webbed straps having ceased to quiver, the curtain is declared to be down and the audience should now go home. The real stagehands are waiting impatiently in the wings, dressed in overalls, not in black coats, and with shovels in their hands. The undertakers, who want everything as painless as possible, still cannot force the bereaved family to go; neither can they indefinitely keep at bay the men, whose working time is regulated by union rules, waiting to whip the fake grass covering off the pile of earth and shovel it into the grave and get the job done.

This time nothing untoward happened. Aunt Jean showed no sign of leaving, though everything was now finished. We couldn't see her face or her eyes, hidden behind her heavy black veil, but we could see that she was leaning forward and peering intently down into the grave. The rest of us, aware of the undertakers' anxiety or simply of our own desire to get away, drew back a little farther and stood aimlessly; a few on the fringes began to tiptoe off. But we didn't like to leave Aunt Jean alone. Perhaps the gravediggers, union rules or not, would have let her stand there as long as she wanted, for this was not quite an ordinary funeral to them either. In a few minutes, however, her brother, Cousin Alec, went up to her and touched her shoulder and whispered something. She raised her head and, taking his arm, walked slowly but firmly away.

At that moment I realized that Uncle Cooper had been the head of the family, and that he had left no successor.

Part Two

Part Two

FOUR SCHOOLS

I WENT TO FOUR SCHOOLS and two universities. Every one of them was a private institution; for, although my parents paid their taxes and thus subscribed to public education, they would not have dreamed of sending any of us to a state school. My father's career took him to various places, so I went to various schools. My second university I chose myself, partly to get away from my family, partly to put off the evil day of starting my own career.

The first school was very private. Shortly after we moved from Cincinnati to Glendale, Charlotte, Mary Ann and I began lessons with Miss Emily Spooner. Miss Emily was governess to the three youngest Clevelands, our first cousins, who were just our ages: eleven, eight and six. Our schoolroom was on the top floor of Oakencroft, a gingerbread Victorian house that had once been my Grandfather Matthews' and was now my Aunt Grace's. We looked out of dormer windows to the treetops.

Our school with Miss Emily could only have lasted two years, but I remember it as a long, slow, calm time that flowed on and on. She and the schoolroom went well together; both were as neat as a plain pin and both gave off the same invigorating air of sharpness. She was spare and rigidly erect; she wore old-fashioned steel spectacles, hair parted in the middle and drawn back to a tight bun, and a dress of invariable dark gray, with white collar and cuffs, and a shiny leather belt with a square steel buckle. She seemed ageless; I suppose she may have been in her 40s.

We each sat at our own desk, facing the blackboard and Miss Emily behind her table. In one corner stood a pot-bellied iron stove, which was lit only on chilly days. We always began with prayers, followed by a writing lesson; after that Miss Emily set us different tasks and expected different things of us. She never gave up and she never let up. None of us were stupid children, but Johnny Cleveland was odd; he was really delicate and wore queer shoes because of his arches; he also had a small wen on his left temple which interested us, though we had been told never to speak of it. Johnny was excitable, and sometimes he would fall into sulky despair or a tantrum and have to be removed by Miss Emily. That made us feel important, like eyewitnesses at a street accident.

Miss Emily was no innovator, and her plan of study was based on the three Rs, but the lessons I particularly remember are the Psalms and Greek history. Thanks to her belief in learning things by heart, I can still recite most of the 19th, 23rd, 95th, 100th and 121st Psalms, and scraps of some others. I think it was her secret ambition that eventually we should learn the entire Psalter—with the possible exception of the monster 119th, which has 176 verses and runs for two and a half days in the Prayer Book.

Because Miss Emily was literal we gave her back what we got from her. There must be worse ways of beginning an education; and, for such reverencers of authority as we were, it was the only conceivable way. She encouraged us to be precocious and priggish, as witness this nine-year-old essay of mine: "Although Socrates was such a good man he had many enemies, who were jealous of his wisdom, and hated him because he was so good, so they falsely accused him of giving bad advice to the young men, and speaking ill of the gods. The judges, blinded by prejudice, condemned him to die the base death of a criminal. He was chained in prison for a while and his pupils were allowed to visit him and when the jailer entered the cell, bringing the cup of poison, Socrates drank it all and lay down upon his pallet, and kept on teaching his pupils till he died. And, to use Plato's words, 'Thus died the man who, of all with whom we are acquainted, was in death the noblest, and in life the wisest and the best.'" Who did I think I was—John Stuart Mill?

We had all the books that well-brought-up children had in those days, and read them all: the usual collections of fairy tales, Grimm, Hans Andersen, the Andrew Lang books and Howard Pyle's; *Alice in Wonderland* and *Through the Looking-Glass* and *The Hunting of the Snark; The Wizard of Oz*, and all its diminishing descendants; Lear's *Nonsense Book* (some of the drawings I thought alarming rather than funny, and some of the verses and limericks just silly); *The Jungle Books* and *Just-So Stories; The Water Babies, The Prince and the Pauper, Captain January, The Little Colonel, Uncle Remus* (which Uncle Mortimer, at his own suggestion, would often read to us aloud); the E. Nesbit books and Beatrix Potter; the George Macdonald books about the Princess and Curdie and the goblins.

The first books I remember reading "all by myself" were animal stories by Ernest Thompson Seton, and from them I got the idea that the lives of animals—which I thought of as lesser and less fortunate kin to human beings—are sad and always end sadly. I can still repeat the words (which I could never read without a sob) that close the story of *Bob, Son o' Battle*—or perhaps they were printed under the last picture: "Dry-eyed the old man sat there, nursing the dead dog's head." When I fell under the spell of Kipling, and made the acquaintance of animals who behaved and talked like gallant or villainous cowboys in the grip of a code, I was half aware that the truth and I were both being bullied. In some of the *Jungle Book* stories—in *Kaa's Hunting* or *Red Dog*—I felt something truer and stronger: primeval fear.

I read in any direction, though of course not in all, and with no real choice in the matter. With a few exceptions, like the forbidden Russian fairy tales, all these books were put in my way. I don't like to think I could have found Jacob Abbott all by myself. That was Miss Emily's doing. Jacob Abbott was famous in my father's childhood for his didactic stories about a little paragon named Rollo; Jacob and his brother John also wrote for Victorian children a whole shelfful of biographies, thoroughly scrubbed, rinsed and starched—all the "great ones" of history, from Genghis Khan to Napoleon. Reading them was a chore, but I liked the feeling of a chore accomplished.

Another historical writer soon made me forget all about the Abbotts. G. A. Henty too wrote about history, but always as a story of high adventure, in which you naturally and inevitably took sides with the hero. This led me into some perplexing situations. When it came to the American Revolution, how could I be "true to the old flag," or be expected to sympathize with the "loyalists" (whom I had been taught to call "Tories") against the American "rebels"—patriots to me? And how could I, the grandson of a northern colonel, be asked to admire and uphold the Confederate cause in the Civil War, however dashing it might seem to be *With Lee in Virginia*? In Henty's company these great quarrels were not only oversimplified but sometimes, from my point of view, turned inside out. This left me with an uncertain view of history, as a story which could be told from at least two different points of view. And that was not a bad thing. Henty put the germ of skepticism in my head.

It was still only a germ, however, when I was being hornswoggled by Horatio Alger, Jr. Why didn't I recognize him and his rags-to-riches stories as the direct if degenerate descendant of Jacob Abbott? Anyhow, I didn't. The only Alger book whose title I can remember now is *Andy Grant's Pluck*, but I must have read at least six of them. The hero was always a poor boy, the son of a widowed mother. There was always a scene in which the boy manages to make himself useful to a rich man. Then the young hero, with antlike industry and Yankee thrift, got to work, adding dimes to quarters and finally multiplying silver dollars, until he rescued his mother and married the rich man's daughter. The effect of these stories, if not their aim, was to whet the appetite for money and for the kind of success that can be translated into money. Heady stuff for a poor boy. I wonder how many self-made millionaires got their first revelation from Horatio Alger. I wasn't a poor boy, and the false appetite these books whipped up in me was fairly soon overcome by boredom and then shame that I could ever have liked them.

When a child begins to read, his taste is neither catholic nor omnivorous: he doesn't know enough to be catholic, and he reads only what he bumps into and what also appeals to him. Even now it's no use my telling myself reprovingly that Macaulay is not even a second-rate poet; all I have to do is to remember the opening lines of *Horatius*:

> *Lars Porsena of Clusium*
> *By the Nine Gods he swore . . .*

Four Schools

Or *The Battle of Naseby:*

It was about the noon of a glorious day of June
That we saw their banners dance, and their cuirasses shine;
And the Man of Blood was there, with his long essenced hair,
And Astley, and Sir Marmaduke, and Rupert of the Rhine . . .

and my skin bristles as A. E. Housman's did when a line of "pure poetry" came into his mind.

Most of the poems I knew and liked as a child sounded to me like the bray and pound of a military parade. There's softer and better music, but that's a kind of music all the same. Likewise with prose (a depressing word I never liked); my name for that was stories, and I liked best the ones that spellbound me: Barrie's *Peter Pan*—the one in Kensington Gardens, not the later pantomime Peter; Stevenson's *Treasure Island* and *The Black Arrow;* Pyle's *Men of Iron, Otto of the Silver Hand* and *The Garden Behind the Moon.* These were all magic. *Tom Sawyer* and *Huckleberry Finn* were not: they were too real and too close to home.

When I was ten, my father took us to England for a year. Was the censorship on my reading not yet in force? I don't think it could have been, or I would never have been allowed to read those bound volumes of the *Graphic* I found in the billiard room at Shrub's Hill. The pictures drew me in to the pages, and soon I was reading instalment after instalment of the serial stories—none of which were meant for a ten-year-old reader. I had never heard of Rider Haggard, H. G. Wells or Thomas Hardy, and didn't know till much later that they were the authors of those stories I first read on the billiard-room floor: *King Solomon's Mines, When the Sleeper Wakes,* and *Tess of the d'Urbervilles.* Perhaps I was discovered reading *Tess,* and that started the censorship; I shouldn't wonder.

At any rate, this first experience of the grandeurs and miseries of grown-up stories started up a precocious taste for reading that was beyond my years and of course to a great extent beyond my understanding. I couldn't have said what these books were about, nor given a coherent report of the stories they told, and many of their words—no doubt whole paragraphs or pages—must have been incomprehensible to me; nevertheless I understood enough to keep me going, and some of their scenes left such an etching on my mind—the clustered assegais of Chaka and his Zulu *impis;* the enormous glassed-in vaults arching over Wells's London of the future; Stonehenge at dawn, with the cordon of police advancing on the doomed lovers—that they stayed with me for the rest of my life. From this too-early initiation I went on, always out of my depth but always keeping up somehow, until at fifteen my favorite writer was Joseph Conrad, and *Heart of Darkness* and *The Nigger of the Narcissus* the books I liked the best.

These earliest encounters were accidental, but the later ones had something dogged and deliberate about them. Though I knew I was diving in over my head without really being able to swim, I couldn't resist doing it; I enjoyed the sensation and risked the half-drowning. When I was about twelve I found a book whose enchantment exactly suited me. The book was really two books but I made no distinction between them: *Dream Days* and *The Golden Age,* by Kenneth Grahame. They were all about children but they were written for grown-ups, by a grown-up who actually remembered what it was like to be a child, and who therefore stood simultaneously at two vantage points in time. The wonderful thing was that I understood him perfectly (or thought I did); while I was reading the book I could borrow his ability to be in two different times at once. It was as if I too were remembering my own childhood—as if I were projecting myself years ahead and looking back at the present.

I knew this was magic, in a literal sense. It could not be induced simply by reading, although certain passages had more evocative power than others. To start the charmed ball spinning required at first the blend, the just right blend, of word and picture. The Grahame books were illustrated by an artist, Maxfield Parrish, whom I considered a sorcerer in his own right. The most effective way of summoning up the spell was to read a page or so from the essay called *Its Walls Were as of Jasper,* and then stare hard at the accompanying picture: a small truant boy looking out over meadows at a turreted city climbing to the sky. Eventually I found

that all I needed was the picture; and after a while not even that—
remembering it did just as well.

Where did I go on the magic carpet of these trances? Not always, or even usually, into the future, where in any case I was sure
to lose myself without my grown-up guide, for everything recognizable there was made of the memories of his past, not mine.
I cannot say with any certainty where I went, except away. I went
out and away from the present, from my childhood. Perhaps I
went into a childhood that I wished I could have, and dreamed
myself into the boy I wanted to be, brave enough to be myself
and lucky enough to be happy.

England in 1911. How far away it seems now; how present it
was then: solid with life, sure and permanent, of an authorized
security; unaware of brinks and imminent catastrophes. The air it
breathed was an air of quiet certainty, a deep conviction that the
rest of the world existed to supply England with the raw materials
of empire, a respectful audience, and a retinue to follow its moral
lead; the unspoken faith that England was not only the embodiment but the culmination of history.

England in 1911 was an impressive place; to a ten-year-old
American boy, overwhelmingly and unforgettably impressive.
From the first moment of landing at Tilbury, in a chilly January
fog, I was enthralled and attentive. I regarded everything I saw
with equal reverence: the Abbey, the Underground, Nelson's column, St. James's Park, Madame Tussaud's, the Crystal Palace, the
hansom cabs. I particularly noted "Sir Landseer's" pictures of animals at the Tate; the Turners there seemed to me "awfully queer."

It was Coronation Year, to cap everything, and later (I remember it as a glorious day in June; even so, I suppose it must have
rained a little now and then), from seats in a stand near St. Mar-
garet's we watched the pomp and circumstance of the procession,
with George V and Queen Mary almost visible in the royal coach.
We were also taken to the naval review off Spithead. As our
crowded little excursion steamer spanked over the waves, I saw
with duller and duller eyes the long lines of England's great navy

stretching out into the distance, with a visiting warship from every other fleet lending its complimentary presence. The American battleship (was it the *Delaware*?), conspicuous with its basket-work masts, was pointed out to me, and then, while the thunder of the saluting guns shook the deck, I wriggled desperately to the rail through the indignant crowd, and was sick.

But all that came later. In January we went into lodgings at Bournemouth while my parents looked for a house. They found one in Lyndhurst, in the heart of the New Forest. Shrub's Hill was like everything else in England then: solid, comfortable, roomy, well provided. There was a butler named Veal, a coachman named Holes, a gardener named Golden—ten servants altogether. Those were spacious days for the rich.

A mile outside the village there was a small preparatory school, Park Hill, which I entered as a day-boy. The school had only fourteen boys; all but myself and one or two others were boarders. The school building must originally have been a country house of moderate size, square-built in the early Victorian style. The grounds spread over two hundred acres, and included a playing field and a pond, where we swam in the summer. Those of us who were still learning to swim were suspended at the end of a line tied to a pole.

The first thing that happened to me at Park Hill was that I was re-dressed. Everyone was horrified at the thinness and sleaziness of the American suit I was wearing, and a tailor was immediately called in to make me "some proper clothes." I was then assigned to the Third Form, the lowest of the school's three forms, seated on a wooden bench (also, confusingly, called a "form"), an open book was put into my hands, and I was told, "Learn this."

Though no one bothered to tell me that the book I had been handed was a Latin grammar, that Latin was a dead language now considered a useful tool for drilling openings into the heads of schoolboys, and though it seemed surprising to me that *mensa*, a table, should be followed by a list of words quite a lot like it but subtly different, and though it had never occurred to me that any-one might want to *speak* to a table ("O table!" the book said)—

nevertheless, since I had been told to memorize this mystery, I tried. Gradually, after some days and certain cautious inquiries, it dawned on me that Latin was a kind of dry game whose rules, once you discerned them, could eventually be mastered. My teachers were not, I think, notably stupid, and according to their traditional lights they were kindly men; but that was the way they had been taught, so that was the way they taught us.

I was the only American in the school; the other boys were English, from all over the Empire. The youngest was only eight. My three great friends were Willie Hombersley, from Trinidad, Harry Dale, from Ireland, and Harold Sandwith—I can't remember where he came from. We soon made common cause against the foe, an older boy (perhaps twelve) in the Second Form, named Barker-Hahlo. He had white hair and teeth like a rabbit, and grinned a lot. I'm not sure that Barker-Hahlo ever actually knew he was the foe, or that he ever did anything hostile, beyond an occasional lording it over us; but we were sworn to bring about his downfall, and were always plotting it.

I remember my year at Park Hill as a time of extraordinarily innocent bliss. I was so happy there that I was almost conscious of it at the time. Even now certain winter smells, of damp gravel paths and rhododendron bushes, and certain sights, like misty sunlight over still pasture land, bring back the happiest year of my childhood. I suppose this serenity was due partly to being constantly with boys of my own age—the older boys, who seemed a different generation, paid no attention to us—and that I found them companionable because they were as sheltered in their Englishness as I in my family upbringing. In spite of the difference in nationality we had a good deal in common: I think the greatest thing was our innocence. We knew nothing about sex, nor that there was anything to know. As I remember, we weren't even curious about it. We had our off-color jokes, and knew they were off-color, but they had to do with other bodily matters. We thought farts were uproarious (though we were not sure of the word itself; for years I thought it was spelled "fort") and were always exchanging news and rumors of the latest and loudest. And a quiet apple-cheeked boy named Richards was for some time famous in the school for having "stuck a Relief up his bum." (A Relief was the kind of stub pen-nib we used in our lessons.)

I had my rebuffs, but they were not wounding. It was inevitable that the topic of America should sometimes lead to arguments, which sometimes led to fights, but they were more like scuffles, never desperate affairs. I didn't much mind being regarded as an incompetent authority on my native land. When I was asked if people in Cincinnati lived in log cabins and did we ever see Indians in the streets, I learned to shake my head with an ambiguous smile, as if I were not telling all I knew. On two occasions I went too far. Once I announced that I had seen a hummingbird in Ohio (later I was to see them much farther north than that, in Rhode Island). When I stuck to my story, a master was appealed to: "Please sir, Matthews says—" The master settled my hash in short order, ruling with quiet firmness that hummingbirds were never seen north of South America. And another time I ventured to say (though I was not really quite sure of this one) that in baseball the pitcher could throw the ball so that it would curve in the air. The master was appealed to again, and again threw me out of court.

The masters were kindly men, as I say, according to their English lights; and it occurs to me now that their distaste for America and their distrust of the American mind, some of which came out in their dealings with me, were not signs of hostility but of complacency—the maddening characteristic that makes England so little, but that, transmuted into pride and courage, makes Britain so big.

The summer term at Park Hill, which, in the English custom, lasted half the summer, was a heavenly time for a small boy. I never tasted such physical happiness again until summer term at Oxford, an equally heavenly time for a young man. Besides swimming in the pond, and occasional school outings to the sea, we had the run of the countryside. There were no definite school boundaries, or if there were, they were not taken seriously, and we had as much of the New Forest to roam in as we could reach in an afternoon. Sometimes we went butterfly-hunting, chasing fritillaries and Purple Admirals and big moths over the gravel pits and clumps of furze; but our favorite sport was bushwhacking, a game in which we stalked each other through the forest, opening fire with cap pistols (we had a crude model of repeater, with a roll of caps in the magazine) whenever we could see an enemy head exposed, or an arm or leg.

Once, returning sweaty and thirsty from one of these long, creeping and running summer afternoons, I was caught at the water cooler by one of the masters. The water cooler stood in the hallway of the school and must have been entirely for show, for I never saw anyone take a drink from it. I learned now that such a thing was in fact against the rules, and the master improved the occasion by reading me a lecture, the point of which was that the Americans were a nation of dyspeptics, and no wonder; we drank "iced water" and wore belts instead of braces. I might have told him, but of course knew better, that the water in the cooler was a long way from being iced, and might have reminded him that all of us at the school wore belts when we were playing any kind of game outdoors. Instead, I learned to save my thirst for tea.

One feature of the school meals which much impressed me was the sight of Mr. Ridout, the headmaster, downing his pint at lunch. He sat at the head of the long table, and always began by taking a solid pull at his tankard, after which he would carefully wipe his drooping mustaches. As he tipped up the tankard you could see through its glass bottom the level of the beer sinking, like an hourglass running out, but faster.

At the beginning of term we were allowed to bring a box of candy, from which, as long as it lasted, we could take a daily ration. When I was a boarder, in my last term, Hombersley and Dale and I, who shared a bedroom together, used to bribe the matron with sweets from our boxes to tuck us in at night. We were all slightly ashamed of this practice, which showed that we missed our mothers, but we persisted in it. The matron would probably have tucked us in without a bribe, but we didn't want her to tell on us, and thought we would make sure of her.

We were to be friends for life, Hombersley, Dale, Sandwith and I. We were full of schemes and plans, stretching every which way, and far beyond the downfall of Barker-Hahlo. Dale had a Gaelic primer whose very possession, he gave me to believe, was some-how illegal. He and I decided to learn Gaelic, studying it after lights-out. Why? I have a feeling that we thought there was some-thing revolutionary about it. A couple of years later, when my family had moved to Minnesota, I had a letter from one of them (I think it was Harold Sandwith), saying that he was coming to New York for a few days and could I meet him at the dock? He gave me no address in New York, nor the name of the ship, and the letter didn't reach me until after the date of his arrival. I never saw or heard of him, or of any of them, again.

Nine years later, after the war that had wiped Edwardian Eng-land off the face of the earth, I revisited Lyndhurst with my father. The school had been sold, the Ridouts had moved away to the Isle of Man. No one knew anything about any of the boys: which of them were still alive or where any of them were.

In the summer of 1913, when I was twelve, we left Glendale for good, and moved to Minnesota. My father had been elected dean of the cathedral in Faribault, a small town of about 10,000 people in the southern part of the state. Faribault was named after a French *voyageur* who had explored those parts and is still pro-nounced in French fashion by Minnesotans; other Americans are apt to miscall it Fairbault.

In 1913 Faribault seemed a very settled place. The town's liveli-est memories were of the Jesse James boys, who, a generation be-fore, had held up a bank in Northfield, twenty miles away. Since those days nothing had happened worth mentioning. The town itself was strung out along one bank of the Straight River. On the other bank, a high bluff, stood a series of institutions: St. James's, a military school for little boys; Shattuck Military Academy, its older brother; St. Mary's, a school for girls; a school for the deaf-and-dumb; a home for imbeciles (known locally as "the Imbies"); and Seabury, a theological seminary.

I first saw Shattuck, where I was to spend two happy years, in the peaceful, deserted drowsiness of summer. The ugly rough-stone buildings, most of them Victorian, some of them mercifully masked in ivy, the cement walks, the sweep of the parade ground, seemed to me venerable if not aged. The waiting buildings were full of interesting smells: the clean, sweet redolence of oil in the gun room, where the long ranks of racked rifles told me instantly: "You will be a soldier!" (My heart leapt, my back stiffened, I never bothered to say good-by to the bishop I had planned to be); the sickly odor of oiled leather hymnbooks (that was banana oil) in the gloomy little chapel; the airless, watery exhalation from the indoor swimming pool; the fumes of arnica and old sweat in the locker room. I gazed worshipfully at framed photographs of the Crack Squad, of the battalion passing in review. I could hardly wait to get into uniform.

Shattuck was an old school, for that part of the country. It had been founded in 1858, only a few years later than my father's school, St. Paul's, which I thought of as the oldest and grandest in America, and to which I knew with dim dread that I was some day fated to go. And Shattuck too was a "church school"—the boys had to go to chapel every day, and the services were Episcopalian. I am sure that my parents had no idea of the real quality of Shattuck. Neither had I until some time later.

I was twelve when I entered, the youngest boy in school and the next-to-smallest. Varney II was the smallest, a good half-inch shorter than I was. We were equally puny, and our puniness was soon shamefully advertised. The rifles which had so excited me when I saw them in the gun room were Krag-Jorgensens, the kind that had been used by the Army in the Spanish-American war. From butt to muzzle they were nearly as tall as Varney II or me, and almost more than we could handle: the manual of arms was a wrestle for us. There was one movement, "inspection arms," we simply could not perform. At the command, you were supposed to throw the rifle smartly up to the position of "port arms"— diagonally in front of your body—immediately pulling back the bolt to open the cartridge chamber *and* (this was the catch) pushing open the magazine box at the side of the rifle. This magazine box had a flange for the thumb and opened against the pressure of a heavy steel spring. Varney II and I were not strong enough to open that box with one thumb: we had to take two hands to it.

This caused such scandalous confusion in the ranks that a Special Order was issued, excusing Cadet Privates Varney II and Matthews from carrying out this thumb motion.

The older boys were in my eyes completely grown-up men. They were certainly older and hairier than the run of Sixth Formers nowadays. The athletes were of course the school heroes. There was another big boy who became a temporary hero, though he was no athlete. Bagley was addicted to chewing tobacco, and may have started a fad for it in the school; anyway, one day there was a surprise inspection: the Commandant strode down the ranks, glaring into a rippling series of opening mouths. Whoever else was caught, it wasn't Bagley. The news was all over school in half an hour: *Bagley had swallowed his quid.*

And there was a middle-sized boy with puffy, red-rimmed eyes and the kind of nose known as a rum-blossom; he was popularly supposed to get himself drunk every night by filling an atomizer with grain alcohol and then inhaling the stuff.

I knew enough not to say a word about any of these goings-on to either of my parents: the inevitable result would have been my instant snatching away from such corruption and wickedness. And I didn't want to be snatched away. This, I felt, was real life, the kind of life that had so far been carefully walled apart from me.

It never occurred to me that the actual scandal at Shattuck was the teaching. With one exception the masters I had were drill sergeants who marched us up and down their small parade grounds in close order, barking commands and counting the step. A falsely jovial, round little man with a face that was all freckle and with dry, springy hair like a wig, drilled us in grammar; his grins and shouts masked sudden leaps of ferocity. Another, whose open, hopeful face shone like his spectacles, drilled us in ancient history, reducing that enormous unmanageable myth into tabloid outlines, an orderly chart of human progress.

The exception among the masters, who was much more out of place at Shattuck than I was—and who knew he was out of place, as I didn't—was George Hastings, a shy man of unprepossessing appearance and uneasy manner, who was what is known as a born teacher. He taught English, and he made me feel hungry, as only two or three teachers in my life ever have. His uneasiness, I think now, came from a perpetual dissatisfaction with himself and what he was able to do. That dissatisfaction was felt and partly understood by some of his pupils, and woke in them too an awareness that they wanted more than they had, and a desire to get it. George Hastings was an easygoing man and no disciplinarian, but he had no trouble keeping order in his classes. The boys liked him, even those who didn't understand him or feel the pulling of his mind; he gave them a fair shake, so they gave him one. I didn't understand him either, but I felt the pull, and must have made some sort of answering tug. He was the first grown man who treated my mind seriously.

The fact that I was the youngest boy in school put me in a special position at Shattuck. Soon I had the added distinction of being known as the brightest, or very nearly. I had a rival, and I have not forgotten his name: Dave Bronson. The boy with the highest marks for the year had his name emblazoned on a wooden shield above the entrance to the dining hall. The first year it was Bronson's; the second year mine. The odds were always in my favor, for Bronson was two years ahead of me and his subjects were harder.

Other boys had to fight for their place in school, but not I: I was a kind of mascot. Besides this favored position, I had the protection of an older boy. Stanley Johnson, the son of my father's oldest friend, was a big, handsome sixteen-year-old, good at all the manly sports and clever in a lazy way. When we had first met, on a visit to the Johnsons' island camp in northern Minnesota, Stanley hadn't thought much of me, except that I was a nuisance, a little city-bred shrimp who didn't know anything worth knowing. He took me out fishing; I didn't know how to fish, or even how to handle a boat. Besides being at home in the woods, he played football and baseball as a matter of course, had smoked since he was ten, and when he was fourteen had once tried to down a glass of beer in every saloon in Bemidji, a lumbering town that had a lot of saloons. There were still a few more to go when he keeled over or folded up, he wasn't sure which.

I thought Stanley was wonderful, and he tolerated me as an

admirer. Then we met again at Shattuck, which we both entered at the same time: I in the Third Form, he in the Fifth. Our friendship became mutual—intense, shy, ridiculous and invaluable as such affairs often are. Even at the time I felt there was something slightly embarrassing about it, though looking back through forty-five years to get a sight of those two boys "as they really were," I can see nothing wrong with us except that we were young.

My forebears, the Victorians, had scared themselves into thinking that close friendship between boys or men is always dangerous and may be dirty. The shade of Oscar Wilde, the pilloried pervert, hung heavy over their heads. Yet the ancient Greeks, who had more than one word for love, kept their best one for the love of friends. Score another triumph for that Victorian invention, progress.

It was my elders who first put into my head the idea that friends should not love each other, because love is a dirty game played with sex, and only to win; therefore your opponent must be a woman. I certainly didn't invent that savage horror all on my own. It had been dinned into me that I lived on the brink of badness and had to watch my step, and be watched. Though no one had ever told me about the doctrine of infant damnation, no one needed to; I knew I would never get to heaven, or even grow up to be a decent person, without a great deal of luck or better management than I had shown so far.

When I was thirteen, in my second year at Shattuck, I was put through a scene that was like a blow to the stomach. My family had gone east to New Jersey, where my father had just been consecrated bishop, and where I was to join them at the end of the school year. I was convalescing from a light case of mumps, not at the school infirmary but in Dr. Rumpf's house, across the river in the town. Dr. Rumpf was the school doctor, and our two families were on very good terms; the youngest Rumpf boy, Chuck, was my roommate at Shattuck. Chuck and I, who were the same age, had started by being great friends but had fallen out. Though we avoided each other's company as far as roommates could, nevertheless he was to come east with me next summer, to spend a month with my family on the New Jersey shore. I wished he weren't coming, but he was obviously going to hold me to my invitation.

During the week I spent at Dr. Rumpf's house, Stanley and I wrote to each other every day. What on earth did we find to write about? "Everything," I suppose, or what seemed everything to intense adolescents, which of course included some strong references to current events—i.e., school gossip. I was sitting in the Rumpf's living room, writing my daily letter to Stanley; I think this one contained some contemptuous remarks about Chuck. Dr. Rumpf was sitting in the same room; it must have been a slack time of day for him, or perhaps it was Sunday. Out in the hall the telephone rang, and Dr. Rumpf answered it; it was for me. Stanley had called up to see how I was.

When I came back into the living room, Dr. Rumpf was standing in the middle of the floor, red in the face, holding my unfinished letter in his hand. He shook the letter at me and shouted, demanding to know what I meant by it, demanding "an explanation." No doubt I should have been the one to be angry, for I knew it was wrong and sneaky to read other people's letters. But he was a grown-up man, and the law, whatever it was, must be on his side and against me. I felt guilty and sick and ashamed. It was the first time I had seen a man lose control of himself, and the first time real fury had been directed against me. But there was something worse in his anger than the words he was shouting. Something not-quite-said about the friendship between Stanley and me. "Unhealthy" was the word that came through to me, and it flooded dark hints all through my consciousness. The whole world seemed then and for some time afterwards "unhealthy." I got out of the room somehow, packed my clothes and went back to school. I was never easy in Dr. Rumpf's presence after that; nor, I think, was he in mine.

In my second year I was promoted from rear-rank private to corporal, the ranking noncom in my form. At this rate I would end up as major of the battalion. But next year I would have to leave Shattuck and enter St. Paul's. I dreaded the prospect, and I thought Shattuck the best school in the world. Even so, I was not sorry that my military life was ending. I had had enough of bugle calls and assemblies and moving by-the-numbers. And Stanley was leaving too, to enter Harvard.

The Great War, as they called it in 1915, was rumbling on the horizon—far off and foreign, nothing to do with me. We took sides, of course, as in any sporting event; I bet Harold Hildebrand, a classmate whose father was German Consul in Belize, fifty cents that the Allies would win. He never paid up.

One of the things I used to hold against my parents was the bad management that landed me in St. Paul's in the middle of the school year. So few new boys arrived then that those who did were painfully conspicuous and couldn't help knowing that they were getting off to a bad start. My father had put my name down, he said, when I was only six weeks old, but it turned out that the school had no record of it. So, instead of entering St. Paul's in September 1915, I had to wait till the following January.

It was just as well that I had a few months' reprieve, for St. Paul's standards were much higher than Shattuck's. I not only had to drop back a year but needed intensive tutoring to catch up with the form below. Every day that fall I took the trolley from Trenton, where my family was living, to Princeton, to be tutored in Latin, Greek, French, algebra and geography in various undergraduate rooms. My tutors all seemed to me tremendous men of the world, and I liked these glimpses of the free and easy college life I would some day inherit myself.

But at last, shortly after Christmas, the grim day came. My trunk lovingly packed with all the wrong clothes and the wrong kind of skates and a little red morocco *The Imitation of Christ*—which Aunt Jane had given me as a talisman against the world and which I had promised to read, a chapter every night—my father and I took the train for Concord, New Hampshire.

My gloomy imagination had made a picture of St. Paul's: a looming, rectangular, penitentiary-like building settled bleakly on a hilltop in the iron landscape of winter. The school as a whole turned out to be quite different, more like a decorous though fancied-up New England village with quiet tree-lined streets and an overlarge and very un-New England church in the midst of it. But my first view of the barracks where I was to live confirmed my pessimistic picture to the last detail. It has now been torn down, but in those days it housed the Third Form and some of the Fourth. Most of the Fourth Formers had tiny rooms to themselves on the top floor, known as "Nigger Heaven"; the rest of the boys slept in alcoves in two T-shaped dormitories. As a new boy I was assigned an alcove on the second floor, halfway down the spine of the T and facing a line of washbasins. These alcoves were identical —about seven feet by four—and furnished alike: a dresser, a wooden chair, a narrow iron bed.

I was numb with horror and expecting the worst. The numbness wore off and the worst, whatever that was going to be, didn't happen. I was treated as any intruder is treated who is unlucky or stupid enough to come alone and at the wrong time into a closed society. If he has a clown's effrontery or the coolness of a hero he can perhaps swing prejudice in his favor and win acceptance by a single outrageous or admirable act; otherwise he must serve his novitiate as an outcast until his contemptible newness and differ-ence are no longer noticeable. Then he is not so much accepted as taken for granted and forgotten. I was neither a clown nor a hero.

One evening before lights-out I was visited in my alcove by a grinning group. Their leader was Ken Drummond, a Fourth Former who had entered only the term before but whose effron-tery and coolness had already won him the status of an old boy. I was in bed, conning my nightly chapter of Thomas à Kempis.

"What do you think you're doing?" said Drummond.

No reply.

"Look at him! He can't even speak."

Silence. (Nothing to say.)

"What a horse's ass! Look at him!"

They all looked, and laughed. Drummond seized me by the shoulders and shook me back and forth like a rag doll. I made no attempt to defend myself. This made them laugh some more. After a while they got tired of it and went away.

I was shamed and afraid, but I continued to read a chapter of *The Imitation of Christ* every night before lights-out. I didn't understand much of it, and I knew my continuing to read it was an incentive to further attacks, but I'd promised to read it so I did. Drummond and the others returned once or twice, but my non-resistance must have made it small fun for them, and pretty soon they left me alone.

And one afternoon, when the dormitory was almost deserted, I was approached by a boy named Tom Robb. He said, in low and hurried tones, "Aren't you a new boy?"

"Yes."

"Then you've got to do what I tell you." And he gave me to understand that as a new boy it was my duty to submit to a beating. I was quite ready to believe him, especially as he was bigger and obviously stronger than I was; so I obediently inclined myself while he gave me three light, almost ritual taps with a shoe brush. His furtive manner seemed to show that he was running some risk, as no doubt he was; hazing was strictly forbidden.

Why do I still remember Tom Robb and Ken Drummond with shame? I think I know, now: it's because I owe them, and myself, something I have lost the chance of settling, a score that had to be paid on the nail or never. When Drummond led his gang into my alcove I should have jumped out of bed and hit him as hard as I could, and been willing to go down overpowered by force of numbers, ridiculously but furiously weeping; instead of submitting meekly to Tom Robb, I should have hit him too and taken my chances on a real licking.

Hazing by the boys was forbidden, but I was a witness to a scene of public brutality by a master. This man, Mr. M., was the only master in school who was respected as well as feared by all the boys. He looked rather like a more muscular Eugene O'Neill, and taught English to the lower forms, in laconic, man-to-man fashion. But his chief fame and usefulness lay outdoors, as a coach in football and hockey. Mr. M. lived on our floor, in a room strategically placed where the arms of the T crossed the spine, whence he could keep an eye and an ear on three dormitories at once.

One night, when the lights had been out about fifteen minutes and I was just dropping off to sleep, a slight noise outside my alcove made me raise my head. Silhouetted against the faint light from the windows was the round, catlike head of a boy named Ham Williams. In complete silence, after the small scraping noise that had roused me, he worked busily away at the washbasins, bending and straightening up again. At last I made out what he was doing: he was stacking up a tower of chamber pots (we called them thundermugs), fixing them so they would topple over. I knew that his alcove was in the dormitory around the corner, and that he would somehow manage to set off his salvo after he was safely back in bed. His silhouette drifted silently away; he must have been carefully paying out thread as he went.

For several minutes there was not a sound in the sleeping dormitory. Then it came—a cascading tinkling crash like a whole china-shop falling off its shelves. Everyone woke up. Shouts, questions; someone crowed like a rooster. The lights came on, and a moment later Mr. M. appeared, striding purposefully to the scene of the crime. If Ham Williams had hoped to divert suspicion on to the nearest alcoves, he failed. Mr. M. hardly threw me a passing glance, and the same for my neighbors, big boys he knew and trusted. He beckoned them curtly out, added a couple more, and led his posse to the cubicle almost directly behind mine. It belonged to a boy named Willoughby Sharp, small but tough and amazingly dirty-minded; he resembled a thick-lipped ferret. As Sharp saw what was coming he let out an animal scream of terror and protest: "No! No! I didn't do it! I swear!"

Mr. M. smiled ferociously and waved his posse into the alcove. "Get him, boys!" he grunted. "Tramp him! Tear it apart!"

In they went, and down went Sharp and his bed in a smother of stamping feet. The dresser was overturned, the chair broken, the pictures and pennants ripped from the walls. In a few minutes it was all over, the lights were out and the dormitory quiet again, except for the slow gasping sobs from the wrecked cubicle.

Another act of cruelty, which I was invited to witness but was able to avoid, was also presided over and encouraged by a master. On Sundays when there was nothing particular to do it was his habit to take a group of boys in to Concord, to visit the lunatic asylum—not for any serious, let alone charitable purpose, but as entertainment, like going to the zoo. I had heard that some Londoners in the eighteenth century used to go to watch the inmates at Bedlam, just for fun; but it sickened me to find the same sort of thing in the twentieth century, and at a school with the pretensions of St. Paul's.

Some of the school's claims I accepted at face value, at least while I was there. For example: that the Christian faith (imported from England and aged in an Episcopalian cask) was the essence of its teaching—and of our learning. *Ea discamus*, said the school motto, *in terris quorum scientia perseveret in coelis:* "Let us learn here and now the kind of knowledge that will stand us in good stead in the hereafter." Whatever that kind of knowledge might be, I never encountered anything in the school curriculum or the school life that seemed even plausibly like it. As for what we learned . . . well, there was something—something lasting: to get up a good sweat and to take a hot bath every day.

The forms of religion were there, in daily chapel (twice on Sundays) and Sacred Studies; the headmaster himself, Dr. Drury, was an ordained clergyman. Dr. Drury, known behind his back as "The Drip," was an impressively ugly man. With a few slight rearrangements he might have been passably good-looking or even handsome; as it was, his face was a caricature of virile beauty. His small eyes smoldered on either side of a bottle nose with a wart like Cromwell's; deep furrows enclosed his long upper lip and wide mouth in a mournful parenthesis; and his great ears stretched out like an alarmed elephant's. His manner was grave to such a degree that most of us felt abashed in his presence. His voice was his fortune: low, vibrant, thrilling. He might have made a good actor. One morning in chapel—it was St. Crispin's Day, but no one except Dr. Drury knew it—he rose in his rector's stall and launched into the famous speech from *Henry V:*

> *"This day is called the feast of Crispian:*
> *He that outlives this day, and comes safe home,*
> *Will stand a tip-toe when this day is nam'd,*
> *And rouse him at the name of Crispian. . . .*

And gentlemen in England, now a-bed
Shall think themselves accurs'd they were not here,
And hold their manhood cheap whiles any speaks
That fought with us upon St. Crispin's day."

No one who heard that performance could ever have forgotten it.

As a speaker, Dr. Drury was easy and carefully informal. His writing was a little too mannered, a little too consciously Emersonian. He cared about style, he abominated clichés and jargon, and in all he said and wrote he showed a constant concern with learning, as the proper adornment of a Christian gentleman.

Dr. Drury made it his business to know all the boys' birthdays, and whenever one fell in the school term he would summon the boy to his study, make him a little speech and present him with a book. I spent three birthdays at St. Paul's, and thanks to Dr. Drury's misapprehension about me, he never gave me the entertaining kind of book the other boys got; mine were always small, evilly printed pious tracts—*The Meaning of Prayer*, and things like that.

Sacred Studies was a required subject in all forms, but only for an hour a week, and nobody took it seriously, like Latin or geometry. I invariably won the prize in my form. In Sixth Form year we took Sacred Studies with Dr. Drury, reading the Gospels in Greek, and for some reason he held these classes in the Old Chapel—perhaps to emphasize the difference between this and profaner studies. Once his restless eye spotted a boy who was using a King James version as a crib. In two strides he had seized the malefactor by the ear and yanked him to his feet. He motioned him toward the door, as into outer darkness, and said, his rich voice shaking with soft but terrible thunder: "My house shall be called a house of prayer; but ye have made it a den of thieves!"

This impressive scene, manifesting the kind of religious action that I understood and appreciated, reminded me of my father and the impious choirboy in Cincinnati. Like my father, Dr. Drury was not popular, but he was feared.

On Saturday evenings in my last year I was sometimes summoned alone to his study, where he would expound the Gospel for the following day, and would often say to me as he bade me good night that he was "counting on" me. I knew only too well what he meant: he was counting on me to enter the ministry. St. Paul's had formerly turned out a respectable quota of bishops and lesser clergy, but of late years the supply had dwindled to almost nothing. I was now the most likely candidate in sight. Why didn't I tell Dr. Drury that he was mistaken? I hadn't the courage to declare myself. And what could I have declared? That my adolescent mind was like an enormous cavern, echoing and dizzy with the conflicting eloquence of my demigods—Walter Pater, Trotsky, H. G. Wells, Carlyle—and that I was hesitating between the only two possible careers: to become a hero of revolutionary politics or a great writer.

Moreover, as I have said, I accepted as a fact the school's claim to be a church school, and as yet saw nothing ludicrous in equating a social sect like the Episcopal Church with its near-antithesis, the Christian faith. I thought of myself too as both an Episcopalian and a Christian, though an increasingly bad and increasingly restless one. If my father had not already confirmed me before I came to St. Paul's, would my growing doubts have kept me from becoming a full member of the Church? Perhaps; but I rather think not. The Anglican Communion is famous for its latitude in accepting conformists of all sorts.

Boys at St. Paul's were usually confirmed at the school by the Bishop of New Hampshire—in those days a nearsighted old man named Bishop Parker, with a chanting manner of speech. As he passed down the line of kneeling boys, the Bishop laid his hands on each bowed head in turn, lifting up his eyes and intoning: "Defend, O Lord, this-thy-child with thy heavenly gra-ace. . . ." The altar rail in the school chapel was terminated at either end by a head-sized wooden knob, and it was widely believed that both these knobs had several times been confirmed by the Bishop.

In the sense in which Episcopalians generally take religion, St. Paul's was indeed a church school, and I think left a certain kind of religious imprint on most of the boys who went there. These Philadelphia lawyers, Long Island stockbrokers and Boston merchants remember all their lives the dim religious light and sound of Evensong on Sunday nights in the school chapel, the tune (if not the words) of the Last Night Hymn; and when two or three of them are gathered together and drunk, will almost infallibly attempt the solo from the school anthem, *O pray for the peace of Jerusalem.* There was one boy at St. Paul's in my day whose aesthetic sense was so developed that he even enjoyed chapel at the time. He would smuggle a bottle of sherry from Concord and sit through Evensong, half-seas over, with closed eyes, smiling and nodding to the music and humming to himself.

Eventually I did impress some of my teachers at St. Paul's—but not all—with the fact that I was a bright boy. I became a prize pupil in English, Latin, Greek and history, but in mathematics and science I only limped along. Once, when I was getting extra tutoring in algebra from Mr. Monie, who was not an emotional man, my stupidity brought tears of vexation to his eyes. I never stood better than third in my form.

The forms at St. Paul's were divided into classical and scientific divisions. In my division, which was classical, we came to regard the science and mathematics masters as our natural enemies and the subjects they tried to teach us as an unnecessary bore. Algebra we didn't mind, and we all liked Mr. Lay, not only because he still kept on producing children at the age of 70 and spread a really satisfying feast when he asked us to tea, but because he was so kindly and absent-minded a teacher. Sometimes he would half-cover a blackboard with an attempt to work out a quadratic equation, scratching his head and pursing his lips; then, turning to peer at us over his half-moon spectacles, he would appeal to one of us to finish the problem, grumbling apologetically: "I've forgotten more algebra than you boys will ever learn."

Many of the masters had their favorites and even friends among the boys, and these relations naturally sprang up among the most popular and successful on both sides. I dare say the unpopular men felt lonelier and suffered more from the pecking order than the most miserably unsuccessful boy. I was never on most-favored terms with any master, but there were several whose friendship

I coveted, one or two who influenced me more than they knew, and only one whom I hated.

Not all the masters at St. Paul's belonged there. Among the younger men there was a constant, quiet turnover as some of them decided—or the school decided about some of them—that they were out of place. Two odd fits who arrived in my day and didn't last much beyond it were both radicals in clergymen's clothing; I suppose they would have called themselves Christian socialists. Whatever brought them and St. Paul's together I'll never know. They might have had the naïve notion that a church school should be good ground in which to sow the seeds of Christian socialism. They were mistaken, of course, but they did find a few small arable and stony patches—in me and one or two others.

The outstanding master at St. Paul's in my day was "Chappy" Scudder. He was a snob and a dandy. In any other surroundings he would have been a figure of fun, but he was as much at home at St. Paul's as a lizard on a sunny Mediterranean rock. His manner was pompous but dignified—above all things he valued "presence"—he wore the right clothes for every occasion and as if with a faint sneer at later and less exacting styles; and he had two mustaches. He had a patch of hair high up on his bald head that was carefully combed to match the curve of the mustache below.

Mr. Scudder was housemaster of the Middle, a comfortably creaky old frame house, painted white, to which I was assigned at the beginning of my second year. He ruled over the Middle, as in his classes, by his obvious assumption that a gentleman could never behave unbecomingly, and that we were all gentlemen. This bland pretense worked quite as well as more evident forms of tyranny, and the Middle had the reputation of being a pleasant but well-regulated house. The cruder disorders were dealt with by Chappy's assistant, Mr. Hodgins. As a teacher Mr. Scudder applied a variant of the same principle: he taught us English literature by raising his eyebrows. We learned from him that no really first-class poetry had been written since 1798 (the date of Wordsworth and Coleridge's *Lyrical Ballads*) and that no living writer could possibly be considered anything but a hack. Mr. Scudder made a kind of exception for F. Marion Crawford and Owen Wister, both old St. Paul's boys. As for journalism—and almost all the books published nowadays were a form of journalism—that was beneath contempt.

He had a lasting if not a profound influence on me. It took me years to unlearn what I learned from him, and I shall never unlearn it all. A pitying entry in my diary at that time notes of one of my friends that "I am very much afraid Rummy Marvin is going to be nothing but a journalist." Long afterwards, when I was nothing but a journalist myself, my managing editor was also an old St. Paul's boy. He once said to me: "What I would give to have Chappy Scudder writing for me, just for a week. God, if I wouldn't blue-pencil his copy!"

To be approved socially by Mr. Scudder was the highest mark of distinction at St. Paul's. He conferred this honor by inviting a few boys, never more than four or five, to have coffee in his rooms after Sunday lunch. This was worth far more than an invitation to tea from any other master, not excepting the Rector. Mr. Scudder once asked me two Sundays in a row, which made me light-headed with brief delusions of grandeur; but I was not one of his regulars. I had always hated even the smell of coffee because it reminded me of the train-sick days of my childhood, but Chappy's coffee won me over. It was made in a thick-bubbling urn like a samovar, and flowed out rich, strong and odorous of success. We drank it in big cups, with cream, and the conversation was urbane.

On Sunday nights in his study, in carpet slippers and his scarlet Halcyon blazer, he kept open house for all the boys in the Middle, reading aloud stories from Kipling, M. R. James, W. W. Jacobs or Algernon Blackwood. He read well, rather theatrically but with complete unself-consciousness; when he came to a verse in a Kipling story he always knew the tune and sang it in a deep bass:

> *I'm sorry for Mr. Bluebeard,*
> *I'm sorry to cause him pain;*
> *But a terrible spree there's sure to be*
> *When he comes back again.*

I made no friends among the masters but I had my hero. Like most of the St. Paul's boys of my generation, I admired John Gilbert Winant just this side idolatry. Winant was one of the younger masters and still unmarried. He was gaunt, intense, awkward and shy, with a lock of hair that fell over his right eye; his clothes were baggy and needed brushing. In his room, in a small house called the Farm, there was no place to sit; the few chairs were covered with toppling piles of books, books overflowed the shelves and stood in perilous columns in the corners; there were even books on the bed.

He taught us American history, in its dryest aspects and most forbidding forms; all I can remember now is some dreadful stuff about the tariff and early decisions of the Supreme Court. In class he was even shyer and more embarrassed than elsewhere, and spoke in such low tones that he could hardly be heard. His words came as his mind worked, slowly, and in his painful search for the next word he would ram his big hands down inside his trousers, teetering from side to side, with a look of distress on his face as if his belly hurt him. He had one other gesture: he would sometimes retreat into a corner of the room where two bookcases formed a right angle and seem to be trying to climb up the shelves on his elbows.

With all this or in spite of all this, he was an incredibly inspiring teacher. Where and how, in his shy stammerings about Chief Justice Taney or the protective tariff, did he manage to convey to us his burning conviction that the United States of America was a wonderful country, the most gloriously hopeful experiment man had ever made? I don't know, but he did; and from his slow smoldering we took fire. With his encouragement I entered the competition for a prize essay—based on Theodore Roosevelt's *Winning of the West*. I wrote the essay at least partly with tongue in cheek, but as resoundingly as I could. One unforgettable day Gil Winant took me for a walk beside the school pond and told me with shining eyes that I had won the prize; that he was proud of me and more than that, grateful, for what I had written had moved him very much. I was almost unable to speak, I was so ashamed of myself. This brought home to me for the first time how easy it is to fool the good—and how miserably cheated you feel when you do. I vowed to myself that I would make him prouder of me, and with better reason.

I was sure, as a lot of us were, that Gil would some day be President of the United States. When he went into politics and rose higher and higher, but never to the height he should have reached, I began to hear skeptical remarks about him: that his Lincolnian looks were a conscious pose, that his shy idealism masked a coldly shrewd ambition, that his slow sincerity was in fact simply a bumbling lack of ability. I saw him very seldom after St. Paul's, but when I did the old magic was still there, strong enough to dispel all such malicious whispers. Besides, we had known him as schoolboys, and schoolboys can infallibly spot a phony. When he changed his party and in effect ended his political career to follow President Franklin Roosevelt, whom he admired to the same extravagant degree that we had admired Gil, it was a blow to my hopes but I sympathized and forgave him.

When he ended his life by putting a bullet through his head I found his despairing act harder to understand. It seemed to me that he, of all people, had no right to resign. It was as if he were saying that life had fooled him, after all; and that he had been mistaken in the faith he had held and imparted to us. Or was it simply that for a moment he forgot America, he forgot us, he forgot everything, in an overpowering access of misery or pain?

I didn't like St. Paul's, but I found my own level there, among other misfits. Only three of them were considered outright eccentrics: Jim McLane, a mincing aesthete and a steely snob who drank green tea and published slim books of plaintive verse; H. M. Ward, who was strong as an ox but disliked organized games, read books on chess and won every school prize he went in for; and Chanler Chapman, who looked and acted like a violently life-loving Italian (his inevitable nickname was "Charlie Chaplin"). Of the half-dozen I counted as my friends, only two distinguished themselves later: Jack Wainwright, who died heroically, in character; and H. M. Ward, who became a professor of pure mathematics. In the world of high salaries and "big" jobs, I turned out to be the most successful of this little lot. But at school I was the least among them, and grateful that they accepted me.

By the leaders of the school, the athletic heroes and the socially mighty, I was tolerated or ignored. I did eventually attain a position as a minor intelligence—second prize in debating, one of the lesser names on the editorial board of the *Horae Scholasticae;* that kind of thing. It was a wobbly position, and I felt that it was. I would much rather have been a little less bright and a lot better at games. But as an athlete I knew myself puny and inept, and the competition seemed to me overwhelming. Unlike Shattuck, where only a few boys were expected to be good enough to make the team, at St. Paul's everyone was on a team of some sort.

As soon as a boy entered school he was assigned to one of three athletic clubs—Delphian, Isthmian, Old Hundred—and to one of two rowing clubs, Shattuck or Halcyon. My father, it appeared, had been an Old Hundred and a Halcyon, so that's how I was enrolled. There was no actual rule that every boy had to play football in the autumn term and hockey in the winter, but unless he could show cause why he shouldn't or was an extraordinarily independent character, he was pretty well compelled to. By entering school in January I had succeeded in missing my first football season, but there was no way of avoiding hockey. I was quickly sized up by the Old Hundred coach and assigned to the lowest team in the club, the tenth.

Hockey, as I and my fellow incompetents played it, bore small resemblance to the expert and blood-rousing contests on the black ice of the SPS (St. Paul's School) rink, where the demigods of the first teams swooped like falcons and clapped together like fighting cocks. It is mainly those games, not ours, I remember: the windless, nose-numbing cold, the clear gray light filtered through a leaden sky, the hushed, crowded lines of boys packed along the breast-high boards of the rink, the sudden thunder of hockey-sticks clattering applause of a thunderbolt shot or a gallant save by the goalkeeper.

My record in hockey was ludicrous, but in football it was disgraceful. My mother didn't want me to play football, which she regarded as brutal and dangerous; she may even have written a letter to the Rector to get me excused. But I didn't really want to be an outcast, and at the beginning of my last year, when a delegate from the School Council took me aside and gravely reminded me that Sixth Formers should set an example to the school, the nudge was all I needed. As usual, the coach put me on the lowest Old Hundred team, with boys two and three years younger than I. In the school football picture, taken at the end of the season, I should have sat on the ground with my teammates, but wormed my way up a couple of rows so that posterity should see me in a better light.

The only games I liked were tennis, at which I became the second best in school, and squash racquets, which I learned to play fairly well. Neither game was highly regarded at St. Paul's in my day.

In 1917 the faraway war came nearer. By that fall, some of last year's Sixth Form had already gone to meet it halfway. One morning in chapel the Rector announced the death of Pete Conover, killed in action with the Canadians at Vimy Ridge. He had been the hero of the school, captain of the SPS hockey team two years running, a name to be mentioned in the same breath with the legendary Hobey Baker. There were rumors of a School Battalion. In the spring term appeared a gruff young Canadian officer with a bad limp; he posted a notice that a School Battalion would be formed immediately, and called for volunteers.

According to the sporadic diary I was keeping then, I had come to two seventeen-year-old conclusions that winter: that my having to go to the war was practically inevitable, and that I loathed the prospect. I was sitting up late that winter (Sixth Formers' privilege) reading and writing till the small hours, mixing up—or together—the French and Russian revolutions, H. G. Wells and my first secret attempts at poetry. The result, I thought at the time, was a whispered but passionate No: "the dreadful conclusion that war is indefensible, conscientious objectors right, and patriotism utterly wrong." I also added that "I was incapable of practicing or proclaiming my views, through cowardice. . . . I have no firm belief in anything."

What I did was just the opposite to what I thought I was thinking. I volunteered for the School Battalion. I expected that my Shattuck training would make me instantly visible among these military innocents, so that our commanding officer would pluck me gruffly from the ranks and set me above them. I started as a rear-rank private, and I stayed there.

Except for the Battalion, however, my last term was my happiest time at St. Paul's. The late New Hampshire spring softened the bleak angles of the school and warmed the cold memories of long winters. The masters, even the hostile ones, seemed to regard us in a new way, speculatively but kindly; we felt the stirring of a specious fellowship with one another and with the school. The dreaded exams came and went, and we were now, most of us, college men at last. The final days drifted by in lazy succession.

And we could look forward to the delights of an even lazier summer. No. A week after I had said goodbye to St. Paul's I was enrolled as a volunteer in a military training camp at Princeton, which would last nine weeks. Why? I had not been a success at school, and I knew it. Once again I elected to do something I didn't really want to do, partly because that was my misconception of virtue but mainly because I wanted to *show them*. I felt a growing determination to prove that I was somebody, to make the successful people I envied and despised admit that I was as good as they were. As good? Better!

TWO UNIVERSITIES

LOOKING BACK AT MY LIFE, I used to think that in a way it had reached its highest point when I was seventeen. For at that age, since I hadn't yet accomplished anything at all, I had purer feelings about accomplishment than at any time afterwards. I had only very misty notions about what I was going to do and was much more concerned with how I was going to do it. Whatever it was to be, I would pursue it with my whole soul. That meant, of course, that only a really noble undertaking need apply. I wasn't thinking in terms of a skilled profession but of a dedicated life.

What happened to that feeling? I'm not sure that I know, but I think it went off to the island of Molokai and left me behind. My courage failed me. When I first heard of Father Damien and his work among the lepers, it was like a tap on the shoulder; but instead of my heart leaping up at the summons, my heart sank. The way I put it to myself was, "Do I have to go?" For a bad short time I thought I did have to, and then I realized I wasn't up to it. If that was the way I responded to the prospect of a noble and dedicated life, obviously I'd better be thinking about something much less noble.

But there was more to it than that. Until action settles the argument about what to do, there is always more to it than that. I spent the next six years at two universities, studying for my future, preparing to live. I might have been, perhaps I should have been, circling as purposefully as a hawk winding down on its target. But my attention was distracted and the target partly hidden by two people, a girl and a friend. During my university years they took up most of my time and attention. Love and friendship were of more concern to me than the studies that were to fit me for my place in the world and also guide me to it.

At the very start my hopeful dreams, which had nothing to do with military glory, were temporarily dulled by the threat of war. The war, nearly over in the fall of 1918, had been going on so long that it had begun to seem the permanent background of our lives. We must have read the papers and heard the rumors, but we were sure it would last our time, and were in no hurry to join it. It had turned colleges into armed camps; Princeton was very different from the undergraduate paradise I had hoped for. Instead of sporting a little black freshman cap, sleeping late, lounging to lectures and sitting up till all hours, I was herded through a medical inspection ("Bend over. Pull apart your buttocks."), issued a khaki uniform, assigned to a barracks, and put under the chafing discipline of the Students' Army Training Corps.

It was like repeating the Third Form for the third time, and with some added disadvantages. All the "men" in my company were under eighteen, which meant that we were not, like the others, inducted into the U.S. Army, paid and given free equipment, and eventually an honorable discharge; we had to buy our own uniforms, pay for our board and lodging, and were (unofficially) expected to desert on our eighteenth birthdays and enlist somewhere else, preferably with the Marines. The brand-new second lieutenant who commanded my company was an almost complete ignoramus in military manners; he was impressed by my drill-book protocol and made me a sergeant.

I first saw my future friend Schuyler Jackson (although then I didn't know his first name) at bayonet practice. He was usually my opposite number when we practiced long points and jabs. He too was a sergeant, and we were to be instructors later on. As he crouched and feinted, grim-lipped and stripped to the waist, I remember admiring the muscles of his chest and shoulders, and wondering whether my bayonet would slip into him as if he were butter, or whether it would hit a rib. We never spoke to each other, and we didn't become friends till the autumn of our third year.

In the Victory Parade in New York, when the battalion marched up Fifth Avenue at the tail-end of the long procession, as a file-closer in "D" Company I had the distinction of being the last man in the parade. That was an appropriate way of expressing how close I had come to the war.

With the disbanding of the S.A.T.C., our postponed college life overtook us as a flood; I was carried away and half drowned in freedom. Three of us had been cooped up in a single room in the crowded dormitory that had been our barracks; now my roommate and I had two bedrooms and a sitting room to ourselves. My roommate's definition of work was "what you have to do that you hate." He worked continually. Whenever a visitor came in, he would retire to his bedroom, slamming the door, and leave me to waste time. I didn't mind; in fact, that was what I thought I wanted.

I had brief bursts of ambition, however. I entered the freshman competition for a place on the college newspaper—and quit when a friend persuaded me to go to Trenton for an evening's drinking.

Still smarting from my athletic failure at school, I went out for football. The coaches usually kept me on the bench and thus may have saved my life. I turned to a field where I felt more at home: the Théâtre Intime, for which I wrote one-act plays and occasionally acted, and the college literary magazine. In my senior year I was made chairman of the editorial board, which enabled me to publish my own poems.

Though I had won a prize of $400 for getting the highest marks in my form in the Princeton entrance examinations, I very nearly failed to get my college degree. My old enemies, science and mathematics, met me like Apollyon in the way and almost prevented me.

I made some friends, in a desultory way; some were drinking acquaintances and some were "bright boys"; in general they drifted into my circle from curiosity and stayed from inertia. I became a kind of leader of a small set, whom I took with me into one of the less desirable clubs. My position in college vaguely dissatisfied me; I felt that I was not being recognized as I should be, so about this time I started two clubs of my own.

The first was political. I wanted to call it the Socialist Society: I considered myself a socialist and thought I would collect some kindred spirits around me. About a dozen, I think, came to the first meeting, from which, after a sharp hassle, I emerged as president. Then the college authorities stepped in and made us change the name to The Society for the Study of Socialism. In those pre-Communist days "socialism" had almost as deep a Red tinge about it as "Communism" has now. Our membership was small and got smaller, and the club couldn't have lasted very long; but while it did it caused a certain amount of talk. I used to import speakers, usually radical professors from other colleges, and advertised these meetings. Since the club had practically no funds, I had to pay the speaker's expenses out of my own pocket—the main reason for the club's short life. One meeting did draw a fairly sizable crowd because I had Norman Thomas as the speaker. He was the perennial Socialist candidate for President; he was also a Princeton graduate, and was generally regarded in those days as a renegade to his class, a disgrace to the university, a Bolshevik, a Red. One right-wing professor went to the president of Princeton to try to stop this meeting, and wanted me expelled from college for my part in it.

The other club I started was literary. The Tuesday Evening Club had half a dozen members and met in each member's room in turn; it was hoped that the host would supply something to drink. This club too might have petered out soon, if it hadn't been for Schuyler. At that time he was known as the most brilliant member of our class but an absentee who took no part in college life. In our first two years I hardly knew him to speak to. He was a handsome boy with a brilliant mind which he was now just beginning to use. He had been a good athlete at his school—"a red-blooded American boy," as he described it—now he lived off the campus with an old bachelor who was a connection of his, and did nothing but read all day and most of the night.

We were in several classes together; one I particularly remember was George McLean Harper's course on Wordsworth and Coleridge. Schuyler was absent from the first four or five classes, and Mr. Harper complained to the registrar, feeling quite properly that anyone who had put his name down for the course should either come to classes or be dropped. Schuyler did finally put in an appearance, and it didn't take Mr. Harper long to recognize the caliber of his mind. Thereafter, whenever Schuyler was present, Mr. Harper always called our attention to the fact, saying—without any intent of irony—that we should be grateful that he was among us.

Not all professors were as generous or as tolerant but, grudgingly or not, they had to recognize his excellence. What could you do with a student who cut required lectures, ignored set papers and quizzes, and then wrote a brilliant final examination? You could deplore him but you had to give him high marks.

Unlike the rest of us, Schuyler studied with intensity, aim and purpose. For, again unlike most of us, he knew what he wanted: to be a poet. At first I felt only his intensity without knowing what he was after, and it made me uneasy. When I asked him to join the Tuesday Evening Club he refused, saying he had no time for that kind of thing. Finally he agreed to come to a meeting, where he sat and smoked his pipe in silence. Our lame and sophomoric discussion went wrangling on. All of a sudden Schuyler burst out in a torrent of talk—about poetry, the subject we had been niggling at. None of us had ever heard anything like it. From then on he was the acknowledged leader of the club, which lasted the rest of our college days and ended by publishing (at our expense) a thin book of our own poems.

When this first meeting broke up, we went into the town to get something to eat, and afterwards Schuyler walked back with me. That was how our friendship began, but it was a long time before we were on really friendly terms. And he had to do the running; I was suspicious and uncomfortable in his presence and never sought him out. I remember one evening when he came into our room; I was reading, or pretending to, in a chair in the corner, and for a while he talked to my roommate about some assignment. Then an increasingly brittle silence fell, broken at last by Schuyler crying out, "For God's sake stop sitting there being so tense and pretending to read!" After that I think we went out for a walk.

We often went for walks in those days, long, aimless tramps through the countryside, and sometimes at night—when life seemed very black to me, as it often did. We would walk for a long way in silence, and then I would begin, monosyllabically, incoherently, gradually ridding myself of all the adolescent bitterness that had collected in me, like bile. Schuyler would hear me out in silence, and when I had finally coughed it all up he would begin to talk. I don't remember what he said, except that it seemed at first irrelevant to what I had been cursing about but usually ended by giving me peace of mind.

When I finally nerved myself to show him some of the verses I had written he amazed and heartened me by taking them seriously. He was severely critical of them, but the thing he criticized most sternly was my pretense that they weren't serious. He astonished me by the flat statement that poetry—all poetry—is written with passion. My doggerel, as I called it even to myself, had only the passion of anger, bitterness and self-pity. I was inclined to regard "beautiful" poetry as dispassionate and insincere. I thought of some of the simpleton poems of Wordsworth, and said, "What about 'We Are Seven'?" For answer he read me "We Are Seven" aloud, with passion. I saw that it could be done, or at least that he could do it.

Toward the end of senior year the class made the traditional judgment on its members, voting on "the man who has done most for Princeton," "most likely to succeed," "most desperate fusser," etc. Schuyler, hands down, was voted "the most brilliant," and very nearly "the most scholarly." I was overwhelmingly elected "worst poet."

Schuyler was proud and passionate; he was not sentimental. I have always admired people who aren't, feeling a shameful proneness to sentimentality in myself. One evening when Schuyler and I were drinking in my room we were joined by an extraordinary character named Johnny Martin. Johnny had lost his left arm in a shooting accident when he was fifteen; in spite of this handicap he was a first-rate athlete (golf and soccer), became an expert wing shot and once held the North American record for landing the biggest game fish of the year. He was then chairman of the *Daily Princetonian* and afterwards my first boss on *Time*. I didn't know him well but he was an extreme admirer of Schuyler's. And it was Schuyler he had come to see.

He wanted to talk about a girl. Johnny was in love with the girl, but that was not what he wanted to talk about. The girl would have none of him, she was too good for him, he would always love her, but that was the way it was. All he wanted was that the two finest people he knew in the world—Schuyler and Helen—should meet; they were made for each other. That would make him happy. It took some time and several drinks for Johnny to state his case, and when he reached his final plea we were none of us sober. Johnny was so moved that his harsh voice broke and an occasional tear crept down his craggy face. Though neither Schuyler nor I had ever laid eyes on Helen or seen her picture, I was so carried away by Johnny's tremendous self-sacrifice and his eloquence that I wept too and joined my maudlin urgings to Johnny's. Schuyler was quite unmoved; in fact, he got colder and colder. He seemed to be refusing even to meet her.

My parents did not share my enthusiasm for Schuyler. I felt and resented their coolness toward him without suspecting that they warmly disliked him and feared his influence on me. The antipathy between Schuyler and my father was obvious if not openly expressed, but my mother did the best she could to like him for my sake, though she could never successfully pretend that she believed in him as I did. I can imagine the discussions they must have had on the subject: my mother worried, my father indignant. Once, during a summer hot spell, I got their permission to have Schuyler stay in our house, which was cooler than his. He started one night by going to bed on a window seat and woke next morning on the floor of another room, having rolled there in his sleep. Neither of my parents liked that. And years later, when he consented to be godfather to my first son, he appeared at the christening in the family chapel but stood with his back to the altar and closed his eyes while he made the required responses.

But the girl came first; years before I met Schuyler I had fallen in love with her. Her name was Julie. She was three years younger than I, and she also lived in Princeton. Her family were impoverished but socially impeccable and with more worldly connections than my own. She was the only girl among four brothers. The two older ones, who were my friends, gave me what sympathy and help they could. There wasn't much they could do, and I could do nothing for myself. Julie was pretty and a flirt; what she liked was gayety, and all I could show her was a morose dull-doggedness.

When I first knew her I was sixteen, she was thirteen. She was too young to have a heart, and I was too young to love anybody properly. She could no more help being cruel to me than a baby can keep from pulling a puppy's ears. As generally happens, I had fallen in love with her pretty face and her charming ways without taking much note of her as a person, as she really was or would be—for in any case, she wasn't a person yet. Her mother, whom I loved with more reason, was a gentle, vague woman with a kind of

167

let-well-alone wisdom, and I banked on Julie's growing up to be like her, though in fact Julie's temperament and her charm had much more in common with her willful and peppery father's.

At first she was pleased that I was in love with her. Then, as she began to attract other boys, many of whom were handsomer or more amusing or surer of themselves than I was, I became a nuisance and she got bored with me. From being a nuisance I gradually turned into a worry and at last a minor preoccupation; eventually she had me so much on her mind that she agreed to marry me. That slow evolution took nine years.

When I first knew her, her family lived in a pleasant old wooden farmhouse about a mile outside Princeton. The house had two stories, with a pillared porch along its front, and reminded me of a much smaller and more dilapidated Oaks. My first memory of Julie is of sitting alongside her on the branch of a tree—is it possible?—with both of us chewing away on opposite ends of a piece of string to reach a marshmallow tied in the middle. Her mother had invited me to a party, and this was one of the games we played. I am sure Julie got the marshmallow, because she would have been the fiercer chewer and I would have been held back by shyness at our lips coming so close together.

Life at the Farm captivated me from the start, and I went there as often as I could. It was as free-and-easy as at Cousin Ellen-and-Patty's, and with even less supervision. You never knew exactly what was going to happen next, or when. Meals were never on time, and if something went wrong with the dessert or the main dish was a disaster, as often happened, the children were likely to make a scene, uproarious or otherwise interesting. Mr. Cuyler, Julie's father, was usually absent, a fact that in those early days I also put on the credit side, for I mistook his gingery, odd humor for bad temper. Mrs. Cuyler, when she was there—but she wasn't always there either—was placid and inattentive amidst the chaos except when things got really out of hand; even then her scoldings were mild. It couldn't have been a greater contrast to my own family's icily disciplined and clockwork-regulated household. I loved it.

There was no electricity at the Farm, no proper screens in the windows (both the screens and the windows were the sort that had to be propped up, and never quite fitted), the furniture was rickety and some of it couldn't be sat on, it was simply for show. These chairs and sofas were known as "the tapestry furniture," and were said to have come from the Tuileries: the reason no one was allowed to sit on them was that they were supposed to be worth vast sums of money which would salvage the family fortunes if worst ever came to worst. Instead of an icebox there was a well in a little cupboard off the kitchen; meat, butter and such things were hung in the mouth of the well and often fell in.

One of the most attractively bohemian aspects of the bohemian life at the Farm, it seemed to me, was the sleeping arrangements. Though all the children had their own rooms, none of them knew where they were going to sleep until Mrs. Cuyler, after vague thought, had told them. I don't know what her decisions were based on; I think they had something to do with the direction of the wind, her guesses about the weather during the night, and the children's supposed states of health. In spring and summer she herself usually slept outdoors in a tent, with the youngest. The tent was not waterproof and invariably blew over in a thunderstorm or a wind of any force.

Julie, I thought, was given the most Spartan treatment. In fine weather, whatever the time of year, her bed was pushed almost entirely out of a window over a sloping roof: the head of the bed stayed inside the window, while the foot was propped up on two little pillars of bricks piled shakily in the gutter. The reason for this was that she was thought to be delicate and needed all the fresh air she could get. However well-meant this prescription was, it gave her a lifelong fear of falling out of the window in her sleep. For years, whenever she slept in a hotel room even a few floors above the street, she tied her big toe to the bedstead with a piece of thread, to wake her up in case she walked in her sleep— a thing she was never known to do.

She must have been delicious as a small child. I have seen photographs of her at that age, and all dark-haired little girls—if they are pretty—put me in mind of her. She was the darling of her family, but not a spoiled darling. Her brothers teased her into tears and sometimes shut her up with the goat to keep her from tagging along after them. Most of what she had to wear was their hand-me-downs and secondhand clothes that had been given to her mother. As a very feminine little girl, she hated that. But I don't think she was an unhappy child. She was high-spirited, like her father, and had something of his humorous imagination. She named her favorite doll Z. Vazinir Brinsby—some of her others were Jane Buffle, Jack Wigglelolly, Ragdraggle and Feather-huncas—and once announced that what she wanted to be when she grew up was "a long green feather that tickles." And she always remembered the time when she and one of her little-girl chums walked sedately down Nassau Street, each with an alarm clock in her bloomers that was set to go off in front of the Nassau Inn.

The casual, hit-or-miss quality of life at the Farm, which was like a fresh breeze to me, was hateful to Julie; she pined for order and electric light and an up-to-date kitchen, for clothes that hadn't been worn by somebody else, and a house that wasn't held together by tacks and glue and bits of old string. I was amazed to discover that she envied *my* life—or rather, the smooth, well-regu-lated comfort of my family's household. The Farm was in constant need of paint and repairs, and in its run-down condition it was a hopeless job to keep it tidy or really clean, but with hammer, paint brush and broom Julie tried. These crusades became more intense as she grew older, and she often dragooned some of her brothers and even me to help, but our hearts weren't engaged to the fierce extent that hers was.

When she was fifteen she went away to an Anglican convent school, St. Mary's at Peekskill. She was so homesick at first that her schoolmates called her "the Weeping Willow." I was some-times allowed to escort her on the train, but had to say goodbye to her at the Peekskill station. St. Mary's frowned on boys, unless they were brothers, and I had to smuggle my letters to Julie in-side one of theirs. Though I thought I missed her terribly, I soon found that it was worse when she came home; then my self-con-sciousness and jealousy kept me in a constant state of misery. At parties when she was dancing with someone else I suffered tor-ments; when I danced with her myself I was clumsy and tongue-tied. And I was always being "cut in on" when I danced with her, for she danced beautifully and was in great demand as a partner.

Then suddenly she was seventeen, finished with school and home for good. Now she was less mine than ever. If I hadn't realized it before, I did now: I was in a queue, and nowhere near the head of it. My one consolation in those days was that the favorite beau changed from time to time, and that I was never at the very bottom of the line. It was then, however, that I first began to learn about timetables and budgets and margins of safety: all my schemes and plans about her had to be revised and revised again. I saw that it was going to be a long haul.

I invited Julie—very unfairly, at least two years in advance—to be my partner at the last "prom" of my senior year. I put great hopes on this occasion, and decided that at some point in the evening I would ask her to marry me and that she would say yes. As it turned out, I saw very little of her at the prom; after a few steps someone would cut in, she was having such a good time that she wouldn't sit out a dance with me, someone else took her to supper, and once I lost her completely for nearly an hour. By the end of the dance I was in a glum fury and in no state of mind to ask her to marry me, which was just as well, for she certainly would have said no.

This period, which I look back on as a time of trouble and misery for me, I suppose may have been the happiest part of her life. She was heart-whole and much sought after, one of the most popular girls in Princeton, with a whole college of girl-hungry undergraduates to pick from. I must have been an unwanted interruption and a nuisance. When I did get her to myself, what sort of company was I? All I did was recite poems—mine or Housman's, it made little difference—which she disliked and thought morbid, and talk, or sigh, like a gloomy furnace half choked with clinkers. I'm surprised now that she gave me any time at all.

She didn't have much time to give me, however, and the meetings I set such store by were subject to postponement at short notice. There was one humiliating occasion I never forgot. She had promised to take a walk with me one afternoon; I hadn't seen her for days, and as usual my tottery hopes had risen high; I expected great things from that walk. We had just started; we may have gone a hundred yards—I remember we were halfway along the iron railings in front of Trinity Church—when a sports car pulled up alongside us. It was a Model T roadster, stripped down and streamlined, a very sporty number for those days, and the driver was a campus hero, quarterback on the football team, a barrel-chested little fellow with a body like a baby gorilla's. I knew who he was, of course, and of course he didn't know me. But he knew Julie. He boomed at her:

"Hi, Julie! Come for a ride!"

Do I have to say it? She dropped me like a hot brick, scrambled in beside him, and off they went.

She knew she shouldn't have done it, but she had been tempted beyond her strength. She apologized to me later, and like a fool I swallowed my hurt pride and my anger and meekly accepted it. If I wasn't exactly getting what I deserved in those days, I think I was getting what I asked for.

There were other times when I went nearly crazy with jealousy for no reason. Once an upper-classman who was a friend of mine and a club-mate took Julie to the movies. I knew I had nothing to fear from him—on the contrary, he would put in as many good words for me as he could. Yet I trusted nobody, and by now I had a feverishly exaggerated notion of Julie's seductive powers, and I didn't trust her either. I bought a flask of applejack, and hid in the bushes outside her house. By the time he had come to call for her I was half drunk. I trailed them all the way to the movies, keeping well in the shadows, and taking heartbroken swigs of applejack behind numerous trees; they never saw me. When the flask was empty I went to call on Mrs. Cuyler, with some drunken idea of demanding an explanation of her daughter's behavior. If Mrs. Cuyler was either shocked or amused she concealed it beautifully, and shooed me gently off to bed.

My behavior was not always good, and worse, it was not effective—or so it seemed to me then. But the thing about queues is that they do move, though there are times when you think they never will. By the end of my last year at Princeton, to my astonishment I found myself fairly near the head of the line. I was not Number One, but neither, it appeared, was anybody else. And because I was about to go far, far away to Oxford and not come back for two long years (that was the idea) I was temporarily the most favored.

My train for New York, where I was to board the ship for England, left very early in the morning. As a last favor I was allowed to wake Julie and kiss her goodbye. She had her mother's blessing on this arrangement but neglected to tell her father anything about it, so that when I pounded on the front door at the Farm, shortly after dawn one bright September morning, Mr. Cuyler, in his nightshirt, was obviously surprised to see me. I was so full of emotion that I couldn't speak, and brushed past him up the stairs to Julie's room. I had never seen her in bed before: she was ravishingly pretty. She held out her arms to me, I gave her a quick, awkward hug and a kiss and ran downstairs and out of the house, my eyes streaming.

Of course I didn't stay away for two years, though of course I should have. Six months was the limit of my feeble endurance. After that, while my fellow Americans at Oxford spent their vacations getting acquainted with Europe, I commuted across the Atlantic to court Julie.

On a mild October afternoon in 1922 I presented myself at the porter's lodge in New College. The porter, a majestic man who looked like my idea of the Archbishop of Canterbury, did not welcome me very warmly. He found my name on a list, frowned at me over his spectacles, and said I was two days early, there was "a gaudy on." That meant, I discovered later, that New College was indulging in one of its sedate reunions; "gaudy" being the Oxford contraction for *gaudeamus igitur*. He waved me in the general direction of an archway, and added a few grumbled directions.

Eventually I found my rooms, at the top of a tower (102 steps), and when my scout (college servant) found me, he gave me some more incomprehensible information about "J.C.R." and "the rears" and "Hall." All these places were ingeniously hidden, and it was necessary to know where they were: Junior Common Room was the place to get breakfast, read the papers and have coffee after dinner; "the rears" ("can" was my American word for it) were in one large outhouse; you had to eat dinner in Hall every night, or pay for it, unless you crossed your name off a list before a certain hour in the morning.

At my first breakfast in J.C.R., after working my way through a soup plate of porridge, a dish of kedgeree and two mugs of tea, I was hovered over by a white-haired man with sweeping mustachios, a generally villainous aspect and an unconvincing smirk—the college butler. He had been hissing fiercely at the other servants, but his voice to me was treacly. He said: "Maaarmalade-jam-or-'oney-suh?" Somehow I knew I was damn well supposed to say "Marmalade," so I said it.

"*Very* good, Suh. Light *or* dark, Suh?"

"Dark, please."

Again the right answer. I had passed his test, and he never treated me with the open contempt he showed for some of the "young gentlemen." I despised myself for truckling to him, but the British undergraduates admired and liked him, or pretended to. They knew he was cleverer and more ruthless than they were, and they were wordlessly grateful to him for shoring up their vanishing world; if they had been capable of saying so, they might have said that he dropped his h's deliberately in order to keep the Empire going. Why did he make me so uneasy? I think because Americans don't like servility, even insolent servility.

The most feared man in New College, the man everyone scuttled from, was the Warden, a little aged albino with gleaming false teeth who blinked and smiled and ruled his roost. His name was Canon Spooner, and I thought he had died in the eighteenth century. I had heard about him since I was a child as the kind of nonsense-monger who appealed to the Matthews sense of humor. I had read articles about him in the *Strand Magazine;* I had seen an example of a Spoonerism in the Oxford Dictionary—"For real enjoyment give me a well-boiled icicle." In my two years at New

College I never once heard him put his tongue wrong, and I believe the whole legend was made up out of whole cloth.

I remember him for other reasons. Once in chapel he fell asleep in his thronelike stall. The service came to a standstill. Finally the porter tiptoed forward and respectfully rattled the curtain rings above the old man's head. He woke with a start, toddled up to the altar, pronounced the benediction, knelt down—and fell asleep again. We all went quietly out and left him. I was not present when he preached his famous sermon on Plato and St. Paul; he left the pulpit, regained his stall and then thoughtfully announced: "In my sermon, whenever I said 'St. Paul' I meant Plato, and when I said 'Plato' I meant St. Paul."

Thanks to Cecil Rhodes, Americans were as common as colonials at Oxford; they were rated a little below Canadians, Australians and South Africans and a little above Greeks, Hindus and Senegambians. The Spoo did his British best to keep an eye on the two or three Americans in his charge. He used to send for me once every term or so, and our colloquy was invariably the same:

"Let me see, let me see. You're an Ameddican, an Ameddican. Aren't you?"

"Yes, sir."

"An Ameddican . . . Did you ever know Felix Morley?" (Felix and his brother Christopher had both been at New College; the Spoo was sure of them.)

"No, sir."

"Ameddica, Ameddica. *I* was in Ameddica once."

"Yes, sir?"

"Mmmm-yes. I was in Paterson, New Jersey."

In my second year I had a servant named Dickens, an old hand but not in any sense a good scout. He used to wake me by opening my bedroom door and announcing: "Seven-thirty, sir, and another 'orrible morning." He sometimes varied this formula: "Seven-thirty, sir; don't turn over, it's fatal." He would then close my door and set about tidying up my study. I kept all my bottles in an unlocked cupboard, and it seemed to me that they were dwindling faster than they should. I marked the bottles: each one went down half an inch a day, as if it were evaporating. Naturally I suspected Dickens. And one evening when I brought a friend in for a glass of port and found the decanter empty, I swore that his thieving had gone too far. Two nights before, the decanter had been almost full, and I hadn't touched it since.

That afternoon, when Dickens came in to clear away tea and fill the coal scuttle, I stated the facts about the decanter—no direct accusation, just the facts. Dickens cleared his throat, put down the tray, straightened a picture on the wall, flicked a corner of the table with his filthy dust rag, and suggested that one of my friends might have dropped in and helped himself. I said nothing. A few days later a Rhodes scholar came to see me and confessed that he had drunk the whole decanter: he had been waiting for me, I didn't show up, he looked in the cupboard, one glass had led to another. Did I apologize to Dickens? I don't think I did. Anyhow, though he was off that hook, he'd had a scare, and stopped nibbling at the bottles.

After four years in Princeton I was not convinced that college was a fair copy of the life to come. And while I admired those few classmates who knew what they were going to do next—teach, study medicine or law—I felt only pity or contempt for the majority who were content to drift into "a job." I intended to be a writer, though I knew I wasn't ready yet; the one thing I was sure I wouldn't do was to take a job, sit at a desk in an office. Meantime I would go to Oxford and get another degree.

My precocious reading, luck, and a facility I had developed in bluffing my way through the humaner sort of exams had wangled me my bachelor's degree; but I knew that my smattering of education was far from being the real thing. As the child of privilege I had been given the best schooling, according to the standards of my world, that money could buy; but I had also begun to understand that the penny's-worth of effort that had been my contribution was nowhere near enough.

The process of education—I suspected by now that it was a literally endless process and not a course to be finished nor a prize to be achieved—after some fifteen years of study had only barely begun. And the price too would finally be paid by me. What price? Years later, Churchill's famous phrase gave me an inkling of the only currency acceptable: "blood, toil, tears and sweat." And when do we stop paying? And what examiners will qualify us at last for the ultimate degree—the mastery of art, the doctorate of wisdom?

A university is a chaos, a fecund chaos in which to find or create a world. Though few take full advantage of them, the opportunities for discovery and creation are there for everyone. At least, that's how Oxford seemed to me, and that's why I felt much freer there than I had at Princeton, where everyone was awarded his place in a far narrower channel; it was the difference between a fish ladder and a falls.

If I had not gone to Oxford, I should never have known what a real university is. Princeton, only a generation before my day, had taken to calling itself a university—perhaps to keep up with its football rivals, Yale and Harvard—but it wore the title uneasily; it had remained in fact a college, a closely knit provincial community under the jealous government of "class spirit" and "college spirit." Schuyler, who was deficient in both kinds, was tolerated because of his brilliance and because he "made Ivy" (was elected to the most exclusive club). Nonconformists at Princeton were exceptional and unwelcome.

In the larger air of Oxford, I soon discovered, nonconformity was quite permissible. If you belonged to a particular set, it might have its rules of dress and behavior, but there were other sets that seemed to have very different rules, or none; and you didn't have to belong to a set at all. The university, that vague entity that made itself felt only at examination times and as the whimsical enforcer of archaic laws, apparently didn't care what people did—in the immortal words of Mrs. Patrick Campbell—"as long as they don't do it in the street and frighten the horses."

For the first few weeks Oxford seemed to me a quaint anarchy; then, when I began to discern a kind of system in its disorder, merely topsy-turvy. You had no classmates, simply "the men of your year," and there was no attempt to foist a specious sense of solidarity on them. Apparently Oxford had its clubs, but you didn't have to "make" one; nobody seemed to pay much attention to them, except for the political clubs and the Union, a debating society; at Princeton there was no interest in politics and the only people who bothered about the debating societies were the wet smacks and the meatballs. At Princeton it didn't matter what time you got to bed or whether you slept in it; at Oxford, on the other hand, you had to be in your college when the gates closed at midnight, and if you hadn't slept in your bed it was a grievous offense and you might well be "sent down" (expelled) for it. Inside college you could do as you liked, short of inflicting insult or injury on a Fellow of the college or damaging college property; but once outside the gates you were hemmed in by rules.

The antique discipline of the University was taken like much else in the established flummery of England as part jolly tradition and part joke. Nobody wanted to be sent down, but short of that, nearly everybody liked to give the proctors a run for their money. The proctors themselves must have found their job a boring chore, but they performed it urbanely.

Next to being out of college all night without permission, the most perilous thing was being caught climbing into college after midnight, when the gates closed. The difficulties of climbing in varied from college to college, but I believe none was considered invulnerable and most had traditional routes, made more sporting by the college authorities, who had strengthened all weak spots by putting up added defenses of barbed wire, broken bottles and such. Even if you had had the route explained to you or pointed out by daylight it was better, the first time, to go with an old hand.

I climbed in often and found that it was safer to wait till at least two hours after midnight. As the traditional route into New College is doubtless still used, I won't give it away, beyond saying that the first bit was the hardest; you had to shinny up a closed window, without putting a foot through the panes, and take the next stage from a keystone just above the window that stuck out an inch or so from the wall. From here you hauled yourself up on to a roof, wriggling through several strands of barbed wire on the edge of the roof itself. The first time I climbed in alone I got entangled in this wire and had an energetic two or three minutes getting out of it. Just as I did, I looked down at the street and saw a policeman watching me with interest. He took a step forward and whispered, "New College?" I nodded; whereupon he saluted and marched off.

I found the system of study at Oxford breathtakingly simple and unlike anything I had known. I was assigned to a tutor, Mr. F. P. Wilson, whom I went to see for an hour once a week; he suggested books for me to read and usually set me a paper to write. That was all there was to it. Lectures? You could go if you liked, but nobody had to: and since the lectures were always peripheral to the subject, and with a few exceptions the lecturers—at least in my School of English Language and Literature—varied from dull to shockingly dull, they were mostly regarded as a waste of time. Also, except in a small lecture room, you could seldom get near enough to the lecturer to hear him, as he was generally shy or otherwise inaudible and because the first fifteen rows would be filled with eager girl undergraduates, avid to cram their notebooks with his stammered phrases, under the mistaken impression that this would all come in handy on the final exam.

Nobody did your work for you, and nobody could. It was all done by you, by reading, marking, learning and inwardly digesting. Your tutor could be a great help, of course, and mine was, as a critic as well as a counselor; but in some cases he would be so wrapped up in his own work that he gave his undergraduates only a lick and a promise. In any event you were very much on your own. And I soon learned another interesting fact: most of your reading had to be done in the vacations. Like so much else at Oxford, this seemed at first absurd but was in fact sensible. There was too much to read, and the terms were so short and Oxford life so full of a number of things not to be missed, that during the term there was hardly time to do more than hit the high spots in your course of reading.

I decided to spend my first vacation on Boar's Hill, just outside of Oxford, and to read every word of Edmund Spenser, if it killed me. I chose Boar's Hill because Schuyler was living there. He had come to England too, not to study but to write, and was already in the thick of literary life. J. C. Squire, then editor of the *London Mercury*, had "discovered" him and printed a good many of his poems; he was on friendly terms with G. K. Chesterton and Yeats, whom he visited in Ireland; and Robert Bridges, who was then Poet Laureate, was his friend and neighbor on Boar's Hill.

I grew to love Oxford, even in the winter. Those dank stone buildings, smudged and darkened by age and smoke and weather, their medieval stairs and passageways channeled by the footsteps of my uncountable predecessors, were somber, uncomfortable and certainly out of date; my cell-like bedroom had never had any heat in it since it was built in 1300-and-something, and I learned to dress for bed in woolen pajamas, socks and a sweater; the fireplace in my oversize sitting room was so minute that crouching over it on a cold day I could warm my front but my back still froze. It was a damn nuisance, when your bowels moved you, to have to run a hundred yards through the rain (some had to run much farther) doubling right and left through murky archways and courtyards. And you had to put up with the absence of the sun, sometimes for weeks at a time, and to face the fact that the sunniest day in spring was almost bound to change its mind and give you two or three showers.

Nevertheless, I grew to love Oxford. I was disposed to like it from the first, having the look and smell of England among the happy memories of my boyhood. I soon picked up the trick of wearing weather-resistant clothes, as the natives did. And I was lucky enough to like the beer. My family life had accustomed me to afternoon tea, and in Oxford I got it as it should be: brown from a brown teapot, with milk, bread and butter and jam, and big wedges of Dundee cake. I had little fault to find with English food in general.

My friends at Oxford were an accidental lot, as they had been at Princeton, but they were much more varied. My English pals tended to be on the raffish side, and one or two of them might have been described as wastrels; perhaps they would have described me the same way. I know, from Gareth, that his mother

regarded me as a bad influence on him. There were some
distinguished undergraduates at Oxford then, who have since
come graduates of even greater distinction, but I was not a... ...
of them. I can recall only two of my Oxford acquaintances who
later made names for themselves, both as writers: Harold Acton
and Evelyn Waugh. I got to know Acton because he and a
friend of mine, Alfred Nicholson, started a literary magazine,
Broom, and I did some writing for it. Acton was the outstanding
aesthete of Oxford, a protégé of Edith Sitwell's and the leader of
a macaronic set of exquisites. I was a sight-seeing visitor who went
to an occasional lunch or tea at his rooms in Christ Church. I remember seeing Waugh there; he was very young and shy—in Cyril
Connolly's accurate phrase, "he resembled a small but valuable fur-
bearing animal at bay"—and I don't think we exchanged a dozen
words. Acton was always the center, as host and performer (he
once read a long poem of his through a megaphone, to make it
sound more artificial); Waugh was on the circumference, looking
and listening. He seemed a more likable little creature in those
days, but I don't suppose he was.

In spite of his own notoriety, Acton's set had a certain snobbish
glamor, and like all sets it was exclusive. There was one young
man who wanted very much to belong to it, but he couldn't quite
hit the right combination of outrageousness and flippancy that
would have qualified him. Finally he did it. He went with some
friends to meet a train at the Oxford station. To buy his penny
platform ticket he changed ten shillings into coppers, and went on
to the platform with a double handful of coins. Then, when everyone was looking, he spread his hands in a lordly gesture, scattering
coppers all over the pavement, and said loudly: "For the plebs!"

The most widely known American at Oxford in my day was
Eddie Eagan, who was at New College with me. A famous amateur boxer, he had won the light-heavyweight championship of
the A.E.F., had fought Battling Siki, and had sparred in an exhibi-
tion bout with Jack Dempsey himself. He undertook to teach me
boxing, but luckily for my nose he decided I must first get in
shape by exercises, running in the Parks and shadow-boxing, and
the lessons petered out before we came to blows. Eddie was a soft-

spoken and mild-mannered character of great simplicity and earnestness. His chum was the captain of the Oxford boxing team, the Marquess of Clydesdale, now the Duke of Hamilton; their characters were as similar as their battered noses. For some obscurely cultural reason those two joined me and another American in taking tickets for a series of concerts at the Oxford Town Hall.

On a concert evening we all dined together at the Gridiron Club, the abode of athletes, and on those occasions Eddie and Clydesdale would break training, to the extent of a glass of wine. The vinous dinner and their perfect digestions combined with the soothing music to send them softly but soundly asleep; they always woke up, however, in time to applaud.

Schuyler went back to America before the year was out. One of his reasons for leaving was an unhappy love affair, but he was also full of a hopeful scheme: he planned to start a press and to discover and publish unknown American writers. Though neither of us suspected it, this was the end of his own promising literary career.

I had not liked the girl Schuyler had been in love with: I was jealous of her but I also blamed her for Schuyler's leaving. Their affair had been brief and intense and had made them both miserable. Oddly enough, she was the same Helen whom Johnny Martin had told us about. She was the Zuleika Dobson of my days at Oxford.

Because we were all terribly intense then and equally vague, I saw nothing out of the way in promising Schuyler, though I disliked Helen and hardly knew her, that I would cherish and protect her if the occasion ever arose. The occasion arose very soon, in the form of a cable from Schuyler announcing his engagement to a girl in America and asking me to break the news to Helen. I took my role so seriously and was so worried about the heartbreaking effect on Helen of what I had to tell her that I prepared myself for our scene by going into a church and praying for help. Then I went to meet Helen in the New College garden.

That was the first time I noticed, or perhaps admitted to myself,

how appealingly pretty she was. Even the severe academic dress
with its floppy Erasmus cap, which reduced most girls to the aspect
of a snuffed candle, couldn't hide Helen's rather rapacious charm.
She had a good body and long legs, but her face wasn't beautiful,
it was too square-cut. Her looks were in her dark brown eyes,
extraordinarily large and apparently candid, with sweeping eye-
lashes, her small, beautifully formed mouth, and her skin, which
was luminous. And when I had blurted out my news, which—sure
enough—made her weep, she neither crinkled up her face nor
howled nor blew her nose: she sat there gazing blindly in front of
her while big tears crept out of her great eyes and her little mouth
quivered like a gasping goldfish. She was a beautiful sight, and I
watched her with tenderness and awe.

So my friendship with Helen began, that nearly ended my engagement to Julie. For by this time we were officially engaged.
I told Helen all about her, of course, and she couldn't have been
more sympathetic. She herself seemed to recover fairly rapidly
from her broken heart. There were many who were anxious to
help her. Besides being the most sought-after girl in Oxford she had
left a trail of suitors wherever she had been, and their love letters
fluttered in from every quarter of the globe. She used to read me
some of the best bits, shaking with laughter. This made me uneasy
—it seemed a little heartless of her—but my vanity was flattered all
the same. I was also pleased when she ran away from one of her
beaux to go on a picnic with me. Once or twice we went to Bagley
Wood, where nightingales were supposed to sing, and Helen
would read poetry to me while I lay with my head on her lap.

I felt quite sure of myself, as time went on, in the role of *fidus
Achates;* if once in a while our brother-and-sister relation grew
troublingly warm, I put it down to my own deplorably sensual
nature and was ashamed of myself. By the Christmas holidays of
1923, when Helen and I took the same ship back to America, I
regarded her as one of my closest and most trusted friends. When
we landed in New York, Julie was at the dock, and she and Helen
met for the first time. Somehow the meeting was not a success.
I wondered if it might have something to do with my new bowler,
which of course Julie immediately noticed and didn't like; Helen

had persuaded me to buy it and had gone with me to the hat shop in London.

Back in Oxford again, a month later, Helen was full of praises for "little Julie." I knew she meant it affectionately, but all the same I wished she wouldn't call Julie "little." And I soon knew that something was wrong, for Julie had stopped answering my letters. For five months I didn't hear a word from her. I did, however, get a number of veiled warnings from well-meaning friends, which were no help at all, as I hadn't the slightest idea of what they were warning me about. I began to have inklings of what it might be like to be insane. I suppose I was morally insane, for everyone but me knew what the trouble was. Did Helen? I don't know. The worse things got, the more I saw of her, and she must have figured frequently in my letters to Julie. Toward the end of this interminable time I took to calling on Helen nearly every evening just to kiss her good night, which I found comforting.

Most undergraduates at Oxford had a series of examinations to hurdle before taking the final "schools" for their degree; as a senior foreign student I was excused from all these preliminaries. Consequently it wasn't till my second year that I began to be worried enough to work really hard—particularly at the subjects that had been put in to stiffen the course, Anglo-Saxon and Middle English. I think Oxford's general attitude toward the School of English Language and Literature was that it was ridiculous to give a *degree* for it, as if English literature was something to be specially studied; it was part of the heritage of every educated man, a thing he breathed in, having begun to imbibe it with his mother's milk. But then, Oxford's attitude toward degrees in general was that they didn't mean much, except to Germans.

I passed my finals all right, with a Second Class, which is respectable but not distinguished. And I took my degree, though I never got it. I had to take it *in absentia*, because on the day when I expected to "proceed B.A. Oxon," I still owed some Oxford tradesmen, and the university is very strict about that. So I first had to pay the bills and then give the university an extra fee of five pounds on account of my absence, and a pound to my college porter for carrying my nonexistent gown. The degree was conferred on me while I was on my way home to America, and the only evidence I had of it was my name in a paragraph from the London *Times,* in very small type, sent to me by a thoughtful friend.

The plan had been that Julie and her mother would come to Oxford in June, and I made all the arrangements for their coming, without being at all sure that they would come. But they did; and then, at last, I found out what the trouble was. At first I was thunderstruck, then I was indignant. I was being asked to admit that there was something wrong, or at least not quite right, in my friendship with Helen. And that would mean, I felt, not only that I had been stupid but that Helen had been devious. I wasn't prepared to admit that. At least, not at first. But when it was finally borne in on me that it was a question of choosing between Julie and Helen—or, in effect, of my deciding whether or not I wanted to marry Julie; I never had the slightest idea of marrying Helen— I came reluctantly to heel.

My surrender took place in Paris, where we had gone (chaperoned by her mother) after Oxford and London and a trip through the English countryside, half reconciled and half quarreling all along the way. We were both exhausted by the impasse and longing for a decision. One afternoon I went out for a walk by myself along the Seine, determined to make up my mind one way or the other. I started across a bridge, and stopped halfway over to lean on the parapet. Helen had given me a pair of gold cuff links which I wore, defiantly; they had become a symbol of my faith in her. I took the cuff links off and threw them into the river. Then I went back to the hotel and told Julie. We were engaged again.

HOW SHALL I BE
A POET?

I NEVER INTENDED TO BE A JOURNALIST; I meant to be a great writer. I was pretty sure, even at the age of twenty-three, that you couldn't be both. So when I needed a job in order to get married I took it and kept the great writing for a rainy Sunday.

That first job had nothing to do with writing or with journalism either: it was with a firm of professional money raisers. I had spent long, discouraging weeks making the rounds of publishers and newspapers in New York. The publishers laughed when they heard I wanted an editorial job; the city editors simply asked what experience I could offer and then said, "Sorry." The only reason the money-raising firm gave me a try, I think, was that they had a big campaign in hand for the Diocese of New York, raising fifteen million dollars to finish the Cathedral of St. John the Divine, and hoped to use me somehow to get into my father's neighboring diocese of New Jersey. The campaign was a failure, it raised only ten of the wanted fifteen million, but apparently I was a comparative success, for when I resigned after a year in which I hated every minute of my job the president of the company urged me to stay, saying that I was to be promoted into the publicity department.

I had written a desperate letter to four editors, none of whom I knew, and got three replies and one interview—with Herbert Croly, editor of the *New Republic*. He was a terribly shy man and on this occasion I was completely tongue-tied. After several minutes of excruciating silence he murmured something about the managing editor, and took me into Bruce Bliven's office. Bliven explained the job to me (proofreading and make-up mostly), asked me some questions about myself and then dismissed me, saying kindly that if I later thought of anything I had forgotten to say, to drop him a line. I rushed home and wrote him an eight-page letter.

I got the job, though not on my shocking terms—I wanted to work for nothing, to prove my earnestness—and was paid forty dollars a week to start. The job had about as much to do with journalism as an office boy's with banking, but at least it was in the same building.

The building was not as impressive as a bank: two old brick houses knocked together and painted yellow, on West 21st Street in New York. This was in the Chelsea district, once residential, but in those days down-at-heel. On 23rd Street, where a huge apartment house now stands, the brownstone houses sat well back from the street behind grimy yards that might once have been gardens; in little basement restaurants, with Japanese waiters, you could get a three-course lunch for fifty cents. A few doors away from the *New Republic* office was a home for wayward girls; across the street was the General Theological Seminary. It was 1925, the depth of the Prohibition era, and there must have been several "smoke shops" (places where they sold wood alcohol—poisonous but intoxicating) in the neighborhood, for it was a common sight to see old bums, their faces greenish-gray, sitting on the curb and vomiting while children watched them with great interest and no sympathy.

It was a quiet quarter, far removed from the bustle and boom of midtown and downtown Manhattan, an appropriate home for a journal of opinion that with no middle flight intended to soar above the American plain. I first climbed the *New Republic's* creaking stairs reverently, almost on tiptoe. It was a long time before I could manage to clump in, whistling. For one thing, I was much the most junior of the staff. (An old friend of my family's had cautioned me not to be led astray by "all those young radicals," and the first sight of their middle-aged faces and bald or graying heads was a slight shock.) My nearest contemporary was Edmund Wilson, who was already a great name to me; his blinking, abstracted gaze and high-pitched voice, his long burrowing silences and abrupt breakaways from a conversation that had never existed but had obviously become unbearable seemed to me the earned eccentricities of an older man.

And the others were even more elderly. Herbert Croly, the editor, who gave the impression of never raising his voice above an almost inaudible whisper but whose presence reduced everyone else to inaudibility or silence; Robert Morss Lovett, whose textbook on English literature I had studied as a schoolboy; Stark Young, dramatic critic; George Soule, the economist; Bruce Bliven, the managing editor—all these and the rest, even including the advertising manager (who, surprisingly enough, smelt of cheap perfume; or was it something he put on his hair?), were to me objects of veneration: men to emulate if I could, understand as I grew in wisdom, and follow without question.

My job was simpler than that; in fact, as Bliven had carefully explained to me, it was "purely mechanical": proofreading, sending out corrected proofs of articles to their authors, pasting up the dummy, seeing the paper to press—at first under the eye of one of the editors. I had been so keen on getting the job that I had not only offered to work for nothing but had promised (I think in writing) to eat any typographical errors that appeared in the paper. In spite of me they did appear, and more than once Felix Frankfurter, who in those days served as legal adviser to the *New Republic,* tried to get me fired. He had no personal animus against me and we had never met; he just didn't like typographical errors and thought (like me, in theory) that they were unforgivable.

My office was a small, boxlike room with a window looking on to the street, at the head of the first flight of stairs, and as everyone had to pass my open door, I soon got to know who everybody was. There was one editor, however, who had no office in the building and whose name, I think, was not even on the masthead; he introduced himself in a hoarse, shy voice as Ridgely Torrence, and said he "did" the poetry. He was a gaunt man of indeterminate age and shabby appearance, with a long, sad face and wisps of thinning hair combed wildly across his skull; he gave the impression of being hunted. He accepted poems for publication but apparently had no authority whatever to say when they should be published, and as none of the other editors took any interest in poetry, it was left to me, as a "purely mechanical" matter, to patch a poem into the make-up when it would fit a hole at the bottom of a page. When Ridgely Torrence came to see me, it was always to urge me to print such-and-such a poem of Robert Frost's before a certain imminent date, when the poem would be published in a book.

He never appeared at the office lunches; I think he wouldn't have been welcome. There was a dining room on the ground floor, with a round table and a Lazy Susan in the middle; a quorum of the editors and one or more guests had lunch there three or four times a week. When I was told that I might come too, I was delighted, at first. Mr. Croly usually presided. The conversation, though hushed, was intense and not always in English. That came to be more and more my private complaint. It wasn't so much the Haitian foreign minister—though his pellucid French was incomprehensible to me I admired his profile—as the visiting experts who spoke a language all their own. Particularly the economists. The hours of economic big talk that passed over my head at these lunches, plus the hundreds of thousands of words of economic argument I had to proofread, left me a simple idiot on the whole subject. It was my profound hope that this fact should not be discovered, and in the presence of these economic adults, fear of betraying my ignorance, added to a natural shyness and sense of juniority, kept me from ever opening my mouth.

In time I discovered that other New Republicans shared my view that these lunches were not exactly the jolliest things going. Stark Young, who was the only editor with a real social sense, simply stayed away; once in a long time he would be prevailed on to come and perform, and those lunches were notably entertaining. Edmund Wilson, urging the view that the heavy atmosphere of these meetings was due to the fact that the editors were "just a bunch of hopeless neurotics" and could no longer help themselves or it, exhorted me, as a young newcomer not yet asphyxiated, to break the spell by speaking up, changing the subject, "being natural," etc. I saw what he meant, and even proved his point, vicariously. On a day when no economists were to be present I invited Johnny Martin to lunch. He was not in the least impressed by the company, was perfectly natural, talked a lot, smoked a pipe, and dominated the whole table. It was a great success.

A later experiment, along the same lines, was a success of a different kind. By this time I had been given an assistant. Pauline was an extraordinary girl, who had learned to speak fluent Russian on a six-week visit to China. She too was allowed to come to the office lunches, where she turned out to be even more tongue-tied than I. Nevertheless, she was definitely my junior, and even as I had been exhorted by Edmund Wilson, so I exhorted her. Pauline listened to me with her usual wooden-Indian expression, and said nothing. Some time later, on a day when I was downtown at the job press where the *New Republic* was printed, a distinguished British journalist was the guest of honor at lunch. By the end of the meal he was in full spate. The dessert was chocolate éclairs. When Bliven, who was acting as host in Mr. Croly's absence, discovered at the first bite that his éclair was stuffed with cotton, he tried to warn the honored guest, but in vain: he could not be interrupted even with his mouth full, and downed the whole éclair. Bliven, who saw nothing funny about this, could see at a glance that Pauline did, and if anyone had ever been fired from the *New Republic*, she would have been. This was the last attempt, as far as I know, to humanize the *New Republic* lunches.

It didn't take very long to master the routine of proofreading and make-up, and though I was not bored with the job I was far from being content with it. I wanted to be a writing journalist, not a mechanical helper. I would have to show these professionals that I could write. When William Jennings Bryan died, I thought my opportunity had come. I would write an obituary of Bryan, eloquent, sardonic, with profound overtones—none of your cheap Menckenisms—that would make them sit up and take notice. I wrote it, I felt, in the grand manner; if there were seventeenth-century echoes, even a certain kinship with the best bits in Sir Thomas Browne, so much the better; it was about time the *New Republic* showed that it could soar into the empyrean. I handed this packaged eagle to Robert Morss Lovett, the literary editor, and sat back to wait, with a thumping heart. Two days, three days passed, and no word. Finally I caught him on the stairs and asked him if he had read my piece on Bryan. He admitted that he had. He cleared his throat, looked kindly over my head, and said: "It's not *journalism*, you know." Then: "You've been reading a lot of Lamb, haven't you?"

That, I suppose, was my first lesson in journalism—or the first one I paid attention to. It was also Lovett who gave me my second. Not long after the Bryan disaster he began to try me on an occasional book note—small unsigned paragraphs on novels that nobody else wanted to review. I labored long over these miniature molehills, and some of them were printed. But I knew that they were not very good. Then, one fine day, I got a book by Jim Tully, a hobo turned writer, one of the professional hard guys of the 1920's. There was something phony in his hardness but also something admirable about his aim. My first sentence was: "Jim Tully is so goddam hard-boiled that his spit bounces." Before I lost my nerve I handed the paragraph in to Lovett. Ten minutes later he clattered down the stairs from his room, waving the review and exclaiming, "That's the stuff! That's the stuff! Let's have a page of these and we'll sign your name."

So I became a book reviewer. If I had known I was to remain one for the better part of ten years I might not have been so eager; but at that point it was anything to get into print, and so reassure myself that I was making headway as a journalist. I had no very high opinion of book reviewers or their work—with the exception of a few like Edmund Wilson—and for years I couldn't understand why anybody ever read them. I could see why anxious authors might, and knew by their letters to the editor that a lot of them did, and by published interviews that a few of them ostentatiously didn't. I read book reviews myself just to see what the other fellow had said, to compare it with my own review; but I was never quite able to regard reviewing books as an altogether respectable occupation. I knew just enough about writing to realize that even bad writing is hard work, and to feel that there was something overhasty and wrong in making a one-paragraph judgment of the job it had taken another man a year or more to do. I doubt whether any of this wise hesitation showed itself in the reviews I wrote, however. Like most of my fellows, I had to sweat over the attempt to appreciate a really good book; I had more fun with the bad ones.

Everyone learns by doing, but perhaps doesn't learn as much or as fast as he thinks. It wasn't long before I came to regard myself as a pretty sharp reviewer—of fiction, at any rate. Then I met a literary undergradute. He wasn't the precious sort; genius—innocent, corn-fed genius—was more his line. He was announcing things to a small group, and I liked what he said. I liked him too. I asked him what he was going to do when he left college. He was going to write, of course, but he knew he couldn't make his living that way. He thought he might review books. But if he did, he would write the truth about them. That's what he said.

I took that remark away with me like something stuck in my eye. It was absurd, and ignorant, but it rankled. What did he know about writing the truth? How could anybody write "the truth" about a book? Just the same, whether anyone could or not, I knew I wasn't doing it. What I was doing was following my nose, and trusting it to tell me when it smelt something good or something bad. As far as I could see, that was all anyone did—perhaps even the critics. I used to ask Edmund Wilson about this, and I think his reply was that a good nose wasn't enough, though it was a prerequisite.

The editorial staff that Croly had gathered round him seemed to me then, and still does, a distinguished collection; I also thought them a bowlful of pretty odd fish. Perhaps the most distinguished, certainly the oddest, was Edmund Wilson. Except for Robert Graves, whom I had met only once, he was the first real "literary man" I had ever known, and as such he drew my fascinated attention. I thought him rather disappointing to look at: a short, sandy-haired youngish man, at thirty already inclining to stoutness and baldness, with pale, blinking eyes and a high, strained-tenor voice; his profile as regular as a plump Roman emperor's but his expression like an absent-minded, cantankerous professor's. There was something chilly and withdrawn—"disagreeable" is perhaps not too strong a word—in the set of his face. Years later I saw very much the same proudly peevish look on the countenance of the famous and successful Evelyn Waugh. But Waugh had earned or had cultivated that face, whereas in Wilson's case you felt it had been wished on him without his knowing it—or had he simply earned it at an earlier age?

He was not so much shy as uneasy and awkward with people, and his uneasiness held more than a hint of impatience, as if he felt he was wasting his time in such company and was in a hurry to be off. He had no small talk whatever, but when he was holding forth, as he sometimes did, on a subject that interested him, he seemed perfectly oblivious of his audience, and would go on and on in his rapid-fire, high-pitched voice, gesturing mostly by jerking back his head or wagging it from side to side. When he paused, always at the end of a paragraph, a hearer might wrongly suppose that he had finished, and would sometimes make the mistake of starting a new subject. That this was a mistake was borne in on him when Wilson, having collected his thoughts and regained his breath, broke ruthlessly in at the exact spot where he had left off.

In the first months of our acquaintance I never had any real conversation with him, though I saw him nearly every day. At first he would slip past my office door without stopping, sometimes with a nod and a small whinnying sound meant as a greeting. Then one day he stopped and came in. He had discovered that I lived in Princeton, where he had spent four years at college.

"Tell me. Do you know Christian Gauss?" Dean Gauss was his great friend on the faculty there.

I said I did, and liked and admired him. Between long pauses, Wilson drew one or two other facts from me, and then departed.

After that, he often took to stopping for a minute or two on his way to his own office. The subjects of our conversation were always the same.

"Have you seen the Gausses lately?" The answer to this was always yes or no.

Long pause. "Any skating on the lake recently?"

This was not a very fruitful topic either. During the next long pause, Wilson would leaf absently through the newspapers and magazines on my side table and then, collecting himself, cry, "Well, see you presently!" and dart out.

He had obviously been a precocious little boy, an omnivorous reader whose absorbing passion for books may have saved him from being thought a prig—or perhaps protected him from being aware that he was one. In the only story I know about his child-hood, his parents once tried to lure him out of doors and into the normal companionship of other boys by buying him a complete baseball outfit; he appeared at the baseball field with this equip-ment and made himself popular with the other boys by giving it all away, after which he retired underneath the nearest tree with his book. There was something impressive and something appeal-ing about him—you felt that while his mind was roaming (occu-pied with very serious matters and in awesomely select company) he might not quite realize that it was beginning to rain, and you felt impelled to open an umbrella over him or guide him to shelter.

He did have friends, and his friends felt that way about him; they respected him, laughed at him and called him "Bunny." Not I, however; I was too much in awe of him as "an older man" and a literary figure. In the dozen years I knew him I never spoke to him by a less formal name than "Wilson." And there must have been something about him that appealed to women, for he was married four times. His second wife, who died in a tragic acci-dent, was the only one I knew. She too laughed at him but evi-dently found him lovable. When I first knew him he was divorced and not yet remarried, and I remember the room he was living in —I think it was on Ninth Avenue—a perfect picture of helpless, squalid bachelorhood: an unmade bed, empty gin bottles on the dirty floor, no carpet, one naked electric light bulb. Women too —some of them—wanted to guide him to shelter.

His most famous friend, who had been at Princeton with him, was Scott Fitzgerald. I saw them together only once, but Wilson often spoke of Fitzgerald, and in a surprisingly protective way. He seemed to believe that in some aspects of life Fitzgerald was a com-plete innocent and depended on wiser or more informed heads to guide and tutor him. This may well have been true, but I thought Wilson's evidence unconvincing, to say the least. He told me about a weekend he had recently spent with the Fitzgeralds near Wil-mington, in a country house where Fitzgerald was hibernating with an unfinished novel.

"You know," said Wilson, "Fitzgerald never reads the papers."
"No?"

"No, he never does, so he doesn't know what's going on in the world, and he relies on me to tell him. On this occasion, after I had outlined the world situation for him, he said to me, 'And I understand there will soon be a presidential election? And possibly a change of administration?' I said, 'Yes.' 'In that case,' he said, 'I suppose you will be made Secretary of State.'"

"He was pulling your leg," I suggested.

"Oh, no, no, no! He really believes that anyone who knows as much as I do will infallibly be made Secretary of State."

Once Wilson brought Fitzgerald to the *New Republic* office. They clumped noisily up the stairs—they had obviously had a good lunch—and stopped at my door. Fitzgerald was about Wilson's height but otherwise a lively contrast to him: alert, compact, grinning, crackling with nervous energy. Wilson introduced us.

"What!" said Fitzgerald, opening his eyes wide, "Not *the* Mr. Matthews?"

"Oh," said Wilson, looking at him in surprise, "do you know him?"

"*Know* him! I used to fix his teeth!"

This assertion pleased me but seemed to alarm Wilson vaguely.

Wilson had enemies as well as friends. The printers at the Steinberg Press, for instance, where the *New Republic* was printed, hated him. They had their reasons. Although Wilson had been a journalist, of a literary sort, for years, I don't think he clearly understood or had much interest in the mechanics of printing. Anything he wrote was likely to be rewritten several times before he was satisfied with it; he would cross out paragraphs on his galley proofs and paste in new passages, typewritten, if there was time; if there wasn't, he would crowd the margins with his small but legible handwriting, in pencil. (He had a peculiar way of holding a pencil: he seemed to bunch his whole hand about it, using both his middle finger and his forefinger to guide the point.) Worst of all, he would often make drastic revisions on the page proof itself. As anyone who knows the printing process doesn't need to be told, such eleventh-hour corrections entail a lot of extra work for linotyper, compositor, proofreader and foreman, and hold up the stereotypers as well. All hands in a printing shop take a strong view of "unnecessary" corrections on page proof.

The printers didn't hold me personally responsible for these outrages of Wilson, as they knew I was only a go-between. But one day at the press, when with a sinking heart I had given the foreman some heavily "corrected" page proofs of a Wilson article, he said to me, "This Wilson a friend of yours?"

That wasn't quite the way I'd have put it, but I said yes.

"Well, let me tell you something. Don't ever let him show his face down here. Why not? The boys would kill 'm. That's why."

I think it's a pity that Wilson never knew that; but it was characteristic of him not even to suspect it. I suppose it was equally characteristic of me not to tell him—although if I had tried to, I don't think he would have understood.

My political innocence in those days was complete. I was aware of Theodore Dreiser, Frank Norris, and Upton Sinclair—but only as clumsy and humorless writers with a dreary and irrelevant "message." I had heard of the I.W.W., now a kind of Paul Bunyan memory. I admired Eugene Debs for having gone to jail for his beliefs, felt uneasily that Tom Mooney had been railroaded to prison on a false charge, despised A. Mitchell Palmer for his "Red raids," and hated the Commonwealth of Massachusetts for the judicial murder of Sacco and Vanzetti. I regarded myself as a liberal, friendly or at least sympathetic to all sorts and conditions of radicals—including the Russian revolutionaries. I had no conception of the Communist attitude toward liberals. In short, I had no conception of the Communist attitude.

As for the struggle in the Communist party between Trotskyites and Stalinists, if I was aware of it at all, it appeared to me as much the same sort of schism as the cleavage between the Hicksites and the other Quakers, a matter of theological theory. Wilson did not feel the same responsibility in keeping me informed about this underground world as he did in bringing his friend Scott Fitzgerald up to date on the headlines, and I remained in ignorance of these significant tremors, though I did notice, to a certain extent, their effect on him. He took to writing on subjects far afield from literary criticism: strikes and factories and the politics of the labor movement. I knew he was reading Marx; I remember his saying that most Marxists had read their prophet very cursorily but that he had read him *all*. He learned Russian, and later went to Russia for six months.

Even in his most "socially conscious" period, however, Wilson remained essentially a critical scholar, and I don't suppose he was ever active in politics of any sort, or became a member of any party. But he must have been regarded by the Stalinists as a dangerous intellectual, a liberal, a counter-revolutionary, perhaps even a Trotskyite. At the time, as I say, I was almost unaware of this underground civil war among the intelligentsia, and certainly had no idea of the bitter partisanship with which it was carried on; on one occasion, to my great surprise, I found myself under fire, though I couldn't see why. Wilson was present, but far from well; he was suffering from some sort of strain at the time, and had told several people he was having a nervous breakdown.

The occasion was a dinner given by Otto Kahn, a rich and civilized banker who was a famous patron of the arts, with an attitude of princely indifference toward his protégés' politics. I think the dinner was supposed to celebrate the first season of the New Playwrights' Guild, or some such title, in which Wilson's friend John Dos Passos was involved. The dinner was held in an upstairs room over a Greek restaurant in downtown New York, and since our host was generous as well as rich, each table was furnished not only with wine but also with an imperial quart of Scotch. Early in the proceedings Mr. Kahn made a speech, suave, elegant and brief, and then tactfully left. The evening thereupon became political.

The toastmaster was a young fellow named Mike Gold, whom I had heard of as a Communist—in my ignorance I thought of him as a liberal like the rest of us, only perhaps a little rougher-tongued. First he called on a few people for speeches. Wilson was one of them; he was expected to say something appreciative about Dos Passos, who had written several plays (though I don't think any of them were produced) for the New Playwrights' Guild. Wilson got to his feet, but then said he was sorry, he was quite unable to make a speech, and sat down. Gold thereupon spoke a fiery harangue against capitalism, followed by others equally fiery: many of them were in praise of Carlo Tresca, an old radical war horse who was also present, and nothing whatever was said about Dos Passos. After a while Wilson got up again and caught Gold's eye. He said he thought he could make that speech now. In his high voice, in breathless rushes and with heavy pauses, he said:

"I've recently been—in California. I was very much—struck—by the domestic—architecture—there. Many of the—buildings—have extremely—fancy—façades. I was told that—they are so jerry-built —that frequently—the front—falls down—before the back is—finished. And I just want to say—that in my opinion—the work of Mr. Dos Passos—is not like that."

He sat down, and the meeting went on. After the formalities were over and everyone was feeling comradely on Capitalist Kahn's Scotch—I was, at any rate—I went up to Mike Gold's table to introduce myself, and was much taken aback when, instead of offering me the right hand of fellowship, he burst into a diatribe against liberals in general and the *New Republic* in particular. I took this unprovoked and, I thought, undeserved attack very ill; we both got angry. Then old Art Young, the cartoonist for *The Masses*, made peace between us, and next day Mike Gold wrote me a note which might have been an apology, and saying he hoped we'd meet again. We never did, however.

About this time Wilson more or less took me in tow. I don't remember ever having my copy actually edited by anyone on the *New Republic;* it was either accepted or not; but he must have given me some guidance and instruction. I have a distinct recollection of his saying once, with a sigh, that I was now able to write a sentence, though still pretty wobbly on my paragraphs. He considered me good enough, at any rate, to use as a guided missile against certain popular writers whose reputations he felt should be deflated. On these occasions I was shotted to the muzzle, aimed with great care and fired with a loud bang.

D-day was the publication date of the chosen author's new book, but the target was the author himself and all his works. For weeks beforehand, I read or reread everything he had written, and by the time I was ready to write the review I was fully loaded. I was given a whole page of the *New Republic* to explode in. Two targets I particularly remember, because I felt the satisfying sensation of having hit them solidly, were Christopher Morley and Struthers Burt. In the case of Struthers Burt I was sure of it, for he sent me word through a mutual acquaintance that if I ever showed myself in his vicinity (he had a ranch in Wyoming; or perhaps it was Montana), he would horsewhip me. This gave me my first intimation of the power of the press, and a dim inkling of its true nature.

When Wilson made himself my editorial tutor I naturally saw a good deal more of him than I had previously. In time I might have become perfectly at ease with him, we might perhaps have been real friends. But it would have taken a long time. As it was, I remember spending some evenings in his company, in Greenwich Village and other places in New York, and even went to see him in his house at Red Bank, in New Jersey. That time we drank applejack in such quantities that I drove home with one eye shut, to keep the road from turning into an X. And I remember another evening, in New York, when he and I sat up drinking till a very late hour; I was trying to find out what he really thought about writing, and felt that I nearly succeeded, but not quite.

On the flyleaf of my copy of his *Axel's Castle* Wilson has written: "In memory of André Maurois." This refers to a weekend when Wilson and his second wife stayed with us at Princeton. André Maurois was living in Princeton that year, on some sort of grant from the university. He was a great admirer of Wilson's writing, and when we met at a party and he discovered that I was on the *New Republic* staff, he asked me if I could arrange a meeting. Wilson was no admirer of Maurois, but agreed to my suggestion that I ask the Mauroises to dinner when the Wilsons came down for the weekend. I should have written Mme. Maurois a note, but it seemed simpler to telephone. I spoke to M. Maurois, who was delighted to accept.

I had asked them for Saturday at 7:30. When at 8:30 they had not arrived, I telephoned the Maurois' house, and a maid said they had gone to dinner somewhere else! But they came home early, and about half-past ten M. Maurois was on the telephone, prolix with apologies for the misunderstanding. When I could get a word in, I assured him that all was not lost, as the Wilsons would still be here the next night; would he and Mme. Maurois dine with us then? Delighted, delighted, but meantime they would come this evening—no, no, he *insisted*—to present their apologies in person. They came. They stayed until after midnight. Wilson obviously didn't much like Maurois. Mme. Maurois obviously didn't at all like Wilson. Everything of possible interest that could be said was said. When at last the Maurois' left, we looked at each other and asked how we could possibly go through another such evening. None of us, the Mauroises included, we felt sure, had the slightest desire for a repeat performance. But how could we get out of it? Perhaps the Mauroises, being older and more worldly than we, would have the grace to make their excuses. All next day we spent in gloomy contemplation of the coming evening, asking ourselves if there was no way out. There was none. The evening came, it was as dreadful as we had expected; at last, at last, it was over. We never saw the Mauroises again.

There was another evening with Wilson which was worse, but more exciting. And this one was entirely my fault. I wanted to bring Wilson and Schuyler Jackson together. I was proud of knowing both of them—Wilson the established literary man and Schuyler the not-yet-established poet—and I hoped they would hit it off. If they did, Wilson would become interested in Schuyler's poetry, and then perhaps his ship would come in. In those days I was always catching a glimpse of its topsails coasting along above the intervening headland, preparing to round it and make harbor.

Schuyler and his wife, Kit, were then living in Trenton, trying to make a go of a combined antique shop and tea-room which they called The Water Monkey. Wilson was spending the night with us in Princeton: he had come down to do some reading in the university library for an article he was writing on Woodrow Wilson. As usual, he was full of his subject; as he and my wife and I drove the twelve miles in to Trenton he retailed long, informative passages about Woodrow Wilson's struggles with Dean West and the Princeton trustees, when he had been president of the university. In the pauses between his paragraphs my wife, in spite of my nudges, would sometimes try a new tack; Wilson ignored these interruptions and always came up again at the exact spot where he had disappeared. By the time we arrived at The Water Monkey he was, in his way, in very good form.

The early part of the evening, I thought, went all right. We had more than the usual number of drinks before dinner, and I was soon in that foolish paradise where every prospect is pleasant and all your companions are clever angels. I did notice that Wilson was being a rather long-winded angel and that some of Schuyler's most penetrating remarks were not getting their due, but I regarded them both with fraternal fondness and confidently expected that great things would soon be said. I hadn't long to wait: we had finished the preliminary drinks and had sat down at the table when Schuyler somehow got the floor. He had reached a point of pent-up eloquence; he too was in good form. Almost too good, I began to fear: for he was riding roughshod over Wilson's attempts to comment or reply. It soon became evident that he was on a runaway cavalry charge, attacking the thin red line of literary men; and as he rose in his stirrups and brandished his saber, it was chillingly plain that the single figure he was intently heading for was Wilson himself.

It took Wilson a little longer than the rest of us to realize that he was being attacked. After all, why should he have been? He was a guest at dinner, presumably among friends. But his host was giving him the kind of reception that no one could any longer pretend was friendly. I think Wilson behaved very well. When the true situation dawned on him at last he rose from his chair. His face was white, and beads of sweat stood on the flanges of his nose—an infallible sign in him of strong emotion, and only partly attributable to drink. He made a little old-fashioned bow, and said:

"I'm sorry that such excellent liquor should have produced such a disagreeable conversation, and I shall now take my leave."

We had finished our soup; that was as far as the dinner had gone. My wife and I got up too—he had come with us, so we had to go with him—and left the ruined evening. On the drive back to Princeton we did what we could to explain and apologize for

Schuyler's behavior. But we could see that Wilson was both hurt and puzzled. About a week later he came into my office.

"I know what's the matter with your friend Schuyler."

"What?"

"He's got dementia praecox!"

Nothing would disabuse him of this notion—and if it satisfied him, as it seemed to, what were the odds? I couldn't hope to explain to him what wasn't altogether clear to me—the complex of emotions (anger and pride were certainly among them) which his pedantic and overriding prosiness must have stirred up in Schuyler; he would only have said that Schuyler was betraying the envy and malice of the amateur for the professional. There was no longer any hope of those two becoming friends; and I could see how necessary it was, from Wilson's point of view, to find some rational or at least scientific explanation for what must have seemed to him a deliberately malevolent but otherwise motiveless attack.

The odd thing was that my last meeting with Wilson was a very similar scene, in reverse. It was about ten years after I had left the *New Republic* for *Time*. Wilson's path and mine had crossed rarely, but I was glad when they did, and I thought of him with a kind of affection and watched his career with a certain pride. One night, as my train from New York was pulling into Princeton Junction and the Princeton passengers were putting on their coats, I caught sight of Wilson's familiar, stocky figure in the aisle ahead of me. I overtook him, hailed him, and asked if he was coming to visit the Gausses. He was. I was delighted to see him again. He blinked at me with no change of expression—but then he never did have much expression. His first question to me was about a mutual friend.

"Is Bill Hanson still in the booby hatch?"

I thought this a surprisingly brutal way of referring to a friend's tragic misfortunes, but I let it pass.

"No," I said. "He's out now, and much better."

By this time we had left the New York train and were walking across the platform to the "dummy" train for Princeton.

"*Time* is dirty," said Wilson. "And it's getting dirtier."

What was the matter with him? Was he in a bad temper, or was he trying to bait me? I decided he was kidding me, in rather a rough way.

"What do you mean?" I said, smiling.

"It's dirty about women. And I notice that the higher up you go in it, the dirtier it gets."

This was rough kidding indeed. I began to get irritated.

"Dirty about women? In what way? What women?"

"Virginia Woolf. Martha Gellhorn. Rebecca West."

He was serious. But what on earth was he talking about? Dirty! I supposed he must mean that *Time* was unfair in its reviews of women writers, and he was determined to hold me responsible. By this time I was too angry, and too much taken aback, to argue. We climbed aboard the dummy. I said good night to him stiffly, and went and sat in a seat by myself.

When I got home, still shaken by anger, I told my wife about this little scene, and had a drink, and gradually felt better. But I had to find some explanation for Wilson's behavior. It seemed to me, as Schuyler's outburst had seemed to him, a deliberately malevolent but otherwise motiveless attack. And worse in this case, for Wilson and I had been friendly, if not friends. All of a sudden the answer—or at least a possible answer—came to me. *Time* had recently printed a review of Mary McCarthy's short stories, *The Company She Keeps*. I hadn't read the book but I had passed the review, which had been written by James Agee. It was a severe review, but I knew and respected Agee and would have gone bail for his judgment. He was the last man in the world to write anything "dirty" about anybody. But Mary McCarthy, I now remembered, was Wilson's third (and present) wife. That was it— that must be it. It never occurred to me to think that Wilson must be suffering from dementia praecox. We never met again, and I was sorry for that.

There must have been other reasons, and perhaps better ones, for his animus against me. I think he may have felt disappointed by my giving up writing for the anonymous, executive job of a *Time* editor; besides, he didn't consider *Time* respectable journalism. There was nothing in my accomplishment he could happily take credit for; in a way it was a reflection on himself as an instructor of my youth. He must have felt that the time he had spent on me was quite wasted. I had not only left school too young but had gone to the bad straight off.

As for me, I remember Wilson as one of my favorite professors.

My years on the *New Republic* in a sense came to nothing, or at least ended in anticlimax. But they were assuredly not a waste of time, and they pointed my life in a new direction. In those four years I made the first steps in beginning to learn how to write—in a chastened and much humbler form than the "great writing" I had aspired to; and I broke away from a part, at any rate, of my family pattern, if "break away" isn't too bold an expression for behavior that seems to me now timid and tentative.

At Mr. Croly's suggestion, I did come to New York for a winter, bringing my wife and infant son, "to be nearer the paper." We rented our newly built Princeton house for what I thought an enormous sum, but our hotel in New York cost us even more. It never occurred to me to repeat this daring adventure, or extend it. Why didn't I leave Princeton for good, get out from under my parents' shadow, and move to New York? There were many reasons, that seemed compelling at the time: we were "settled" in Princeton, in a house we had allowed my parents to pay for; Julie had never seriously considered living anywhere else but in her native town—and last of all in New York; most of the people we knew were in the same boat, and accepted it as man's fate to spend three hours of his day commuting to and from his job.

Though I remained a suburbanite and a stay-at-home son, in other respects I didn't fill the bill as a solid citizen. The liberalism of the *New Republic*, to which I wholeheartedly subscribed, was a cause of grief and alarm to my parents; and I not only stopped going to church but joined the Orage group in New York.

A. R. Orage (pronounced in the French manner, although he was British) was a journalist who had had an erratically brilliant career in London, had fallen under the spell of an esoteric religious teacher named Gurdjieff, and was now expounding the word to

New Yorkers. I heard about him from my friends the Jacksons, and Julie and I went to our first meeting with them. Gurdjieff was a man of obscurely Russian origins, whose headquarters were in France, in a large house called Le Prieuré, in Fontainebleau. Here for a while Gurdjieff had conducted his "Institute for the Harmonious Development of Man"—I had heard of it because my admired Katherine Mansfield had died there, of tuberculosis. The Institute was no longer officially in being, but Gurdjieff continued to live there with a handful of disciples, traveling from time to time in Oriental style, with his retinue (he came to New York every year for at least a month). Meanwhile his teachings were presented in London by P. D. Ouspensky and in New York by Orage.

Most of the Orage meetings I went to were held in bookshops or in barnlike lecture rooms, and I thought the people who came to hear him a pretty job lot. One of my friends who was also a regular attendant described us as "the 100 neediest cases." There were a few notables among us: I remember Muriel Draper, Mabel Dodge, and her fourth and final husband, Tony Luhan, a Zuñi Indian. Tony was a massive man who wore his greasy black hair in long pigtails, wrapped himself in a striped blanket and never spoke. It was also a question whether he understood anything Orage was saying. Nevertheless, Tony was taken as a kind of barometer: if it was an interesting evening, he sat erect and watchful; if not, his head sagged and he slept, quietly and solidly as a weathered rock. Perhaps what really affected him was the air.

Orage was a compulsive smoker, lighting one cigarette, with slightly trembling hands, from the butt of another. We often discussed his smoking habits and wondered whether he was completely conscious of them. For consciousness was the lock that Gurdjieff's key was supposed to open. It was Gurdjieff's claim that he had discovered, or rediscovered, a secret known to Pythagoras and handed down to the elect of all later generations: the only possible method of escape from man's doom of "eternal recurrence" and of attaining a real, conscious and lasting identity. This was the Method: "self-observation with non-identification."

As a slogan, it would not have appealed to an advertising man. According to Orage, Buddha perfected this same method; and so, presumably, did Christ.

It was admittedly a laborious process. Buddha had begun by observing his breathing; when he was completely and continuously conscious of that, he went on to muscular tensions, posture, heartbeat, and so on. By the time you had finished the course (so we gathered, at least) your complete and objective awareness of your body had not only put you in absolute control of it but had summoned into wakeful being your hitherto nonexistent (or sleeping) self. The trick was, we thought, to get over the first hurdle. Orage gave us some helpful rules of thumb. One was: be more so—the more like yourself you behave, the more likely you are to catch a glimpse of yourself. "He that is filthy, let him be filthy still" —but a damn sight filthier. We discussed this notion with enthusiasm and at length, and when the bolder spirits among us, like Schuyler, broke into abrupt eccentricities of speech or action, we knew they were practicing.

It remained a constant question, however, whether anyone was actually "able to do it." We eventually decided that no one we knew had yet quite got the hang of it, not even Orage; but that Gurdjieff himself must have mastered the Method, if anybody had. Our own attempts grew more and more sporadic, and finally ceased, but we kept on going to the meetings. Orage was an extremely interesting and lucid lecturer, and there were other aspects of Gurdjieff's teaching which were not so forbidding as the Method.

That is, when Orage himself was expounding them. There were other evenings of an unspeakable dreariness when we got it straight from the horse's mouth, in readings from The Book. This was the Bible of the cult; it was referred to as "The Book" not only out of reverence but because the full title took too long to say: *Tales Told By Beelzebub to His Grandson.** A literal translation into English of Gurdjieff's Russian original, it was a masterpiece of long-windedness and boring repetitions. Even so, it had its

---

* The Book was later published in New York (Harcourt, Brace) with the more modest title of *All and Everything*.

points, its occasional phrases (one I remember is "to go the whole hog, including the postage"), and some of the made-up names were memorable (the Very Saintly Ashiata Shiemash, the Law of Heptaparaparshinokh). Buried under the middens of pretentious verbiage were sly, peasant-shrewd sayings and some pointed fables.

When Gurdjieff visited New York, I noticed that everyone, including Orage, was afraid of him, didn't understand him, and never knew what he would do next. I neither trusted nor worshiped him. He was a massive, bald, heavily mustachioed man in his sixties, with liquid, bull-like, hypnotic eyes. His manner said more clearly than his never-clearly-understood words that he regarded all people as different classes of idiot; his bearing and manners toward them were those of a pasha. His women followers obviously adored him, and some of those who had found favor in his sight had visible mementos: swarthy and liquid-eyed children.

I can't remember exactly when or why we quit the Gurdjieff cult. I suppose it must have been when Orage did. He had a row with Gurdjieff and was fired, in effect; I believe much the same thing happened to Ouspensky. Orage, who was a great man for causes, went back to crusading for Social Credit, and took some of us along with him. He once told me that he had never been able to make up his mind about Gurdjieff—whether he was a completely cynical charlatan, an inspired religious teacher, or a bit of both. Gurdjieff, Orage and Ouspensky are all dead, but the cult still goes on.

In my *New Republic* days I never dreamed that my future held a *Time*-machine in it. All I wanted then was the recognition of the *New Republic* editors that I was one of them, and worthy to be. Book reviewing led to other sorts of writing, and after a while I was doing light satirical pieces, parodies, even an occasional editorial paragraph or a leader. I still had my mechanical job of proofreading and make-up, but now I had an assistant, and I was encouraged to do more and more writing for the magazine—or "the paper," as Croly always called it. My salary was raised ten dollars a week; my name appeared on the masthead. I wouldn't have changed places with anybody in the world.

When Mr. Croly asked me to write my first editorial paragraph, about some judge's decision in Massachusetts, I knew nothing whatever about the case or its background except what I could find in the few newspaper clippings I had been given. Nevertheless, I turned out a ringing paragraph declaring that justice in Massachusetts had miscarried once again. The paragraph was printed; I felt like Casey Jones with his hand on the throttle.

I was convinced that the *New Republic* was the best and most distinguished journal in the United States, and that I was the luckiest young man alive to be on its staff. Such familiarity as I had with the editors had not lessened my respect for them in general, in spite of their oddities, and I revered (there is no lighter word) Mr. Croly as a great editor and a good man. There was an *esprit de corps* in the *New Republic* of those days, of which he was certainly the source and focus. This diffident, ugly, soft-spoken, often taciturn man radiated a kind of moral force, and everyone felt it. It was Croly himself who somehow gave a unique distinction to the paper.

The *Nation* was then the only other liberal weekly in the country, and it was generations older than the *New Republic*. We had a kindly tolerance for the *Nation;* we rather looked down on it. The *Nation* seemed to be in a constant state of defensive outrage; it hurled itself, ax in hand, against tree after tree, and there was no end to the trees. The *New Republic*—Croly's *New Republic*—had an ax too, but used it to blaze a trail through the woods. Croly's liberalism was in support of something unique and positive in American life that perhaps had never yet quite come into existence, and therefore remained indefinable; whereas the *Nation* was against every threat to American liberties—and those threats were inexhaustible.

I think it was in some such distinction between the *Nation's* liberalism and the *New Republic's* that we felt the difference between the two papers. The difference may not have been obvious to the public but it was obvious to us; and it was Croly's doing.

How Shall I Be a Poet?

Can Croly's idea of liberalism, his vision of America, be put more clearly than in a metaphor? Not by me. Nor, I fear, by him either. He struggled all his life to get into words what he wanted to say. Luckily he also had a sense of humor. When the Springfield *Republican* (I think it was) reprinted one of his more turgid passages, with no comment but the headline "*The New Republic* Makes It Clear Again," it was he who passed the clipping from hand to hand through the office, with a silent grin. I will never forget his telling me how difficult it was for him to write, that it never got easier or less painful for him. He had no pride of authorship and almost no talent for writing; he understood much more than he was able to convey. He wrestled with words like Jacob with the angel, and the effort he had made showed honorably in the impressive limping of his phrases.

My cubbyhole was next door to Croly's office, and Bliven's was next to him, with a communicating door between them. This meant that I was accessible to them, rather than the other way about. The office was much too old-fashioned to have bells or interior telephones, and it would have been against the spirit of the place; if you wanted somebody, you went and saw him. Croly and the rest were always coming to me to hand me proofs or other chores, but it was months before I ventured into Croly's room. I was aware of his comings and goings; he usually worked at home in the morning, arriving at the office about noon. Soon after he got in he would sneeze three times, very quietly; it sounded rather like a cat sneezing. His shyness was extreme, but then, so was mine; and after we got used to one another it was something shared.

Croly was incapable of putting an agonized young man at his ease—but, though it was too painful for him to express it, he was really more sympathetic and understanding than Bliven. When I finally got past the barrier of silence and constraint, I discovered that in a very rare sense Croly and I spoke the same language, or were trying to. I never felt that we were of an age or that I was anywhere near his equal in experience or wisdom; but the thirty-odd years' difference between us was not the unbridgeable gulf it generally is between men of different generations. In the four years I knew him, or was growing to know him, I came to regard him as a kind of father—but a father to whom everything might be said. And I know, though he would probably not have put it so dramatically, that he too felt a kinship between us. If he had lived I might have been his editorial heir.

The last time I saw him, after the stroke that ended his days at the *New Republic,* he told me that he had hoped I would one day succeed him as editor of the paper. I would have asked nothing better; but we both knew it would never happen now. I was Croly's choice but nobody else's, and still the youngest member of the staff. With Croly gone, and the succession and even the continuance of the paper in doubt, the centrifugal aims and animosities that Croly had held together would reappear and break the place apart. In the years following his retirement and death, the *New Republic* became a battleground of personal politics, further confused by the raids of left-wing guerrillas, and one by one almost all the editors I had known withdrew or disappeared. But this is getting a little ahead of the story.

Felix Frankfurter must have vanished into the Supreme Court when I made the most horrible typographical error of my proofreading career. Two successive lines, both containing frightful errors, made gibberish of the leading editorial paragraph (Mr. Croly's work). Reading the new number of the magazine on my way to the office, I spotted this horror at once. Should I resign before they fired me? I thought I would be fired; I knew I ought to be. Sure enough, the office was in an uproar. But some time in the course of that awful morning I learned, to my intense relief, that a crime so much worse than mine had been committed that in effect I had been reprieved. The advertising manager had succeeded in selling two whole pages ("a double-page spread," in the lingo of the trade) in the center of the magazine, and had been feeling proud of his almost unprecedented feat; it was difficult to sell advertising space in the *New Republic.* Unfortunately the advertisement was of two notorious pornographic publications, *Casanova Jr.'s Tales* and *Two Worlds Monthly.* The *New Republic*'s editors were thunderstruck and aghast. No one, with the exception, I think, of Stark Young, thought it was funny.

I said that in those days I would not have changed places with anybody; that is true. But not even an enthusiastic young man of twenty-seven could go on indefinitely believing that the *New Republic* was the best of all possible worlds. I knew that there was jealousy and bad feeling between some of the editors, much as a child knows when his parents are at outs, though he sees no open quarreling; for I was not taken into my elders' confidence and was well below the level of office politics.

As time went on, another fact of *New Republic* life bothered me more and more, though I wouldn't admit it: that the paper did not pay its own way and was supported by a liberal-minded millionaire. I had heard the story, probably from Bliven, of how Croly, then the editor of an architectural journal, had met a young and idealistic businessman named Willard Straight, and that Straight had put up the money for the liberal weekly that Croly had always dreamed of editing. Straight's early death must have raised a question about the survival of the *New Republic*. Would Mrs. Straight continue to pay the annual deficit? It turned out that she would. Though she also supported or helped to support three other magazines—*Asia, Theatre Arts* and *Antiques*—the *New Republic* remained her favorite. Then she married again, and went to live in England. Her British husband was known to have expansive and costly ideas of his own: an academy for Rabindranath Tagore in India; a large estate in Devonshire to house experiments in progressive education, the teaching of music, guild socialism. After another period of uncertainty, the editors breathed again; Mrs. Straight (now Mrs. Elmhirst) would still pay the deficit. But these nervous occasions deepened the *New Republic*'s sense of dependence on its Lady Bountiful and left their mark on its editors. In differing degrees and ways we all, I think, sometimes felt like kept men or babies that don't trust the nurse not to drop them; and nobody likes that.

If we had been supported by an impersonal foundation instead of a rich woman, would that have been better? I think it would. Scientists and scholars are often subsidized and feel none the worse for it. But subsidized journalism is uneasy. Many years later I learned from T. S. Eliot that the highest circulation his once-renowned *Criterion* had ever reached was 900. He was not proud of the figure, and said that he thought even literary magazines should pay for themselves.

And there was no hope that the paper might work its way out of this dependence and pay its own way. The circulation went up and down a little, but I don't think it ever rose above 35,000 in Croly's day. Whatever the "break-even point" might have been, it was far above that. The natural, perhaps inevitable, result was a tendency to settle down into a sort of defensive complacency, an attitude of mind not unlike civil servants', who know they are not in a competitive job and that their pay will be taken care of by the taxpayer.

The process of my disillusionment with the *New Republic* was gradual, and never completed. I still think of Herbert Croly as a great editor and a good man, and of his *New Republic* as different from anything I have seen since, and better.* Like everyone else, I went on getting my education—by successive shocks of delighted recognition or angry surprise. One such shock was innocently administered, mostly by Croly himself, at the first *New Republic* dinner to which I was invited. It must have been in the early days of my apprenticeship, for I remember feeling highly honored at being included. I was told to wear a black tie.

We met, about six of us, in the library at the *New Republic*, a ground-floor room adjoining the dining room. Etienne, the Belgian butler who served the office lunches, brought in a tray of cocktails —one apiece, and Orange Blossoms, a very mild type for Prohibition days. And everyone (except, of course, me) talked. I listened with every pore. I cannot remember what I expected, but I know I expected a great deal. In my eyes these men were not only learned and wise, and tolerant as only the learned and the wise could be, they were aware—who could be more so?—of what it was to be Americans and they were committed to a constant and profound concern for our country. What would I hear them say? What I heard was small talk, very jocose small talk, about the way the New York tabloids were reporting the last hours of a condemned murderer in his death cell.

Yes, I was shocked; more than that, I was bitterly disappointed.

* No, I must admit that Britain's *New Statesman*, for one, now outshines it.

How Shall I Be a Poet?

I too had been reading the papers about the murderer in his death-cell, and I didn't see anything to make jokes about; quite the contrary. It was not the first or last time that the flippancy of my elders outraged me. But these particular elders, I thought, should have managed something better. It never occurred to me that even Socrates might want an occasional night off. In those days I believed that wise men never stepped out of character—drunk or sober, joking or serious. When we went in to dinner, I suppose the conversation must have settled down, or risen, and perhaps words like freedom, republic, traditional liberties, constitution went rumbling through the air. But all I can remember of the evening was its beginning—and that it decided me to write my first book.

The more I heard and read about this murder case, the more disgusted I got with everyone concerned in it except the murderer himself; I began to feel an indignant sympathy for him. Why couldn't people see how alarmingly ordinary, how much one of ourselves, he was? He was no criminal but a victim—a victim of the valueless "values" of our cheap society, of the conflicting codes of decency and passion, of the cold-hearted mistress who had used him as an instrument to kill her hated husband; finally, of an unscrupulous press which had pilloried and exploited his last days to rush into print the "sensational true story" of his life (obviously untrue, obviously unsensational, the cheapjack work of sob sisters and hacks). A publisher had brought out a book allegedly written by the murderer in his death cell. At the sight of that shabby counterfeit I thought: "I could do better myself."

But of course I didn't. I botched the opportunity by a lazy underestimation of its difficulties that now seems incredible; I wrote the book in ten days. My excuses for this were equally lazy and incredible: I had to write it fast because I had put it off until my two-week vacation from the *New Republic,* and then the weather was so inviting that I squandered the first four days on the tennis court. The book was very short, only some 40,000 words, but even so I had to turn out an average of 4,000 words a day to make the publisher's deadline. The book got a few kind reviews, and was also published in England, France and Brazil, but never earned its $500 advance royalties until twenty years later, when an enterprising agent sold it to a company that published paperbacks. Then it brought in a windfall of $2,000.

That such a hastily written book should have been publishable at all was a fact to be credited, or debited, to a man who taught me some useful things about writing—not Edmund Wilson in this case, but Orage. After leaving the Gurdjieff cult, Orage started some evening classes in which he taught would-be writers how to write; for some time I went regularly. If you wanted to write a narrative, Orage said, it was absolutely necessary to tell it to yourself over and over, until you were letter-perfect and there were no gaps in it—like a crook committing to memory a watertight cover story. Then, when it came to the actual writing, that would almost take care of itself. This is the somewhat simplified gist of what he told us. I tried to follow his advice, and found that it happened as he had said; by the time I sat down to write, all I had to do was transcribe what was already in my head.

Orage also taught me something I was less willing to swallow. At every meeting of the class he would read aloud some of the homework we had handed in, and often as not he read with malicious gusto, making as much fun of it as he could; he never gave away the victim's name but you could usually spot him by his expression. One evening Orage read aloud two or three parodies I had handed in and then remarked that the writer of these pieces should give up all notions of "serious" writing, at least for some time to come, and stick to parodies and light, satirical stuff. This wasn't at all what I wanted to hear; but Orage was proved right when shortly afterwards I began to get such trifles published, and was asked for more.

Those days on the *New Republic* were hopeful and exciting; they also seemed slow and settled and full of promise. Then came Croly's stroke, and the whole future was suddenly in doubt. Again the question circled through the office: was this the end of the *New Republic?* Gradually the rumor spread and at last was officially confirmed that Croly was finished but the paper would go on. Though nothing official was said to me, I knew that I too was finished. Bruce Bliven was to be in charge until a new editor was appointed, and I guessed (correctly) that that meant a long and indefinite interregnum. I don't know what Bliven really thought of me—except that I was sure he wasn't nearly as sympathetic toward me as Croly was—but I could tell that my young-David days were over. And for my part, I wanted no *New Republic* but Croly's. That was gone, so I must go too. But before I resigned I needed to find another job.

After four years on the *New Republic* I regarded myself as a full-fledged journalist, or pretty near it. No newspaper man would have said I was a journalist at all; I had never been a reporter nor worked on a newspaper. I had done a few reporting jobs for the *New Republic*, but they were the kind of personal reports that my *New Republic* training, such as it was, had encouraged me to do. Without really knowing anything about them, I looked down on newspapers as crude and primary training schools, from which a few of the better newspapermen eventually emerged as special correspondents, able to do the same sort of work that we did on the *New Republic*, though rather below our level. What a lucky break it had been, I thought now, that when I had tried for a newspaper job I had been unable to get one. All those years of pointless drudgery by-passed (a daily round of the morgue, the lunatic asylum and the jail, as one newspaper editor had expressed it); I had started at the top, where I wanted to be. Now I had to scramble down and begin again.

HOW SHALL I WRITE IN RHYME?

IF WILSON WAS ANNOYED AT ME for joining the staff of *Time*—abandoning the respectable failure of serious journalism for an upstart success you couldn't take seriously—I was not proud of myself either. I felt both cynical and bewildered. It was like what had happened to me ten years before, when I had been a white-hot pacifist and then, all of a sudden, found myself a volunteer in a military training camp. This time it left a bad taste in my mouth.

I made excuses; I said, "If Croly had lived . . ." I asked myself how long the boy was supposed to stand on the burning deck. Was it wrong to give up the complacency of failure for the anxieties of success? Not that either *Time* or I was a howling success at that point, in the fall of 1929; but I knew that *Time* intended to be, and was already showing alarming signs of progress. I had thrown in my lot with *Time*'s; that was what bothered me.

Well, what else could I have done? Tried to get a job on a newspaper, I suppose. Or applied to the *Nation*. Or holed up in a garret to do free-lance writing. None of these things occurred to me as a serious possibility. When Johnny Martin telephoned to offer me a job on *Time*, I didn't have to think it over very long; it was almost as if I'd been expecting the call. I felt that I was taking a step down, all the same.

Six years before, two college boys fresh out of Yale had brought into being a strutting little venture which they called *Time, the Weekly Newsmagazine*. Martin was a cousin of one of these founders, bought stock in the paper and joined its staff in its first year; he was now managing editor. After a dubious and struggling start *Time* had turned the corner: its circulation had climbed to 250,000—gigantic compared with the *New Republic*'s, but nothing to the figure it would later attain. Several times in its first few years *Time* moved its editorial offices. They now took up most of a floor in a sizable building on East 42nd Street. The whole staff may have numbered twenty-five or thirty, of whom about a dozen were writers.

I was to write three sections of the paper—Books, Religion and Press—and also act as "late man," i.e., see the final pages to press every week. It sounded like a fairly large order, but it was a pretty small magazine. For this I was to get fifty dollars a week, the same pay I had been getting on the *New Republic*. It was a high starting salary for *Time*, which in those days took most of its recruits straight from college and paid them accordingly; but I had my four years' "experience" to offer, and a name that *New Republic* readers, at least, had begun to recognize. On *Time* I should remain forever anonymous.

Few *Time* writers had a room to themselves. I was given a desk in a glassed-in alcove which I shared with two others. They had been crowded enough before, and with three of us there, no one could come in or go out without disturbing us all. An office boy slapped down a pile of newspaper clippings on my desk, marked variously BOOKS, REL and PRESS. My roommates gave me a cool reception, and neither of them offered any help or advice, beyond telling me, when asked, where the men's room was. Martin gave me no instructions except a small black notebook, headed "Famed Phrases," from which I gathered that all "neophytes" (*Time*'s word for cub writers) were expected to memorize these phrases and use them at every opportunity.

Most of them I have mercifully forgotten; but what *Time* writer of those days could ever forget the invariable formula ("curt" and "clear" perhaps, but certainly not "concise," and *Time* continually vaunted itself on being all three) in which a death was announced: "Death, as it must to all men, came last week to So-&-So." Or the tag that was clipped to Senator Thomas Heflin, a rabble-rousing politician from the Bible Belt: "Senator Tom-Tom Heflin, who mortally hates and fears the Pope of Rome."

Of the other shreds and patches I can recall from this scarecrow "style," some were archaisms dug out of the dictionary—*moppet*, *tosspot* (usually "famed tosspot"), *neophyte*, *tycoon*—some were deliberate rhymes ("the late great" So-&-So), some were cunning euphemisms, designed to avoid libel ("great and good friend" for mistress or catamite). A known suicide's death was always reported as being "by his own hand"—with the instruments ("gunshot" or "poison") in parentheses. Some were new coinages, usually by elision, as *cinemansion* and *cinemoppet*.

One of the most obtrusive elements in *Time* style was the miscalled "Homeric epithet," a trick more reminiscent of Carlyle (whom *Time*'s inventors had obviously not read) than of Butcher & Lang's translation of the *Iliad* (which they had at least looked at). These *Time*-isms never achieved the level of "wine-dark sea" or "seagreen incorruptible" but soon degenerated into such snook-cockery as *snaggle-toothed* and *balding*. Words and phrases like these, plus some eye-catching inversions ("Ghostly was His Eminence's business") and the frequent omission of *the*, *a* and *and*—to create an impression of condensed, breathless writing—were the stuff the notorious *Time* style was made of.

Briton Hadden, the instigator of this ludicrous, exhibitionistic but arresting dialect of journalese, had died, at the unripe age of 32, a few months before I joined *Time*. Martin, who was his great admirer as well as his cousin, developed and cherished this lingo as a kind of memorial to his great shade; it seemed to us more like an albatross that hung heavy around our necks. The *New Yorker*, which was the same age as *Time* but had cultivated a very different manner and tone, gave *Time* style some long and amused stares. In Wolcott Gibbs's profile of Henry Luce the parody caught the flavor: "Backward ran sentences until reeled the mind. . . . Where it all will end, knows God."

A few years later, when a first effort was made to unwind the accursed chain—it had served its purpose of getting *Time* talked about—the iron had so far entered into our souls that the attempt at reform was never completely successful, or never appeared to be. To this day many *Time* readers, and perhaps more non-readers, are convinced that *Time* style still exists. That it was catchy, not to say contagious, is proved by the traces it has left on a large part of the press; many otherwise respectable newspapers now occasionally indulge in inverted phrases, teasing captions and other *Time*-isms.

As I had only the vaguest idea of what a "*Time* story" was supposed to be, and as nobody showed me or told me, I thought at first that every newspaper clipping the office boy brought me must be somehow reworked into a form acceptable to *Time*. The Press section was my particular bugbear. The first week, as I remember it, I sent in more than twenty Press stories (hoping they were, anyway). Martin finally told me to stop; I was swamping him with unusable copy. I felt more at home with Religion, and on Books I fancied myself an expert.

Before I came, the book-reviewing on *Time* had been casually parceled out among the staff or to part-time reviewers—who, I was given to understand, did the job with their left hands. That's the way it looked to me too. And there seemed to be no system for picking books to review. There were two sections of a Globe-Wernicke bookcase in an outer office, where new or fairly new books somehow collected. The reviewer would take whatever struck his fancy from these two shelves. Advance lists and publishers' catalogues were unheard of. At least I brought some order into this chaos.

In general, I was allowed to decide for myself which books to review, since in that ill-read crew I passed for something of an authority. When I was urged to give kindly treatment to an author who was a friend of the editor's or to review a novel simply because it had been written by a Wall Street broker, I stood on my professional integrity. I also pointed out that *Time* would make itself ridiculous (I meant more ridiculous) if it failed to show itself knowledgeable in any department of human affairs. Doctors knew what was real news in medicine, scientists in science—by the same token, professional book reviewers must be presumed to know which books were worth noticing and which weren't. This wobbly argument worried Martin, who didn't want *Time* to be laughed at but on the other hand quite rightly suspected me of wanting to be too literary. The result was that I got away with a good many reviews that were against his better judgment, but I also had to notice (though not very kindly) all the Book-of-the-Month choices.

On the *New Republic* I had grown accustomed to expressing myself as I pleased and then seeing my copy printed just as I had written it, without so much as a comma changed; on the *New Republic* I don't think I was ever "cut for space." Now my copy was hacked about, rewritten, cut to ribbons, rude questions and jeering comments scribbled in the margin; sometimes it disappeared altogether, and I learned later that it had been thrown out as hopeless, "no story." In my first days on *Time* I threshed desperately about to find a toehold.

Martin's plan for me, although I didn't understand it at first, was to load me down with all I could possibly handle, and then some

—the idea being that I would learn fast and soon be competent to write any department in the magazine. No doubt that was why, one black day, I was given a "big story" to write for National Affairs, over and above my regular jobs. It was the famous Gastonia murder trial—or rather, the second trial; I had reported the earlier one for the *New Republic*.

That had been my first sight of a courtroom circus, and it gave me the creeps: the unequal contrast between the calm, dispassionate judge and the clownish savagery of the prosecuting attorneys; the fresh young faces of the prisoners (all of them mere boys and girls, except for the Communist organizer who was the real quarry) and the brutal, believably criminal mugs of the police who sat beside them; the wildly contradictory but apparently vindictive evidence of "eyewitnesses," the fixed, blank unintelligence written on the faces of the mountaineer jury (one of whom went off his head before the case was finished, thus causing the judge to declare a mistrial). The misgivings I expressed about the jury system annoyed the New York *Evening Post*, which said in an editorial that I had better leave such worries to my elders and betters. Anyhow, I had known what to write about that trial for the *New Republic*; I said how it looked to me.

I still hadn't a clue about what a *Time* story was supposed to be, or how to write one. It had to have a pattern, didn't it? And each "big" story had to have a new pattern, all its own? Something like that, I felt sure. Having racked my brains to the point of near-idiocy, I decided to settle for the pattern of "Consequences": the parlor game in which He meets Her at such-&-such a place; they do thus-&-so; He says this and She says that; the consequences are as follows; and the world says—something irrelevant that sums it all up. Then I tried to fit the facts to my pattern. I worked so hard and long over this hopeless game that by midnight on Saturday, when the story was due, I was dead beat and felt sick. I took my copy in to Martin (it was the office rule in those days that you always said good night to the managing editor on Saturday night) and told him it had me licked. He grinned briefly and said to get along home. Next morning I saw his edited version of my story;

with some added sentences, some cuts and a few shifted paragraphs, he had made it into a straightforward and readable narrative.

My struggles to write in *Time* style were as inept and cramped as any other neophyte's—more so, I think—until a great light dawned on me. Why not a parody? I had written parodies before. I began to turn out a Niagara of counterfeit Timese. One day Martin called me in. Speaking *ex officio*, as a friend, he said musingly, "If I didn't know you so well, Matt, I might think you were trying to parody *Time*."

"Who, me?"

A year or so later, when it was decided that *Time* style had served its purpose and that straightforward English would be the ticket, Martin several times called me to order for backsliding into the old ways. By then it had become second nature to me, and a hard habit to break.

There was a deeper difficulty, as far as I was concerned: I couldn't take *Time* seriously. The work itself was hard enough, and the hours could hardly have been longer. In my first three months on *Time* I never got a day off—it seemed to me scarcely a waking hour off; any "spare time" I had was spent in reading books and writing reviews. But what was it all about? "Keeping our readers informed"! That certainly wouldn't wash. The young men and boys who wrote and edited *Time* were not well informed themselves.

A story was told of the late great Briton Hadden, the inventor of Timese, whose editorial technique included the constant chewing of enormous red pencils, accompanied by a low growling that might indicate either ferocity or delight. Some reference to the Crimean War had popped up in the news. Hadden ordered a complete history of the war, two full columns' worth, and added: "And let's tell all about duh crime!" This tale, admittedly ambiguous, was told with pride as showing either Hadden's innocence or his sense of humor—it didn't seem to matter which.

Time's staff were all college graduates and some of them had been big-men-on-campus; that didn't mean they were well educated or in fact educated at all. They were getting their education, such as it was, now; they were informing themselves as hastily as they had crammed for exams, and the result was much the same—slickness, smartness, bluff. But serious? It took me the better part of seven years to convince myself that *Time*'s ambition to be taken seriously was in fact a serious ambition.

The contrast I felt between the *New Republic* and *Time* was a contrast between scholarly, distinguished men and smart, ignorant boys. The *New Republic* did not exist primarily to call attention to itself; it had the nobler motive (or so it seemed to me) of trying to recall Americans to their better senses. The *New Republic* was a failure. And what was *Time* up to? As far as I could see, *Time* simply wanted to succeed, to get bigger, to get all the readers it could collect by exhibiting its bumptious, impertinent, adolescent self. After it grew up . . . but I couldn't imagine *Time* growing up.

In any case, I didn't like *Time*. On every piece of copy I typed I could have written with truth, "I do not like my work." If this was the other side of the coin from being subsidized, it was more unpleasant. The job I disliked most was being "late man." Every Monday night, alone in the office except for the girl who ran the teletype machine, I expected that the President would be assassinated or that some other part of the sky would fall in—and I would have to deal with it. In fact, nothing much ever did happen in my three-month tenure. Once in a while an expected late story would come in, but that was no problem if the right space had been left for it. I remember taking one such story over the telephone from Madison Square Garden, where Niven Busch, the sports writer, had gone to report a fight. I think it was considered noteworthy mainly because Jack Dempsey, who had recently been heavyweight champion, was acting as referee. Anyway, this was Busch's *Time*-ly lead sentence: "Thoughtfully picking his nose, Referee Dempsey strode from the corner."

Most of the late man's job was getting the pages to fit, usually by adding or cutting a few words or sentences. The girl with the teletype machine was necessary because the pages were going to press in Chicago, nearly a thousand miles away. Teletypesetting machines were not yet in use, and this awkward distance between us and the press meant that we never saw proofs, and that the make-up that went to Chicago could never be quite accurate. When Chicago clacked out on the teletype the message that page 32 was six lines long, I would mark the cuts (seven words to a line, approximately) on my duplicate copy, and the girl would then "send the greens" on the teletype. "Sending greens" was an expert technical job. ("Greens" were so-called because all cuts for space in *Time* copy were indicated by brackets marked in green crayon. Cuts marked in red crayon were "kills"—"must kill"; cuts for space were always "greens" because we had to leave Chicago some latitude. They had the proofs in front of them, and all we knew was what they told us.) It required something like a dozen lines on the teletype, in lingo incomprehensible to a layman, to say with exactness that a certain two words should be dropped from a given page.

The job was usually finished by two or three o'clock in the morning, unless we closed late; one of my last chores was to look through the early editions of the morning papers to see if there was anything we should remake for. As the long hours wore on, with periods of silence from the teletype machine, the tension did not so much relax as settle in. To ease the tension (my constant anxiety about the President's getting shot) one night I brought in a bottle of rum. When we considered that the worst was over, about midnight, the teletype girl and I each had a swig. On the following press nights the worst developed a tendency to get over earlier. We usually finished the bottle before we went home, and I ceased to suffer from anxiety about the President's safety.

My friend the managing editor must have seen that I was losing some of my steam, for one Monday night after the magazine had gone to press he summoned me to his apartment. With the help of a bottle of whiskey we talked till dawn. He reminded me that my present miserable condition was a necessary part of my training. He elaborated on his great plans for me—for us. I was to work my way through every department of the magazine and then become his assistant, his alter ego. Then, if he wanted to go to Nassau for six weeks, off he would go, leaving me in charge; when I wanted to go to Bermuda, go I would. And I could look forward, he told me, to making at least $25,000 a year. The prospect didn't appeal to me, even at that price. But I said I would think about it.

The upshot was that I gave up the possibility of getting to Nassau or Bermuda, and retired into the Books page for seven years. In effect this got me a raise in pay, for after some haggling Martin agreed that my salary should not be cut, though I ceased to write the Press and Religion departments, and was no longer permanent late man. Dropping that job was the greatest relief of all.

At first I felt an almost pleasant sense of guilt at having nothing to do but review books. Book reviewing was not regarded as a full-time job. Nevertheless, I found it a fairly large order. I read, on average, about eight books a week, and reviewed about five. I had to fill between three and five columns a week (1,500 to 2,500 words) except on the rare occasions when *Time*'s weekly feature, the "cover story," came my way; then it was seven columns or more. I managed to keep my weekends free by crowding all the reading into the first three days. I wrote my reviews on Thursday, took my copy in to the office on Friday, often finishing a review on the train, waited until the managing editor had passed it, collected the books for the next week, and went home for two free days.

I liked the arrangement, but it had its drawbacks. The principal one was pay. As an absentee writer who spent most of his time in an armchair at home, just reading books—in short, enjoying himself—I was considered to have a very soft job. If I had been at the office, working comparable hours, my industry would have been noted, my presence might have been a reminder that I too existed and that it was about time I had a raise. As it never occurred to me to ask for one, and as I had chosen this withdrawal myself, I suppose the only reason I ever did get a raise (two, I think, in seven years) was that *Time* made more and more money and that my pay began to seem too low even for a book reviewer.

Another drawback was the amount of reading I had to do. Not because I was conscientious but because I dreaded the moment when I would have to sit down at my typewriter, I read every word of the books I reviewed. (There were exceptions, like Sidney and Beatrice

How Shall I Write in Rhyme?

Webb's two-volume history of the Russian constitution. Luckily, that orderly couple put a synopsis at the end of every chapter.) It was absurd, of course, to think that I was in any sense competent to deal with the whole field of books all by myself; but neither *Time* nor I saw anything absurd about it.

I took little pride in the work I was doing, but my vanity received several shocks. Martin seemed to delight in blue-penciling the lead paragraphs I had sweated over most. Still, he could sometimes be argued into restoring the cruelest cuts. A much severer blow came from Orage, whose judgment I respected: he told me flatly that my *Time* reviews were much better than those I had written for the *New Republic*. And Bruce Bliven, meaning it kindly, I think, said that a paragraph in *Time* helped the sales of a book as much as hundreds of dollars' worth of advertising. I didn't like that at all. But the worst was an old Oxford friend whom I hadn't seen for years; she asked me what I was doing now, and when I showed her, she couldn't hide her amazement that I should be paid all of twelve pounds a week for writing the kind of "shorter notices" that people wrote for the *Times Literary Supplement* for nothing.

I am a slow reader, and that was a considerable handicap in a book reviewer's job. I wondered how other reviewers managed. Clifton Fadiman, who was then writing the *New Yorker*'s book page, reviewed only one or two books a week at length, but covered fifteen or twenty in shorter notices. One day I called him on the telephone and asked him if he really read all those books. Oh, yes, he said. But how? Well, he said, there was a book by Walter B. Pitkin—don't laugh—called *The Art of Rapid Reading;* he had found some very useful hints in it. I ordered the book. But I never got around to reading it; there didn't seem to be time.

I still had a desk at the office, though I came in only one day a week. My cellmate was Frank Norris, one of the two men I had first shared an office with. Now, while I was static, he was going up in the world. He had graduated from writing Animals, People, Milestones and Miscellany to Theater, which was regarded as a great plum. He saw all the Broadway shows and knew the Broadway crowd. When he wrote a cover story about an actress, he would get her to autograph the cover and then, as the office custom was, frame it and hang it on the wall. Soon he had four or five such trophies. I of course had none. I think the only cover story I had written then was on James Joyce; the occasion of the story was the publication of *Ulysses* in the United States.

One day I found a message on my desk that Luce wanted to see me. Henry R. Luce, the surviving founder of *Time*, was the editor and boss, and even in those days lived well above the tree line on Olympus. I had had only the sketchiest of dealings with him, and had found him nervous, brusquely shy (not at all like the shyness of Mr. Croly) and stammering. I knew he was the head man on *Time*, but I didn't take him very seriously either. Martin was the sun around which I revolved, and I got the distinct impression that he had small regard for Luce, whom he thought lucky rather than brilliant, the fortunate inheritor of the grand design for which his late partner Hadden should get most of the credit. Since in those days I had barely laid eyes on Luce, and in my lowly position I could see few signs of his direct concern with *Time*, my opinion of him was colored by Martin's.

There were stories about Luce, mimicking his abruptness, uneasiness and alleged ruthlessness. One concerned a man who had been engaged to write the Art department. There was nothing very striking about him except that he was almost entirely bald, which rather set him off from the rest of the staff. He was in his first week at the office, and had just finished sending out notices to all the 57th Street galleries, art museums, etc., that he was now the authorized *Time* representative. Luce darted out of his office, barking, "Who's-doing-Art?" Someone pointed to the bald-headed man. "Too old," snapped Luce. "Fire him!" I believe this story to be quite apocryphal, but it was told as characteristic.

I remember a memo Luce put out in these early days that caused some talk but which no one took seriously. The memo announced that writers were dawdling; it should not take a writer more than an hour, all told, to write a one-column *Time* story. While he was reading the "research" (in those days a little pile of clippings, mostly from the New York *Times*) the lead paragraph should be forming in his head, and as he laid down the last clipping he should turn to his typewriter and *begin*.

The editor had now summoned me. I picked up the telephone and asked for Miss Thrasher, his secretary. Her cheerful voice informed me that the boss (one of her favorite names for him) was busy; she would let me know. Several times that day I tried again; no go. I went home, the summons unanswered. When I came in the following Friday, supposing that the writ still ran, I applied once more to Miss Thrasher. Still too busy. As I remember it, I persevered for a third week, and this time I got a response. Miss Thrasher sent me a neatly typed message: "Mr. Luce—Do you care to see Mr. Matthews today?—C.T." and the date. On this Luce had violently scrawled "Thrasher—NO." I had this trophy framed, at a cost of $2.48, and hung it on the office wall, alongside the Broadway stars.

The weeks wore on into months, and the months into years. On my weekly visits to the office I saw new faces and missed some old ones. Once more I was given a cubbyhole to myself—but this one was a little closet with no window; it was explained to me that the staff was increasing, and as I was hardly ever there, this was the only space available. Several times I was told that, if I were only sensible and "came back to work full time," I would get a better office and a much better job. No, I preferred my comparative freedom, and I had still not made the discovery that *Time* was a serious undertaking. But I was getting tired of book reviewing. Like so many other gorged reviewers, I began to feel that I must regurgitate a book myself.

By this time my friend Johnny Martin had been drafted to work on plans for a new magazine (it eventually emerged as the pictorial weekly, *Life*), and his place was taken by the chief National Affairs writer, John Shaw Billings. In most ways the change was an improvement. Billings was a much easier and pleasanter man to work for; he was even-tempered (which Martin was decidedly not) and appreciative. But as far as writing was concerned he had a narrower field of fire, and nothing would move him to widen it—as I learned when I tried some of my fancier bits on him. He was sensible and kindly, but once he had made up his mind there was no arguing with him.

One day I went to Billings with a scheme for getting a six-months' leave of absence. I wanted, or thought I wanted, to go to Mallorca and write that book. As a substitute for my job on *Time* while I was away I could supply a friend who was much better read than I and a much better writer—Schuyler Jackson. The shift would cost *Time* nothing, since Schuyler would be paid my salary. Billings considered the idea, and pointed out two possible hitches in it: in spite of my high opinion of him, my friend might not turn out to be up to snuff and would have to be fired, whereupon my job would be gone; or he might do the job so much better than I that he would not keep my seat warm for me but make it too hot for me to sit in. I said I would take those chances; and Billings granted me my leave of absence.

The arrangement worked so well on the whole that it gave me a further idea. Why not share the job with someone else who also wanted time off to do his own writing—six months on and six months off? The man I had in mind was a young writer named Robert Cantwell, whom I had never met but whose work, as a novelist and a book reviewer, I much admired. Billings agreed, Cantwell agreed, and for two years we spelled each other in six-month shifts. The unforeseen result was that we both got caught in the machinery, and eventually found ourselves working full time in the office. When we made the first change-over it was borne in on me what an effective covering anonymity can be, like a coat of white paint on a brick wall of various shades. Cantwell had a markedly distinct style, or at least manner of writing, and he was quite incapable of aping *Time* style (which in any case was now officially nonexistent). His sentences were lengthy and Jamesian; he had in fact learned to write by studying Henry James. I on the contrary had gone to school to *Time,* and wrote in short barks and yelps. The contrast between his reviews and mine was so obvious that I was sure everyone would notice it. Nobody did.

I gained a friend as well as an alternate in Cantwell, but it was a bad day for him when he walked into the *Time* office. He had published two novels, the second (*Land of Plenty*) of greater promise than the first, and was obviously on his way to becoming a writer of some distinction. He had also made a name for himself, on the monthly *New Outlook*, as one of the best—some of us considered him the best—book reviewer in New York. He was as out of place in *Time* as a canary in a coal mine. Canaries in coal mines have their uses, however, or did have, and Cantwell's sensitive talent on occasion was invaluable to *Time*. But he never published another novel, and his career on *Time* ended in a breakdown. I was aware, to some extent, of the risk he ran and was even willing to take some of the responsibility for it; in those days I was beginning to evolve the foolish notion that poetry and journalism must marry, to produce clearer poetry and sturdier journalism. By the time I realized that Cantwell was in real danger, it was too late.

In those early days, however, when we shared the *Time* book page between us, we both felt that we were spoiling the Egyptians, and occasionally thought up ways to make the spoiling easier. We had books mailed to us at home, and in the summer appeared at the office only once a fortnight. It was I who wrested vacation pay from the reluctant managing editor; I pointed out that all *Time* writers were entitled to vacation with pay, and since Books never had a vacation, it (we) was being cheated of two weeks' pay a year. It was Cantwell who got us an assistant, a slightly older friend of his named Calvin Fixx, who came from the same part of the Northwest, and who had introduced him to Henry James. Fixx was no writer himself, but he had read a good deal and was remarkably level-headed in his judgments. Fixx stayed in the office and did a great many useful things besides reading and reporting on books; he answered the telephone and mollified editors, kept the lists in order and attended to the mail, and generally made the Books department visible, continuous and respectable.

He had a slow way of talking that sometimes annoyed the impatient, but it was no use trying to hurry him. Years later, when he had had a coronary thrombosis and had returned to *Time* to do jobs with no deadline attached, he and I regularly had lunch together every Monday. I was managing editor then, and Monday being press day, it was not the day I would have picked for a protracted, deliberate lunch; but Fixx insisted, though he knew it irritated me. He said it was a good thing for me to be slowed down, especially on a Monday. We always met at Billy the Oysterman's, a restaurant near the office. Fixx would be at the bar, drinking (very slowly) a dry Manhattan. If he saw I was more than ordinarily nervous or impatient, he would have two. He took his time ordering lunch, and the conversation, which he usually got away from shop talk, was low-keyed and snail-paced. He always kept me at least an hour. He was a clear-sighted man, wise beyond his years, and a good friend. When he died I missed him sadly, and *Time* was a poorer place.

During my book-reviewing years, between 1930 and 1937, *Time* was making the transition, in Luce's words, from "a big little-business to a little big-business." Even to an absentee journeyman like me the signs of growth were manifest. As the circulation mounted, the editorial staff got bigger; writers no longer wrote more than one department, and the "front-of-the-book" sections (National Affairs, Foreign News and Business) now had as many as three writers apiece. The offices were moved again, into larger and loftier quarters, high up in the needled tower of the Chrysler Building. From the fifty-second floor you could look out over the jostling crowd of midtown skyscrapers, and get a glimpse of both Manhattan's boundary rivers.

Time had given birth to *Fortune*, to *Life*. (My successor on the Press page was much annoyed that *Time*, looking for a good name for its new picture magazine, should have bought the title of the moribund humorous weekly; he had been waiting patiently to write a story with the head *Death of Life*.) The bringing forth of this infant Gargantua, *Life*, cost its mother a great loss of blood, and if *Time* hadn't been in such good shape it might have proved fatal. The circulation of *Life*—and consequently its advertising rates—had been reckoned in hundreds of thousands; when it immediately jumped to a million and went up from there, production costs soared over the static revenue. By the time new advertising contracts could come to the rescue, *Life* had lost a packet. After that, as soon as it could begin to collect its own earnings, it was a bonanza.

As for us on *Time*'s editorial staff, our concern with *Life* was smaller and more personal. Our ranks had been decimated to collect recruits for *Life*, but that was to be expected. When we heard that Billings was to be taken from us to be made *Life*'s managing editor, and that Martin was coming back as our boss, there was a general murmur of rebellion and many openly said they would quit. The transfer took place, and nobody quit. But the era of good feeling we had had under Billings was over. Martin's temper was not improved by his disappointment, and he came back to a larger staff, a harder job, more power and more scope for tyranny.

He and I were friends, or had been friends before he took me on as an employee, and I had never had any real trouble with him. One Friday afternoon he summoned me, as he always did—either to say that my reviews were O.K. as they stood, or to raise some point or objection. This time he never mentioned my copy.

"I want to talk to you about your attitude."

"What attitude?"

"Your attitude towards *Time*."

"? ? ?"

"You're supercilious about it. You always have been. You look down your nose at *Time*. You don't take it seriously." (More and more in this vein, repetitious, accusatory, wilder and warmer—and uncomfortably close to the truth. But why this sudden attack, and why such an aggrieved personal tone? Ah!)

I said, "I'll talk to you about it when you're sober, John," and went back to my office. I waited for the telephone to ring, with the message that I was fired. It didn't ring. And that conversation was never continued.

But perhaps it was, in other terms. It must have been a year or so later—anyhow, it was some time in the summer of 1937. This time Martin was in an amiable mood, and no one could be more winning when he cared to be. And this time the assumption, on both our parts, was that I was at least serious enough about *Time* to do a good job. Martin returned to the proposal he had made to me years before. The chores of the managing editor, the single-handed managing and editing of the whole magazine, had become too much for one man to do properly; he needed an assistant. No partnership was mentioned this time, nor was Nassau, Bermuda, nor a top salary of $25,000. Perhaps the prizes were bigger now. He wanted me to start by taking over some of the "back-of-the-book" departments. After that, we'd see.

I was heartily sick of reviewing books, and the six-month leaves had not produced much writing of my own. I was strongly tempted to accept Martin's offer on the spot. But it would mean a fundamental change in my way of living: commuting daily to the office, with perhaps several nights a week in town, and no more weekends with my family and friends. And it would mean a long, perhaps a final, goodbye to any hopes of writing. I knew the job would demand all my time and energy and might even end by swallowing my leisure. It should be thought about. I told Martin that I must talk it over with Julie, and that I would give him my answer in a week.

Long before the week was over my mind was made up; and Julie, who knew what a blind alley I was in, encouraged me in my decision to get out of it. And yet what would I be doing, really, except cutting my losses, choosing the lesser of two evils? However you put it, it was a *lowering* decision. I had thought I wanted to write. I hadn't wanted to, evidently, enough to do it—and there had been plenty of opportunity in the last few years. I tried to salve my conscience by telling myself that my grandfather and my father had both risen to the top of their professions; and why shouldn't I do the same? Nevertheless, it was with an uneasy mind and a not altogether light heart that I took this deliberate first step toward becoming "a success."

I wrote to Martin, saying I was ready to start whenever he wanted me. There were still a few more weeks to run of my six-month leave, but I was anxious to begin. Ten days passed, and no word from Martin. Then Fixx sent me a memo that had just been circulated to the staff (although no copy was addressed to me); translated from the euphemistic jargon of management, it said that Martin was out ("a well-earned year's leave," apparently to be spent in traveling around the world), the top editorial jobs had been reshuffled, and *Time* was now to be headed by a publisher, one Ralph McAlister Ingersoll. In the new line-up my name appeared nowhere.

What had happened? I could only guess, but it was obvious that Martin had either failed to get some necessary approval of his offer to me or hadn't bothered to tell anybody about it. And he hadn't answered my letter (he never did) because he was too busy fighting for his own head. I was angry and disappointed. What should I do now? I did the first thing that occurred to me—sent off a telegram to Ingersoll, as the new head man, offering my resignation.

A soothing reply was wired back, urging me to come in to the office and talk things over. I took the next train to New York. The outraged feeling of having been cheated was still strong in me when I entered Ingersoll's office and blurted out my story. I'm reasonably certain that it was all news to him—although he struck me at first sight as what we called "a smooth operator," and you could never be sure of what he knew and what he didn't. In any case, and although he would have been well within his rights in refusing to honor Martin's check, he didn't refuse. All he wanted to know was when I could start. Next week? And what about salary? I took a deep breath and said, "Ten thousand." That was roughly three times the pay I was getting. He nodded casually. Somehow I got out of his office without exploding, to rush home and tell Julie that I was now a very minor but terrifically overpaid editor of *Time*.

Ingersoll had been put in charge of *Time*, apparently, in much the same way that a Roman proconsul might have been sent to restore law and order in a disaffected and too independent province. It was a role that suited him. He liked power and enjoyed exercising it—to such an extent that his own allegiance became intolerable to him; he was a natural conspirator. He was a tall, stooping man, bald except for an encircling fringe, with a compensating mustache; fleshy nose, full lips, protuberant and mournful eyes that could freeze into a choleric stare. He was a hypochondriac; a battery of pill bottles ornamented his desk, and he went to the doctor several times a week to have his sinuses treated.

I never liked Ingersoll or trusted him, but he said one thing I always remembered. He had been an engineer before taking up journalism, and he had changed trades, he said, because "in engineering you can only make one mistake." For several years he had been on the staff of the *New Yorker*, and for some reason—had they laughed at him? or simply not taken him at his own valuation?—bore a deep grudge against that airy crew. I can't remember whether he himself coined "smartchart" as *Time*'s unvarying epithet for the *New Yorker*, but he certainly encouraged its use.

This same grudge led him into a very childish action. The masthead of *Time* was of great concern to all of us whose names appeared on it, and we were instantly aware of every change or addition—but I doubt whether anyone outside the office gave this list of *Time*-servers so much as a passing glance. When I first joined *Time* I saw on the masthead someone called Peter Mathews, and wondered who my namesake might be. Later I learned that he was nonexistent; in those early days when *Time* couldn't afford to lose a single member of its tiny staff, the editors thought it a good idea to have a scapegoat for emergencies. They never did have to fire Peter, so he stayed (he's still there).* Ingersoll's vengeful scheme was based on Peter Mathews; he would put on *Time*'s masthead the name of Eustace Tilley—the top-hatted exquisite, the spirit of the *New Yorker*, who appeared annually on the magazine's anniversary cover—*as if Time had hired him*, leave him there a month or so and then drop him, *as if Time had fired him*. In spite of some demurrers, it was done. Did anyone notice this elaborate little game? I don't think so.

Not all of Ingersoll's editorial ideas were so pointless. But in general he was more of a hard-driving manager than a stimulating editor; he gave orders to be carried out rather than objectives to be won. As publisher, he wasn't supposed to interfere with the actual operation of the editorial side, but that was not the way he

---

* Danton Walker, a Broadway columnist for a New York tabloid, once informed his readers that *I* didn't exist. He was mixed up.

read his charter. He treated the managing editor like an underling, and summoned him like an office boy. After Ingersoll's time, the relations between publisher and managing editor on *Time* were never like that again, but they remained anomalous and in practice depended on the characters of the men involved. Luce later tried to define the relative positions of publisher and managing editor: almost parallel, with the publisher half a step behind. Nothing like that would have suited Ingersoll.

I had been hired, this time, by Ingersoll, so he must have been the one who figured out what to do with me. Rather to my relief, I wasn't immediately put to editing anything. Instead I was assigned to writing stories for various "back-of-the-book" departments, and then for a month or so given Cinema. I liked going to screenings in the Broadway projection rooms, but the effect on me of the movies I saw rather alarmed me. A grade-C comedy would set me roaring with laughter, and a grade-B tear-jerker make me wipe my eyes and blow my nose. Afterwards, in the hard Broadway daylight, I would be ashamed of myself and pull my critical faculties together. There was one horrible little child singer, Bobby Breen, who was much in vogue then in Hollywood; I never had to harden my heart against him. In fact, those reviews had to be edited for libel.

My own editing came gradually. While I was still writing copy myself I was given occasional stories to look over. Then one day the managing editor, Gottfried, called me in to say that I was being given six departments to edit in the back-of-the-book: Art, Cinema, Theater, Music, Books and Religion. These were known as "the critical departments." Religion was included simply as a hot potato—or a cold one, depending on how you looked at it. It was really only Theater that was too hot to handle; and luckily I'd been tipped off about that. At this point the Theater page was being written by a woman, who never appeared at the office and sent her copy in by messenger. She was also a good friend of Ingersoll's. I knew what to do with that copy: nothing. Fortunately, she wrote good reviews; and she too found her position embarrassing and resigned after a few weeks. Her place was taken by Louis Kronenberger, who was such a good critic and wrote so well that he couldn't be edited either; so Theater was never a problem.

I soon saw what an opportunity I had been given with these six departments; in fact, nothing quite like it ever came my way again. In effect, they formed a magazine within the magazine; as far as I was concerned, the cream of it. I still didn't like *Time*—although by now I had to admit that other people, at least, seemed to be taking it seriously—but these "critical departments" were a special, self-contained part of *Time* that might be made civilized and respectable. That is, if I could do it; if I could get "my staff" to see it the same way.

In Books, Cantwell and Fixx could be counted on, I knew. And Kronenberger in Theater. The rest were strangers or unknown quantities. I was mildly acquainted with Carl Balliett, who wrote Religion. All I knew about him was that he was repressed, competent and conscientious, that he had written the Religion department for years and hated it, and that he had a passion for music. Noel Busch, in Cinema, was an even older *Time* hand; he had begun to write for *Time* when he was still an undergraduate at Princeton. He was a cousin of Johnny Martin and of Hadden, the co-founder, and younger brother of Niven, who had now left *Time* for Hollywood. Noel was good-looking, cool as a refrigerated cucumber, a cat that walked by himself. I soon learned that he didn't much like the movies but that he felt quite competent to express his distaste in a readable and professional manner, and that he could be relied on to get his copy in on time.

In Music I had a new man named Winthrop Sargeant. I don't think he had done much writing of any kind, but he had played second violin under Toscanini. He was a small, defensively belligerent man with stomach trouble, which he treated according to ideas of his own: before meals, several drops of "bull's blood" (I think that's what he said) in water; after meals, twenty minutes of immobility in his chair; at night, six bottles of beer so he could sleep. As a writer on music his problems—and therefore mine—were two: he said he hated music (I could never quite believe this, but it worried me) and he always tended to write about it in terms of food, stomach and digestion. We had many arguments about this, and he would point out, very nearly unanswerably, that when you wrote *about* something you had to put it in terms of something else; so what could be more natural, for him?

The Art man, Robert Fitzgerald, was also new, in a sense. Our paths had crossed briefly once before when he was just starting on *Time;* he had been tried out as my assistant on the Books page. His very first piece of copy had been so literary that Billings, who was then managing editor, had promptly shifted him to the business department, where he languished for two years. Fitzgerald was a poet and a scholar, shy but arrogant, who at times kept his mouth shut and controlled his fury only by grinding his teeth; they were considerably worn down. He said he knew nothing about any art but his own, and had never looked seriously at a picture in his life.

So there we had it: a Religion writer who hated religion, a Cinema writer who despised the movies, a Music man who said he hated music, an Art man who knew nothing about pictures. Thank God for Books and Theater. Golden Fleece, here we come! When I embarked with this crew I was given no sailing orders: they were not considered necessary. Except for one thing—I was told that the Art page was to be kept just as it was, "light, amusing, chatty." I knew what was meant. Under our predecessors the Art page had been a sniggering gossip column retailing racy anecdotes about Toulouse-Lautrec, Gauguin, Van Gogh, etc. Fitzgerald was quite incapable of writing such stuff and wouldn't have done it if he could.

That was the year when Braque's "Yellow Cloth" won first prize at the Carnegie International Show at Pittsburgh. Fitzgerald and I agreed that the aim of the Art page should be to show stockbrokers why "The Yellow Cloth" was a prizeworthy picture. Experience soon taught us that we had set our sights too high, and we lowered them several times in the months that followed, but never to the contemptibly easy target we had been told to shoot at. And instead of getting me into trouble, this flouting of my only specific orders brought Fitzgerald and me unexpected credit. The change in the tone of the Art page, and the raising of its standards, was noted and approved by the editors—and by the readers, which was more important.

Of these seven men who had been given into my editorial charge, several were new to their jobs, but not one of them was as new as I. And if I had picked none of them, neither had they chosen me. I decided that the first thing to do was to get to know each other. I asked them all out to dinner, and encouraged them to drink as much as they felt like. After several such evenings I think we knew each other better, and we had warmly discussed a good many subjects, including the aims and standards of journalism and of our common job. My own aim was simple and crudely expressed: I wanted to make the rest of the magazine look sick.

This was not an admirable viewpoint, and certainly had something vindictive in it. I wanted to show *Time*, as I had wanted to show the *New Republic*, that it was entertaining an angel unawares. But now there was a difference. All I had wanted from the *New Republic* was recognition and an invitation to come inside. In the case of greedy, envious, unadmirable *Time* that recognition and invitation would not be good enough, and I didn't want them (or so I thought then): my ambition was to capture or rescue *Time*'s vital organs—which *Time* didn't know were vital—and make them beat and breathe as they should. I completely failed to see that if I even partly succeeded I would be yanked out and put to work in another, deader part of *Time*'s body. I wasn't looking that far ahead; I was too wrapped up in the exciting possibilities of the present. Those were my happiest days on *Time*.

"Success" is always partial and comparative, and exists largely in the eye of the beholder. We were said to have made a success, and as a reward got praises and raises. And of course our little team was broken up, for various good reasons; we were wanted elsewhere. Only one of us is still on *Time*, and in the same job, too valuable and too canny to be moved. The rest have gone—one is in Italy, one in the Far East; two are dead (one by his own hand).

My suspicions of Ingersoll, it appeared, were well founded; he was not a straightforward character. There was sometimes a note of near-apology in his manner that may have been semi-conscious, and that brought him as close as he could come to being attractively human. Although in office hours he played the autocrat and I think enjoyed treating the managing editor like an errand boy, he wanted the staff to like him, and took pains to make himself as popular as he could.

In his large and luxurious bachelor's quarters, an uptown apartment with a good East Side address, he kept open house for the whole staff, one afternoon a week. Plenty of drink, a poker game —also craps and poker dice, and even a pin-ball machine; late-stayers were welcome, and could help themselves to a lavish cold supper on the sideboard. Almost all of us dipped into his hospitality occasionally; some went every week.

If I had been one of Ingersoll's regulars, I suppose the news of his defection would not have been such a bombshell. But though I mistrusted him I didn't suspect him of anything so definite or drastic. One fine day the news was all over the office: Ingersoll had left, taking half a dozen of the staff with him, to start a New York newspaper, *PM*. He must have been laying his plans for this move for some time.

Why had he been so secretive about it? Couldn't he have resigned in the normal way, and then started working on the plans for his newspaper? I don't know; but his action seemed very much in character, and no doubt he had reasons that seemed good to him. Perhaps it was more convenient to draw up his scheme and make his preliminary arrangements under the cover of his position as publisher of *Time*. The element of surprise must have appealed to him. Perhaps he couldn't face Luce with his decision, or perhaps he had a grudge against Luce and hoped to pay him back like this.

Whatever Ingersoll's reasons, his sudden disappearance, coupled with the half-dozen other desertions, spread consternation through the office. The immediate crisis—getting out that week's issue short-handed—could be met; but what about the future? What would now happen to *Time*? And what was to become of us? We wanted no more Ingersolls; neither did we want an even worse King Stork. Some of us were grumbling over a drink about these changes and chances, and someone must have voiced a wish for "the good old days."

"Boys," said Frank Norris, "these *are* the good old days!"

Well, maybe so. At any rate, by now I was in them up to my neck. I could no longer say that I didn't take *Time* seriously. I now thought it a barbarous magazine that might, at least in part, be civilized. It had possibilities that hadn't been apparent to me before. I liked my job and wanted to go on with it. But not under any and all circumstances, not under any kind of management.

It was high time, I decided, to get acquainted with Luce.

ON THE BRIDGE

I HAVE LIVED AMONG HISTORICAL EVENTS without noticing them, as I think is commonly the case with people who are lucky enough not to be caught in them. The first Great War, the depression that ended the boom of the twenties, were hardly more to me than newspaper headlines. But the headlines in 1939 made everybody stop and look. As the months went by and war came closer, newspapers were not enough, and radios were kept tuned in to the news bulletins.

The Spanish civil war, the dress rehearsal for a Fascist triumph, had cleared the stage for Hitler's crazy and criminal assault. Like most of my friends I had been sympathetic with the losing side in Spain but had done nothing to help them, beyond giving a few dollars and attending a few New York cocktail parties at which fiery speeches were made in their behalf. Now that it was too late, I shared the suspicion of some of my fellow Americans that this might have been the last great public quarrel of our times in which the issues were clear, and that we should have taken part in it; we tried to square our consciences by recalling that nearly everyone else had also stood aside. And now that the Nazi bully-boys were loose there were no issues to think about, only the anxious questions: could Europe survive, and could we keep out of it?

On the Bridge

In fortunate America, in 1939, we could still afford the luxury of private lives and the illusion that our privacy would not be invaded. But for millions of people in Europe and Asia 1939 marked the end of the world, and for millions more the beginning of the end. It was a black year, and history will have to rate it so. It was far from being the end of my little world, but its upheavals were microscopically reflected there in private and personal tremors. I used to think of it, in the small terms of my own life, as "the year of the big wind." Not because of Ingersoll's defection, but because that was the year I lost my friend Schuyler.

In those days of thirty years ago, I was unsure of myself but sure of him. He was to be a true poet, dedicated to the high craft of verse; poetry was his calling. I had neither his singleness of purpose nor his passion of conviction that only the great heights are worth climbing; my ambitions were timider. There was nothing timid about him. He was brave, brilliant and assured; I was none of these things, but he made me understand that I too was a kind of poet. Though he was the leader and I the follower, we were friends whom nothing was to part: we thought ourselves devoted to one another for life. We laughed and wept for the same reasons, or understood them. When we married, each was the other's best man, and marriage was not allowed to interfere with our friendship.

What went wrong? Which of us failed the other? Why did he stop writing poetry; and how did our friendship end? The only answer I can give cannot satisfy me: that he and I told ourselves different versions of the same story, not the truth but our truth. In his version, I was disloyal. In my version, he was mad with pride and literally bewitched.

At that time we were both members of a little circle who considered ourselves, with ludicrous or idiotic complacency, "inside people"—that is, human beings of such intelligence and understanding that we were a different breed from the common run "outside." In that spring of 1939 some ten of us had come together for weeks of almost continuous session. The avowed purpose of our meetings was to draw up a "Protocol" which by the sternness of its thought and the authority of its language would arrest the

241

drift of the world into the war we saw coming. Believe it or not. The Protocol was never finished; instead, three of the families in our group broke up and the friendship between Schuyler and me ended, more finally than if we were dead.

Had my career at *Time* ended too? That depended on Luce; was he the kind of man you could work for, and work with? I didn't know, but I was determined to find out. There were others who said they felt the same way. I suggested that we get Luce for an evening and try to discover what he was like. Some of us had never spoken to him; one or two had never seen him.

Luce accepted my invitation to dinner but then, characteristically, turned it inside out: we were to dine with him, at his apartment in the Waldorf Towers. I think there were five of us, though I may have forgotten somebody: John Osborne, Charley Wertenbaker, Bob Fitzgerald, Frank Norris and myself. (Wertenbaker gave a description of the evening in his last novel, *The Death of Kings*, but he rearranged what happened and of course changed all our names). Our questions at first were hesitant, but Luce took a lot of time and care to answer them. We were all much impressed by him.

I remember the evening also for a comic mischance that befell me. Some time after dinner, feeling in need of the lavatory, I went in search of one. I walked down a hallway and opened a likely door—it was a closet, full of women's clothes. I turned a corner and tried again; this time it was a boudoir, and there was Mrs. Luce sitting in front of a mirror, getting ready for bed. She glanced up as I opened the door. What a stupid thing to have done, I told myself; I must be careful to open no more wrong doors. I tiptoed down the hallway and turned another corner. This must be it. Softly I opened the door—and there she was again, the other side of her! This time she was definitely annoyed. "Young man!" she said. I heard no more. I gave up my search and returned to the high talk in the living room.

There was so much to be said, and listened to—for it turned out that Luce was a great talker—that we could hardly begin to cover

the ground in one evening. When we left, some time aro[
night, we had agreed to meet again the following week[
we had two more evenings; for the final one I insisted t[
should be our guest, and I engaged a private dining room at The
Players'. By this time we felt that we knew him a lot better, and
we had only a few more things to ask. But some of them were
awkward questions—things like "How much is your financial interest in *Time*?" and "Under what circumstances would you consider using *Time* as a political instrument?"

When Luce arrived for this meeting he handed us each a copy
of a memo he had written. As we read it, we saw that he had
anticipated all these final questions and had written his answers.
Furthermore he had lifted the argument to a general discussion of
journalism, its purposes and possibilities, and ended with a statement of his own journalistic faith. He had cut the ground out
from under us. We looked at each other and shook our heads.
There was nothing left to say. Luce stared at us inquiringly, read
the answer in our faces, and started gathering up the copies of his
memo. He said that if we didn't need him any more he'd be getting
uptown; he had a date. I followed him to the door, and asked him
for a copy of the memo, which I promised to return after we had
gone over it again. It was then I got a first hint of one of Luce's
most marked characteristics—in part a love of secrecy and in part
a fear of publicity.

"Well, all right," he said, eying me sharply. "But I'd hate to have
Walter Winchell get hold of it." I promised that nothing like that
would happen.

Having at last discovered Luce, and having found him very different from the plodding, lucky dullard he had been advertised to
be, perhaps I went too far in the other direction. As if I had forgotten that he had at least half-invented *Time* and was therefore
chiefly responsible for its faults as well as its virtues, I jumped to
the enthusiastic conclusion that all that ailed *Time*—its crude
smartness, its horrible lapses in taste, its generally brummagem
quality—all these flaws could be mended if only *Time* and Luce
got better acquainted!

In 1939 Luce was just entering his forties. If *Time* had described him—which of course it never did—it might have called him "brisk, balding, bristle-browed." (He would have objected violently to "balding," and protested that he was only getting a little thin on top.) And the description would have been as coarse and super-ficial as *Time*'s usually were.* Luce was a good-looking man: just under six feet, with strong, regular features, unusually bushy eye-brows, shapely, tapering but hairy hands. His physical endowments were certainly above the average, and yet the sum total was dis-appointing, the general effect cold. Perhaps it was his small eyes, whose usual expression ran a narrow range from the noncommital to the suspicious, peering out at you from under the thicket of his eyebrows; perhaps it was the set of his face, which he could manipulate into quizzical amusement, mock surprise or wary atten-tiveness, but which always settled again into a severe, poker-faced, almost Oriental impassiveness.

---

* Edmund Wilson once wrote (in the *Princeton University Library Chronicle*, February 1944) an acid attack on *Time*:

> *Time*'s picture of the world gives us sometimes simply the effect of schoolboy mentalities in a position to avail them-selves of a gigantic research equipment; but it is almost al-ways tinged with a peculiar kind of jeering rancor. There is a tendency to exhibit the persons whose activities are chron-icled, not as more or less able or noble or amusing or intelli-gent human beings, who have various ways of being right or wrong, but—because they are presented by writers who are allowed no points of view themselves—as manikins, sometimes cocky, sometimes busy, sometimes zealous, sometimes silly, sometimes gruesome, but in most cases quite infra-human, who make speeches before guinea-pig parliaments, issue com-mands and move armies of beetles back and forth on bas-relief battle-maps, indulge themselves maniacally in queer little games of sport, science, art, beer-bottle-top collecting or what not, squeak absurd little boasts and complaints, and pop up their absurd little faces in front of the lenses of the Luce photographers, and add up to a general impression that the pursuits, past and present, of the human race are rather an absurd little scandal about which you might find out some even nastier details if you met the editors of *Time* over cocktails. . . .

I sent copies of this to Luce and half a dozen others, "on the principle that enemies are better critics than friends." No comment from any of them.

He was one of several Americans I knew who had been born in China and whose faces seemed to bear the inscrutable stamp of their birthplace. That may have been my imagination, but in other ways he showed undoubted traces of his early upbringing. His father had been a Presbyterian missionary, and young Luce had had his first education—I think up to the age of fifteen—at a British school in China. This basic fact may partly explain some of his most strongly held convictions: his feeling for America, a kind of fervid patriotism more usually felt by converts or late-comers (in a less intelligent man it might have become chauvinism); his feeling for England, a complex of love and envy, admiration and contempt. If he had been British he would certainly have been an extreme Tory, proud of the Empire, protestingly furious at its liquidation. As an American, with an imperial sense of America's future, he was glad to see Britain's competition dwindle. And as an American trained by British teachers, he resented the fact that British educational methods were superior to American.

His feeling for China I never altogether understood. I believe he loved the country and the people, and I have heard him really eloquent on the subject. And yet, long before China's defection— or kidnapping, from his point of view—into Communism, he must have misunderstood China just as badly as his hero Chiang Kai-shek did. Luce was stubborn and headstrong, but facts and logic could usually persuade him; on this issue alone he went beyond the bounds of reason. At the climax he pitted his faith in the China he had known against the present facts reported by his principal correspondent on the scene; it was a heavy responsibility for a journalist to take, but he took it. When the facts went against him and he was proved wrong before the world, he had to have a villain, someone who could be held responsible for "losing" China to the enemy, and his villain was ready to hand; the Democratic administration in general, Roosevelt and Acheson in particular.

Luce's fidelity to Chiang Kai-shek does credit to his loyalty, whatever it says about his intelligence or his partisanship as a journalist. But Chiang, particularly Chiang-in-exile, could not be his principal hero, for his heroes must succeed. Churchill was the man he most admired. Luce could not quite forgive him for being

British—or half British—any more than he could reconcile himself to the fact that Franklin Roosevelt was American.

Every man is a battleground, but in Luce I think the battle was fiercer and more unremitting than in most of us. As a convinced Presbyterian he knew that there can be no such thing as success and that man is a miserable sinner. As a fervently patriotic American he had an almost religious faith in competition and a striving belief that it was a man's duty, like his country's, to win. He must have been daily (and nightly) torn by the struggle with these apocalyptic beasts, these irreconcilable and mutually hostile convictions. Although his devotion to the Presbyterian creed was not always apparent during office hours, and was certainly not allowed to shackle his progress as a press tycoon, it was there, it was a part of him, and it made both himself and his success more interesting. I finally decided that what most drew me to Luce and made me feel that we had something in common—and has kept me fond of him even when I didn't like him—was his guilty conscience.

There was a period, after his second wife became a Roman Catholic convert and it was known that Father John Courtney Murray, a formidable Jesuit, was a frequent visitor in his household, when some people thought that he himself was "under instruction" to the Roman Church. A man came into my office one day to tell me so; Luce had been seen attending Mass, and following the liturgy in a missal. This news left me quite unmoved. I told my visitor: "The day Harry Luce turns Roman Catholic I'll look out of my window and see streams of pigs flying past." His interest in Catholicism may well have deepened his own faith but could not supplant it.

My acquaintance with Luce's character did not reach this point of sureness in a day, and in fact, although eventually I came to feel that I knew him well, I never felt that I knew him intimately. Very few people, I think, could honestly say that. There was a time when I almost despaired of understanding him—and I thought some degree of understanding was necessary if I were going to work with him the rest of my life, as seemed probable then. He had a sister whose resemblance to him was striking, except that she was warm and lively while he was cold and withdrawn. I invited myself to tea with this lady, with the avowed purpose of getting her to tell me what her brother was like. It turned out that she didn't know either.

I have never succeeded in finding a real short cut to anything. On the other hand, men who work together long enough get to know each other pretty well, and sometimes even develop a kind of attachment to each other which is no less real for being the result of a chance association. In this sense, at least, Luce and I were friends. As far as he was concerned, I don't think he had any other kind. When he came back from a trip—and he was always coming back from a trip, whether it was to Western China or to Washington to see the President—he wanted to tell people about it. (Not for him the Procter motto: "Welcome home and shut up.") He never did anything for pleasure—or perhaps it would be fairer to say that the business of journalism was his only pleasure— so he usually had something to report. There were other times when he hadn't, when he simply wanted to "bloviate," as he called it. We never knew which it was going to be when he summoned half a dozen of us, usually at short notice, to lunch or dinner.

These were not always easy occasions, and as Luce grew older and more garrulous, a more perceptive host might have seen that his guests were sometimes restless and felt themselves an unwillingly captive audience. The reassurance of success gradually cured his stammer, and when he was talking well he could strike off a witty, pungent or even eloquent phrase; but when he was below his best he could be as incoherent and rambling as any club bore.

I began to notice two of his mannerisms which I did not find endearing. One was his uninterruptibility. It may not be polite to interrupt, but among friends it is part of the natural give-and-take of conversation, and not to yield to such interruptions can become mere rough-shod rudeness. Luce was continually guilty of this rudeness. There were some compensations, I found, in being forced to sit silent while he "bloviated": by the time you did manage to get your word in, you had had time to sharpen it to an effective cutting edge.

His other peculiarity was the appropriation of any matches or packages of cigarettes within his reach, no matter whose they were. He never asked permission, and sometimes casually put them in his pocket. I was sure this was only absent-mindedness; all the same, it seemed to me another form of rudeness, an unawareness of other people. I suppose he must have had a strict upbringing as a child, but I sometimes wondered if he hadn't also learned in his mission compound a lordly disregard of servants and underlings.

Was it at his mission school in China that he got the idea that there was something un-American in being a gentleman? At Yale he had been a great success and had been "tapped for Bones"—the most exclusive and therefore the most socially desirable of the secret societies. But he must have been aware that this was an acknowledgment of success rather than the recognition of quality. His attitude toward the quality of gentlemanliness was ambivalent (one of his favorite words) in much the same way as his attitude toward England, where gentlemen were invented: he was annoyed, amused, resentful, grudgingly admiring, a little uneasy.

By the same token he was attracted by rascals, though not as much as he pretended to be. I think it was the streak of flamboyant rascality in Churchill he admired, no less than the more obvious histrionics of "greatness." And Beaverbrook, a purer example of scalawag, fascinated him. He used to enjoy baiting me, during the darker periods of the war, by suggesting that if things got bad enough for Britain so that only a really tough character could save the country, Beaverbrook would become Prime Minister. Eventually he would goad me into the expected retort that no matter how bad things got, the British would never take such a man to be their leader.

Did Luce like me? There was a time when I think I was regarded as his current favorite, and that may have been briefly true; if so, however, it was because of my performance or promise, not because our personalities matched. We had in common a religious background, and that was about all. I know I irritated him—especially when I took (or he thought I took) a position of moral superiority—and his bad manners and devious secretiveness sometimes infuriated me. But at his best there was something engaging, almost touching, certainly likable, about him.

One morning we were driving in to the office together, having spent the night at his house in the country. He smacked his newspaper with the back of his hand.

"This Lindbergh story!" (Lindbergh had just made a resoundingly isolationist speech somewhere in the Middle West.)

"Yes?"

"I'd like to write it."

I was then editing National Affairs, the department in *Time* where the Lindbergh speech would be reported; I had already scheduled and assigned the story. I told Luce so, but he insisted that he wanted to write it himself.

Later that morning his secretary, Miss Thrasher, appeared in my office, beaming, and laid some typed pages on my desk.

"From the boss!" she said.

"Yes, I know."

"It's a wow!"

"I hope so."

Wow or not, it bore little resemblance to the orthodox *Time* story: the lead paragraph was more like a Fourth of July oration. But it was an oration I found moving; I was inclined to agree with Miss Thrasher. I made a few changes in spelling and punctuation, put my initials in the upper right-hand corner and pressed the buzzer for the copy boy. Though I edited and passed all copy for National Affairs, it then went to the managing editor; he had the final say. Later that day I asked him,

"Have you seen Harry's story?"

"Mmm."

"Like it?"

"Well, I fiddled with it a little."

I knew what that meant. When he "fiddled with" a story, it was like an elephant trampling through a cane brake. And sure enough, when the retyped story returned from the copy desk, the lead paragraph had disappeared; the rest had been largely rewritten.

Bright and early next morning, Luce came to my office, to inquire about the fate of his story. I silently handed him the mangled remnants. When he had read it he said, "Well, quite a lot of it got by."

"What about the lead?"

"Oh, did you like the lead?"

"I certainly did."

He picked up both versions and went off to give the managing editor an argument. Ten minutes later he was back again.

"Well, we can keep the lead, and the first sentence of the second paragraph, but after that nothing but plain sense."

In *Time*'s earliest days, Luce and Hadden had taken turns, six months at a time, at editing the magazine. After Hadden died, Luce's name led the masthead as editor, but he was generally an absentee, busy on other enterprises. When, to keep his hand in or to see for himself how things were going, he came back to his old job, it was at long intervals and never for more than a few weeks. These visitations were invigorating but also exhausting for all hands—rather like a strong wind that blew fresh air through the office but also scattered the papers into hopeless confusion. Luce never attempted to understand the complexities of organization and procedure that had grown up in *Time* since the early days, and consequently threw many a monkey wrench into the machinery. Perhaps it was sometimes deliberate. Once when he was acting as managing editor he found an unaccustomed gadget on his desk: a little battery of push-buttons, designed to summon various specialists. When he wanted to see someone, he pushed all the buttons at once, at the same time yelling, "Tack!"—the nickname of a useful factotum who shared his dislike of red tape and could be counted on to understand what Luce wanted and how to do it.

The general outline of the week's issue was planned on Thursday, the first day of the "*Time* week"—or sketched rather than planned, because one thing you could be sure of was that by Sunday the run of the news would have made hash of Thursday's plan. No firm make-up, even of the "early form," could be started before Sunday. Nevertheless Luce would plan a make-up for the whole magazine on Thursday, revise it with renewed enthusiasm on Friday, and so on until the ineluctable reality of the waiting presses on Monday night forced a final decision. These constant changes of plan, calling for sketches of layouts, special pictures, maps and ideas for stories, etc., sent everyone scurrying in all directions, doing twice as much work as usual—or as necessary, for at least half these schemes came to nothing. In the midst of this windy chaos, at its very height, about midnight on Saturday, Luce would put on his hat and go home. Later stayers had to rescue or create some sort of order out of the gaseous genesis he left behind him. There were usually two noticeable results from a week of Luce's editing: the staff got less sleep but their morale went up; and the finished issue, though it might be uneven, had some unusual high spots in it.

As an editor of copy, Luce was very sparing of the blue pencil. He might kill a sentence or so, or even a paragraph, "just to keep my franchise," but in general he either passed the story without change—often with generous words of praise scribbled on the margin—or threw it out. If he didn't like it but thought it might be saved, he would call in the writer and discuss it with him, and send him off for another try. This editorial practice I approved in theory and much admired; but I couldn't behave that way myself. A great part of the copy that came to my desk was so lamely written, and experience showed me that a second or even third version would be so little improved, that my pencil was always interfering, and my words of praise were ungenerous and few. I still think Luce's way of editing was better, and that he was a better editor. But when it came to the quality of writing, I think he was also more easily satisfied.

I was considered to have made such a success with the "critical departments" that I was given more and more editing to do. Within two years, in fact, all departments in the "back of the book"— at least half the magazine—were put in my charge. This load of work was in fact too heavy for one editor to carry, and I didn't have it long, but it was fun while it lasted. My salary was raised several times, and in big jumps. This was the period, I think, when I found most favor in Luce's eyes. I remember at least one occasion when he himself broke the happy news that I was getting a raise. He took me to lunch at the Ritz, where he made me a little speech of congratulation, and then, lowering his voice—for he had a horror of having such secrets overheard—mentioned the amount that my salary was going up. What with the clatter of plates in the restaurant and the other voices, and the figure I thought he mentioned, which seemed incredibly high, and my inability to ask him to repeat this almost whispered confidence, I was left in doubt until my next pay check came in. Then I realized I *had* heard him right after all.

In the next stage of my career on *Time*, as National Affairs editor, my relations with Luce were closer and more abrasive. Luce always regarded me as a political innocent, or at least an indifferent. To this half-spoken indictment I could return the silent answer: in that case, how did I not only survive but manage to get ahead? He, of course, meant national politics, politics as news; my kind of politics was closer to home: street-fighting, not misty problems of high strategy. I had to get rid of enemies, put down incipient rebellions, win and make sure of my supporters; isn't this politics? Sometimes I was forced, or he forced me, into showing my hand, and I learned to resent or regret those mistakes; isn't that like a politician? My strategy was to gather round me a minority that I hoped to make dominant, and for a while I thought I might succeed. Like all politicians, I was too sanguine.

The fact I kept forgetting, or wouldn't admit, was that *Time* was not only Luce's invention but his property. I still won't agree that the one follows from the other. Grover Cleveland had already said it for me: "A public property is a public trust." By becoming a success, and because it was a journalistic enterprise—i.e., with the acknowledged responsibility of keeping its readers as well informed as it could—*Time* in a sense was also a public trust, and therefore must not be subject to the whims or dictates of one man. And, in practice, *Time* wasn't. In practice, no newspaper or magazine ever is, altogether. It was Luce's theory I objected to, much more than to his practice. In my view, the responsibility for *Time* was shared among the men who produced it and their responsibility must carry with it a corresponding share of authority (which, to a greater or less extent, it had to); in Luce's view, the final authority was vested, more or less entirely, in him. Practice and theory on this question frequently clashed. I suppose they should have clashed more. For until the question was settled one way or the other, the theory of Luce's omnipotent authority tended to shackle our responsible practice.

I don't think I truckled to Luce, but neither do I think I opposed him enough. It sometimes seemed to me that nobody stood up to him sufficiently, although they used other effective ways of circumventing some of his bad-tempered fiats, his ill-conceived or impossible notions. On the rare occasions when I did reluctantly force the issue, I always wondered why it had to be me. Except the first time. That was a question of principle, perhaps, but it was also a private matter. It was during the rough-and-tumble of a presidential campaign—Roosevelt vs. Willkie in 1940. Luce called me up at home to complain, in a long, rambling, furious diatribe, about my handling of some political story in the issue that had just gone to press. When I got a chance to speak I told him, with equal fury, that if he ever again called me at home on a Wednesday, or if anyone from the office ever did, I would resign on the spot. If it had been Tuesday, while the presses were still running and changes were still possible, that was another matter; but Wednesday was too late to make any changes, Wednesday was the one day I had with my family, it was a sacred day, and was never to be trespassed on again. He apologized handsomely, and thereafter my Wednesdays were sacrosanct.

Luce's notes and memos to his editors, which he scribbled off at great speed, often had a sting in them. His irony was sometimes amusing and effective, but his occasional sarcasms were apt to be more wounding than I think he realized. Was I too ready to take offense? Or was I too watchful for signs that power was making him tyrannical? Perhaps both. But once I did something worse, in terms of office politics: I wrote an answer to his memo and took it to him myself and stayed while he read it. That was worse than a crime, it was a blunder, for it left him no way out. This was my note:

"There are several possible answers to your memo of yesterday on Harry Bridges: (1) tear it up and throw it in the wastebasket (as Alex did); (2) remonstrate with you (as John Billings did); (3) say nothing; (4) tell you to go to hell—as I have been very strongly tempted to do.

"I honestly think I have listed all the possible answers. No decent human being would answer your memo by accepting it (I mean of course its tone and manner—*not* your views on Bridges). You have written it as if to dogs, not to human beings. And you thus make a great mistake.

"If you're really degenerating into a barking boss, you'll soon have behind you only the anxious, stupid, dishonest subservience that kind of boss can command. But you will no longer command either my respect or my services."

No apology wrested by force is worth getting, and this cornering demand for one was, I am sure, both wrong and foolish. I got the apology, but I don't suppose he could ever quite forgive me for insisting on it. I wouldn't have, in his shoes. In fact, as I look back on those days, I can see now that Luce must have put up with a good deal from me. I've found another of my notes to him, dated six months later, that begins:

"Well! Your memo amply proves that you are not only (1) a busy man but (2) a rude one and (3) an unclear one. . . ."

I can't imagine Beaverbrook, or McCormick, or any press lord you can mention, tolerating that kind of talk from one of his subordinates.

To be promoted to the editorship of National Affairs was an honor but a dangerous one: from that step on the ladder you either went up or down. The department was sometimes known as "the bloody angle," not so much because of the casualties that could be expected there as from its exposed position; the work was hard and taken very seriously, without much fun, and we all felt that we were bearing the burden and heat of the day. I took over the job with some reluctance. I had no flair for political reporting (Luce was right about that) and not much interest in the heavy sort of news the department was loaded with. Furthermore, in taking on National Affairs I had to abandon my attitude that only the cultural side of *Time* could be made to count. And now that I was to be responsible for the most important department of the magazine

On the Bridge

I must consider the possibility that one of these days I might be responsible for the whole of it.

It was like starting all over again—and with an added handicap. I was a newcomer to this field of affairs; my staff were no better off. Of my four writers, two had been newspaper reporters, one had had a brief and not successful career on *Fortune,* and one was a free-lance writer for pulp magazines. All of them were new to *Time.* And before we found our feet, we were in the thick of a presidential campaign. Somehow we got through those months, but at one point I wouldn't have given much for our chances. I was determined to report the campaign as fairly as possible, but in our attempts to be fair we managed to alienate the partisans of both sides. And as private citizens we had our own opinions: two of the writers were passionate supporters of Roosevelt, the other two and I favored Willkie. But as journalists I think we all tried to play it straight. This must have been the last presidential campaign when that could be said about *Time.*

The most violently pro-Roosevelt man deliberately disfranchised himself by failing to register as a voter. A week or so later, in *Life,* Luce published over his own signature a stern reminder to all citizens of their absolute duty to vote, adding that he would not willingly shake hands or sit at the same table with a man who failed in that duty. My overconscientious writer came to me with a pale face, asking whether he should confess to Luce what he had done. I told him: certainly not; he would only embarrass Luce, and he had acted as he thought right.

The first uproar we caused, as I remember, was by a story describing the crowds that gathered to see Willkie in the early days of that amazing campaign, largely out of curiosity—as people would flock to see "a dead whale on a flat-car." The other story that brought the most outraged protests from the Willkie forces was a report of the Willkie campaign train; it was both accurate and indiscreet. This story was the joint work of three hands: our Washington correspondent's, a National Affairs writer's, and mine. Our Washington man had been on the train for weeks (he finally sent a despairing telegram: "Take me off this train. All I can do is sit at my typewriter and write, 'Wendell Willkie is a wonderful man.

Wendell Willkie is a wonderful man' "). The final version of the story was stitched together at the last minute by the three of us, over cups of coffee at Child's, around the corner from the office.

The roars we drew didn't all come from enraged readers; the most frequent and loudest came from Luce. At the height of the campaign he announced that we had made such a botch of it that he would punish us by "exiling himself" from our floor until the election. We breathed a collective sigh of thanksgiving and staggered on. Some months later, after the dust had settled and the heat had died away, Luce made a speech at a company dinner in which he looked back over the achievements of the past year. He referred to us then, this same National Affairs staff, as "a great team."

Over the years I must have heard dozens of Luce's speeches; his improvement as a speaker was extraordinary. He was no more of a natural orator than Demosthenes, and if he didn't actually practice with pebbles in his mouth, he worked as hard to train himself. For a set speech before a large or important audience he always wrote out his address, sometimes making several drafts of it; then he memorized it word for word until he was letter-perfect. The speech itself gave the impression of being extemporized, for he never consulted a note. I know this is how he did it, because he had the habit of sending the final draft of a speech to me, to see that its hair was properly brushed and its tie straight.

I once heard him speak from the same platform with Churchill and Tom Dewey—and Luce was easily the best of the three. Dewey was appalling: ungenerous and bitter about his recent defeat for the presidency, embarrassingly fulsome in his references to Churchill. That old war horse felt obliged to rise and protest that "there are some things that should not be said about a man until he is dead"; and his own speech was only rumbles and flickers on the horizon; he had come to make an oration in Boston a few days later, and was conserving his ammunition. When Luce got up to speak, he was brief, pointed—and some of his phrases were Churchillian. He certainly out-Churchilled Churchill that evening. Instead of the fawning and near-blasphemous compliments Dewey had made, he compared the great man as a war correspondent to Julius Caesar, and as a historian to Macaulay.

But it was a speech of his at a company dinner that I remember best. It began something like this: "You know, I too sometimes venture into polite society. The other evening at a dinner party I was sitting next to a charming young lady, and did my best to make myself agreeable. When our hostess took the ladies from the table, my partner turned to me and said, 'Why, you're quite nice!' How much of a son of a bitch does the managing editor of *Time* have to be?"

That was his text. As I had become managing editor only a few months before, I was perhaps more interested than most in what was coming next. He paid his respects to each of *Time*'s managing editors, from the beginning. When he came to my predecessor he said: "Now, how does Gott qualify for the son-of-a-bitch club? In theory, yes. In practice, no." An accolade, no less. What would I draw? Well, here it came. "And now Tom. How can he possibly be admitted to this club? Perhaps it depends on who is in charge of the pearly gates when he gets there." I thought this then, and still do, a characteristically ambiguous Lucean "compliment."

Luce's ambiguity was more than verbal. He liked keeping people uncertain about his actions, he was naturally secretive, and if he didn't actually shy away from clear-cut decisions, he preferred the kind of ingenious compromise that often "solved" a problem by doubling it. As an administrator I think he had more than a little in common with his pet hate, Franklin Roosevelt—who also inclined to settle arguments by seeming to favor both sides and waiting for the stronger to emerge—and problems of jurisdiction by appointing two men to share one responsibility, leaving the authority of each in doubt.

Luce's own position might have seemed ambiguous to an outsider. The title he chose for himself was editor-in-chief of *Time* and his other publications; but he was actually the publisher, in the usual sense of that word—a publisher who actively intervened in editorial affairs. He was also the business head of the company; although for convenience he gave to other men the titles of president, chairman of the board, executive vice-president and so on, he had the final say on every business decision. Nevertheless he managed to infuse a general belief among the editorial staff that he was primarily on their side; they believed that as long as Luce was there the "business side" would be kept subordinate to the editorial (as I used to put it: "in the servants' quarters, where they belong").

People were fired from *Time*, and eventually I had to do my share of that disagreeable job, but I don't know that Luce ever personally fired anybody. His forte was the reshuffle. When he was arranging his hand for one of these complicated maneuvers, he always kept his cards under the table. Sometimes it took him a long time—several months—to get his hand arranged to his satisfaction. I figured in one of these reshuffles. It was in 1942. By then I had the title of executive editor. I was a kind of assistant and deputy to the managing editor. The war was going on and on, and I was becoming increasingly restless; I wanted at least to see some of it—though I was not at all tempted to join the desk-soldiers in Washington, where my age and experience would inevitably have landed me, if I had enlisted.

I must have voiced my complaint several times to Luce, because he finally asked me where I wanted to go—Moscow? I said no, not *Moscow*. Well, what about London? Yes, all right. Soon after this he took me out to lunch at one of his clubs, and in a corner of a nearly deserted room, where no enemy ears could overhear us, he put this proposition to me: I would go to London and run the bureau there for three months, and get the war out of my system; then come back and be managing editor. This last was to be just between the two of us, as while I was away he would have to arrange a number of rather difficult and complicated changes in the *Time* staff. I agreed, and went off to London with my secret—which was so well kept that a good many of my colleagues in the New York office thought my mission was in fact an exile and a sign that my days were numbered.

During the three months I was in London not a single bomb dropped; I never once saw a German plane nor heard an anti-aircraft gun. One week-end night when I was in the country, there was a small raid on Canterbury, nearby, but I was asleep with my deaf ear turned up, and heard nothing. The dozen or so times the sirens wailed an alert were all false alarms. Nevertheless, London was at war, and the signs of the last blitz and the expectation of the next were all about me: the blackout, the bomb scars, the barrage balloons—one misty day I saw one on the ground, like a monstrous, wetly shining silver sea cow, nestling among the bushes of a park— the sleepers in the Underground, the rationing, the steady confidence.

It seemed to me a blissfully natural place to be, and I walked whistling along the grimy, greasy streets, feeling delighted and at home among people who had stripped life to its good essentials. I had never been so happy. From this hurricane's peaceful eye I returned to New York—not because I wanted to but because it was expected of me.

I tried to explain to Luce that London had changed my mind about New York, and that the prospect of being managing editor of *Time* no longer seemed so inviting. I would rather be something else: editor of the *Atlantic Monthly*, perhaps. I would still like to have the experience of the *Time* job but, feeling as I did, I supposed he might like to reconsider his offer. He gave me a hard look and seemed to agree. After ten tenterhooked days he took me to lunch, and shot me questions about what I thought and would do about this, that, him and it. As we parted I said, "Then you do want me to be managing editor?" He said, "Of course!"

I was managing editor of *Time* for six years, from the beginning of 1943 to the end of 1949—a record then, but since surpassed. It was a good job, regarded by some as one of the best in American journalism; and it had its moments. There were other times when I felt I wouldn't have inflicted it on a dog. Since I am a slow learner and always have a lot to learn, it took me four of those six years to acquire the knowledge and the confidence that I was doing all right; during the last two I felt I was performing fairly well—which may have been a sign that I wasn't.

And what did I accomplish in those six years? Nothing tangible, visible or lasting, as far as I could see. I picked up a brief and local reputation as a hard editor, "a slow man with a kind word," who had some ludicrous blind spots, taking too little interest in important news and getting overenthusiastic about news that was off-beat and minor. I was neither popular nor beloved, and I made some enemies. I was sometimes told that I had "changed the tone" of *Time*—which I am quite sure I didn't—or at least had left some ephemeral impress on the magazine. I could never see any signs of that myself, much as I should have liked to see them.

In moods of depression I thought of most *Time* writers as Yahoos, or of myself as the aged Ulysses condemned to rockbound Ithaca, where I must "mete and dole unequal laws unto a savage race"—or as a governess who has taken on the hopeless task of improving the guttersnipe accent and incorrigible rudeness of a spoiled, rich, foul-mouthed brat. One change in *Time* I was determined to make, and it is sufficient evidence of my general failure that I couldn't or didn't make it: to root out *Time*'s notorious technique of innuendo—often ineptly and even clumsily done, but poisonously intended:

> *Damn with faint praise, assent with civil leer,*
> *And without sneering, teach the rest to sneer;*
> *Willing to wound, and yet afraid to strike,*
> *Just hint a fault, and hesitate dislike. . . .*

Pope's lines are too good for *Time*, but they apply.

And how can I exonerate myself from membership in this son-of-a-bitch club? I can't; in fact for six years I was the chairman, and must take the responsibility (under Jove) for everything that appeared in *Time* in those six years. That record is incontrovertible and perhaps damning. The only scrap of indirect testimony I can cite in my own defense is a scene in my office, when one of my infuriated lieutenants shouted at me: "The trouble with *Time* is, it's too f----- fair, and you're the one who does it!" Being angry, he exaggerated, of course; *Time* was no more f----- fair in those days than it is now.

I had friends among the staff too, and perhaps some of them shared my hope that, once I was on the bridge, we could take over the vessel. Where did we hope to head it? At all events, I soon discovered that it was all I could do to keep it plying back and forth on schedule, on its regular run. My hands were so full of daily problems and weekly crises that there was literally no time left to think of anything else. Besides, it wasn't "my" ship. It belonged to the company, and I worked for the company. That obvious situation became clear to me only after I was actually in it.

My mother once embarrassed me by asking me what it was I did, exactly, in my job. I thought for a minute, found I couldn't answer her question, and said coldly, "Well, I manage to keep busy." My work week was then about seventy hours, packed into five days.

Around midnight the following Sunday, just as I had at last got my desk clear of copy and was reaching for the pile of Monday morning newspapers, my mother's question came back to me. What *did* I do? I knew exactly what I did, and if anyone really had the patience to listen I could tell him: it would take some time. Where should I start?

The job began again every week—that was one of the best things about it—on Thursday, when the editorial staff came to work, and ended every Monday night, when we went to press. There were all kinds of fancy reasons why it had to be Monday, but no good reason except that you have to go to press some time. The issue was dated the following Monday, although it reached the newsstands and subscribers the Thursday before. That was something I wouldn't have attempted to explain to my mother or anybody; it never made sense to me, and the only reason we did it was that everybody did it. A magazine that was postdated gave the reader a feeling of being ahead of the game, whereas it would depress him to see that the magazine was dated the day he bought it, or even a day or so before. At least that's what the advertising-promotion-circulation boys said. They were always saying things like that.

Anyhow, our week began on Thursday. In the early days the Thursday story conference was held in the managing editor's office, and it lasted all day. The managing editor acted like a combination of judge and prosecuting attorney: he would cross-question the prisoners and then sentence them. The prisoners were the writers, who were summoned one after another, and came in with lists of suggested stories for their departments. The managing editor's idea seemed to be to turn down every suggestion he possibly could; once in a while he would grudgingly make a note on the big chart spread on his desk. It was such an exhausting, boring and one-sided business that when I became managing editor I changed the system: instead of one day-long meeting presided over by one man I had a series of small meetings, each in charge of a different editor. In a few years, of course, these small meetings had grown so that they had become nearly as large and one-sided as the old one, but at least they didn't last all day.

Instead of trying to describe this, however, wouldn't it be better to show it happening? The material I would need would be a nuisance to collect, but it could be done in one week. To get what happened on Thursday, for instance, all office telephones would have to be monitored, all scribbled notes and memos rescued from the waste baskets, stenographic reports or wire-recordings made of conferences and conversations—maybe even at lunch; the talk there, when it wasn't strictly business, was mostly shop talk. Besides that, you'd need all the cables and marked newspaper clippings, and the first tentative story list. That would give you Thursday.

And each of the next four days would be another chapter, each one showing the week's issue gradually taking shape, from the first draft of a story, the edited version, the checking of facts, the re-edit, down to the final cuts for space and the captions under the pictures, then the make-up, and the setting and sending of the copy over the teletypesetting machines. The last chapter would be the printed issue—with an appendix of all the overset material that had to be left out. It would be a sizable book. Expensive to make. But it should answer my mother's question about how I managed to keep busy for five days a week.

I mentioned this idea to a couple of other people in the office, and they took it seriously. One said it would make just the handbook he needed for beginners in his department. The other, who was a vice-president of the company, thought the idea had great promotional possibilities; a book like that should make a hit with our advertisers.

Luckily there was a paper shortage just then, or something might actually have been done about it.

But supposing the book had been made and my mother had read it, would she have thought it a satisfactory answer to her question? I doubt it. I would have shown her a blueprint of a complicated machine, but only that; what she really wanted to know was how I was spending my life. What was it like to live most of my waking hours in that office, sitting at that desk?

This question would not be so easy to answer. I might start with my office door, which was almost always open because it was a large part of my job to be interrupted. Besides the open door, I could be interrupted in other ways: by telephone and the "squawk box"—the interoffice phone, like a small switchboard, that stood next my desk. Most of the time I rather liked the state of being continually interrupted; you never knew what was coming next.

In between the interruptions there was the regular job to be done: reading several hundred thousand words a week of cables and reports, morning and evening newspapers and weekly and monthly magazines (all these for points bearing on stories past, present and future); keeping an eye and a finger on the important stories for that week (and my unimportant favorites); reading and if necessary re-editing all the copy (about a third more than could possibly be printed) that came, at first in a trickle and then in a flood, to my desk. With no interruptions at all, it would have taken a lot of time. Even though I carried work home, the shortest day in the office was eight or nine hours, and when the crescendo reached its peak on Sunday, the day might stretch to 16 hours. We got two days a week off, and we needed them.

Then there was the Weekly Crisis. There may have been some weeks when it passed us by; if so, I can't remember them. This crisis was not always or perhaps very often caused by some great external event, like the Sunday morning of Pearl Harbor or the week Hitler disappeared—more often it blew up suddenly from some apparently slight shift in the news or from some failure of the news to make an expected shift. Monday was its favorite time to strike. That was press day, when everyone was tired, and everything should be flowing smoothly and rapidly to a stop-watch finish. That was the day the top brass, the vice presidents, the super-editorial intelligences, came back to the office refreshed from their weekends, full of ideas, opinions and suggestions.

Another thing my blueprint book would not have explained, except by implication and to the expert reader, was the internecine warfare of the office—known locally as "politics." It was always going on, although usually below the surface, and it ran the scale from the Florentine to the infantile. The way the paper was organized, in self-contained departments, encouraged rivalries and cliques, and the layout of the offices, in which each petty war lord had his followers grouped around him, was just what was needed to keep the campfires burning. Since I had to preside over this loose federation of mutually suspicious satraps, of necessity I learned something of the art of governing nomads—or at least some of its rules of thumb. Like the esoteric teacher who divided all mankind into various classes of idiot, I came to regard everyone on the staff, without exception and varying only in occasion and degree, as a "personnel problem." Dealing with them successfully was another question. In my years of trial-and-error I made a lot of mistakes, and learned a little. If I had known beforehand that I would be called on to be a combination of foreman, teacher, confessor, nursemaid, judge and psychoanalyst . . . but I didn't.

I did learn to distinguish between two kinds of outburst: the plausible protests of the sluggard who considered himself over-worked and the safety-valve explosion of the good man who really was—and the good men always overwork themselves; they have to, on account of the sluggards. I learned to shut my ears to the often impressive but always fishy demands of the buccaneer who wanted something at the expense of another buccaneer. But when a small, shyly determined lady named Louise would appear in my doorway on a Monday evening, I would say, "Come in, Louise. What have I done now?" She never bothered me unless I had done something wrong.

Other rules of thumb, although I learned them in theory, I was never able to apply. It took me years to reach the conclusion that an editor's principal function is to be an encourager of the others, and that consequently he should do as little editing as possible with his pencil. As a writer myself I had always resented having my copy cut or changed. And yet, when I became an editor, I found my pencil running away with me. With a few, a very few exceptions, the writing on the paper was shockingly bad; much of it would have disgraced an eighth-grade classroom in a public school.

A large part of my weekly problem was to get the paper to press on time; another large part was to try to make each issue a good one. Sometimes these two parts of the problem seemed incompatible, like Mary and Martha. On Thursdays everyone tended to be an optimist, and it seemed as if we had all the time in the world. By Sunday it was obvious to the growing number of pessimists that we would never make it. After it was all over, on Monday night, I often felt, "If we had only had one more day!" Nevertheless, if we closed on time, my Martha-half felt successful.

I learned to value the steady man, the slogger, the writer who got his copy in on time and did what he said he would. If it had not been for him and his kind, we should never have got to press. I often thanked God for him. But my real Te Deums were reserved for the uncertain performance of his unsteady brother. There were never more than three or four (out of fifty-odd) of this breed on the staff, and I suppose that was about as many as we could safely carry. In many cases, they were "hard to work with"—touchy, suspicious, arrogant, unpredictable. Their working habits were spectacularly individual. When they worked, they often worked all night, then disappeared for indeterminate periods. They were not only subject to temperamental tantrums but prey to fits of despair; and they had absolutely no feeling about going to press, one way or the other. They sometimes missed the target completely, or failed to pull the trigger. But when they did make a hit, it was often a bull's-eye. They were regarded by the rest of the staff with mingled contempt and awe. I loved and cherished them.

They sometimes took a good deal of cherishing. I remember one who was supposed to be writing the lead story that week for National Affairs, our most important department. It could and should have been written on Friday. It was not written on Saturday. All day Sunday I let him strictly alone. On Monday morning I went into his office to see what had happened. He was not there, of course; he had worked all night. There was no trace of the story, however. Except for the usual disorder, his desk was bare of copy. In the crammed waste basket I found the results of his labors: eight crumpled pieces of paper, with the same first sentence written on each. He was nearing the end of his tether. It must have been about this time that he used to come into my office on Monday evening, staring wildly, and announce that he was resigning. This happened for six weeks in a row, as I remember, and always ended the same way: when we had gone to press, I would take him to a nearby bar and gradually argue him out of it.

The problems of these problem-writers took up a good deal of time, but on the whole I did not regard them as an interruption: they made a lot of my drudgery worth while, or at least seemed to justify it. It was mainly they who encouraged me to feel that, however prosaic the result, the effort we made sometimes approximated the poetic. I could never be proud of any particular number of the paper, or even satisfied with it, and could never admit that it might not have been better done, but sometimes I felt that we had given it a first-rate try. There were more frequent occasions when, shuffling home to bed at three in the morning, I would ask myself, "What am I killing myself for?"

When that question began to recur in broad daylight I finally realized it was what my mother meant.

Did I know what I was doing? I thought so, but how could I be sure? What I hoped I was doing and what I was actually doing might be very different things. I hoped I was engaged in trying to find out what is really news (i.e., what is worth trying to report) —if not what news really is (i.e., the truth about human life that is beyond the scope of journalism)—and how to communicate it to several million people. I knew that few of my colleagues would agree with me. Most of them were quite sure they knew what news is, and their chief concern was in getting the news told, according to well established techniques. Nevertheless, one of them had once said to me that journalism does more harm than good. That had shocked me; if he really thinks that, I said to myself, what the hell is he doing here? For myself, I considered journalism a blunt instrument, often ineptly handled or mishandled, but a necessary tool of democracy. In the process of "telling the news" we lay about us with this bludgeon and occasionally crack the head of an innocent bystander; but democracy can no more get along without journalism than an omelette can be made without cracking eggs.

I had tried to believe in journalism as a partly successful experiment which was still in an early stage of development. In so far as it has succeeded, I told myself, it seems to be a crude but fairly effective means of keeping a democracy awake and self-conscious. The press is not a completely satisfactory means of getting the word around, I admitted, but among those who have the proper hearing aids to hear with and the right spectacles to see with, it does spread the word. Now I found myself wondering about the necessity for those hearing aids and those spectacles—and about the validity of the word itself.

Is journalism really necessary? And is it actually trying to inform people about what is going on in the world—or just trying to sell them a bill of goods? Can anyone, including any journalist, say for sure? The more I thought about it, the more it seemed to me that journalism was actually doing both at the same time. But most of its real earnestness went into salesmanship; its hypocrisy was particularly evident when it protested that all it was doing and all it wanted to do was to inform its readers. No matter what successful editors and publishers thought or pretended to think, wasn't it obvious that people bought their papers because they had learned to like the taste, as with a habit-forming soft drink? Journalism was really a part of the entertainment business.

And the more the techniques of journalism were refined and developed, the more evident it became that the men supposedly in control of the press were in fact at its mercy; they were being run away with. No matter how much they paraded themselves as molders of public opinion, in fact they were actually accepted as entertainers, side-show barkers, vendors of patent medicine. The stuff they peddled might indeed be harmless, but I had begun to doubt it. I could no longer flatly disagree with my friend who had said that journalism does more harm than good. I still hoped he wasn't right, but he might be.

I hadn't quite reached this dubious conclusion, it was only knocking about inside my head, when I became certain of a lesser fact; that there was something seriously wrong with the machinery of *Time*. I couldn't put my finger on it, but I felt it as a kind of fatal complacency. Everything was going much too smoothly. This worried me so much that I tried, again and again, to convey my feeling to Luce, as well as my sense of urgency that something must be done to combat the self-satisfaction. I think I only succeeded in irritating him. In any case, he finally told me that if I really felt that way, why not take some time off—say, a year—investigate the possible causes for alarm and make a full report on what should be done? As I had said myself, everything was going smoothly; my deputy could run the magazine while I was away.

So I did. Halfway through this sabbatical I took my wife and our four sons on a long-planned trip to Europe. The year before, she had had a minor operation which revealed a slight trace of cancer; she then had a much bigger operation which, the doctor assured us, not only removed all signs of cancer but would certainly prevent any recurrence. On the voyage to Marseilles, although she was a good sailor, she felt increasingly ill and weak. In Rome, the doctor gave her a salve. In Florence, the doctor gave her a pill. In Venice, the doctor prescribed rest and quiet. In Geneva, the doctor put her in a clinic for two weeks, and diagnosed a tumor, definitely not cancer. In Paris the doctor refused to come to the hotel to see her, put her through a painful examination, and repeated (as he disdainfully pocketed his unearned fee) that there was no possibility of cancer. By this time she was so weak and in such pain that I decided to fly home with her. We took a plane to New York the next day.

There, as soon as she was strong enough to bear it, our own doctor operated on her. The operation should take, he told me, about an hour and a half, but he reappeared much sooner than that, to say straight out that nothing could be done; she had cancer and would soon die of it. She woke up from the anaesthetic long before she should have, and immediately asked me whether they'd found cancer. I did the best I could to pretend that everything was all right. Next day when the doctor came, she asked him. He said, "You won't have to have any more operations." She understood immediately. For two days she didn't speak. I think she was struggling to accept the fact of death, making her peace with the world. And she did it. From then until she died, four months later, she lived as I think few people succeed in living. I had the impression, I couldn't escape it, that in those four months she grew in wisdom by at least twenty years. I am certain that no one who was with her during those days will ever forget her.

That fall of 1949, I spent all my time in Princeton with her. I did go to New York one day in September, however, to see my deputy about matters connected with *Time*. While we were having lunch I said to him that I would almost certainly never come back to *Time* as managing editor; he was handling the job all right, and after my wife died my first duty would be to my children, so that I would have to have a work week that would leave my weekends free for them. I said, "I think I'll go and tell Harry that, right now." He urged me strongly to do no such thing. He said, "You know what Harry's like: if you don't go to him with a scheme all worked out, he'll think up one while you're away. Don't tell him till you come back—or at least not until you've got a scheme yourself you can go to him with." So I agreed to say nothing to Luce as yet.

About a week later I got a letter from Luce, a very cold letter. He said he was sorry to hear that I had resigned, but that of course he must respect my decision; and what did I propose to do now? I replied, quite warmly, that I had *not* resigned; and that when or if I did he would hear about it from me, not from somebody else. His answer was to summon me to New York.

We had lunch, alone, at his apartment. For the first forty minutes or so he talked, at his disarming best, about various matters; then he casually let drop the fact that he had given my job to my deputy. Well now, what were we going to do about me? That seemed to me his problem, not mine, and I said so. He talked on, and finally suggested, or seemed to suggest—it was not always easy to tell, with him—that he might be willing to vacate his title of editor of *Time* in my favor. I said that would suit me, even though I didn't know what kind of job could be worked out of it. He said he would have to talk to various people, but he would, as soon as he could—he gave me the impression that it might be that very day—and would let me know.

I heard nothing more from him for the next six weeks. During that time I wrote him a one-sentence letter—which, however, I didn't send: "Dear Harry, aren't you getting tired of bending over that hot stove?" On December 18 I got a telephone call from New York. It was Jim Linen, *Time*'s friendly publisher, bubbling with "glorious good news" for me: Harry had generously decided to make me editor of *Time*. "Be sure and tell Julie!" said Jim. I said, God knows why, that I would try. She was very weak by that time, but I whispered the "glorious news" into her ear, and she smiled as if she understood. Next morning she died.

And that's how I got to be "editor" of *Time*.

After New Year's I went back to the office and the empty title; it was empty all right. But I searched it for three years to make sure, and found nothing worth looking for. As managing editor I had had great responsibilities and enough, or almost enough, authority to carry them out; the "editor" had to invent his own responsibilities and could whistle for his authority. The title should really have been in quotation marks; Luce was still the editor.

I might perhaps have learned to be content with my lot—though I doubt it—but there was another reason why I found *Time* an increasingly unpleasant and finally impossible place to stay: its political partisanship. In theory (which grew yearly more canting) *Time* was always "51% against the administration"—whichever party was in power. In its practice, however, *Time* had become very nearly 100% Republican. Though the lower ranks on *Time* were overwhelmingly Democratic or at any rate anti-Republican, *Time*'s management, almost to a man, followed Luce's Republican lead. There were one or two highly placed crypto-Democrats who either found it wiser to keep their opinions to themselves or were in no position to influence editorial policy. This put me in an opposition of one. And my opposition was as ineffective as it was isolated.

I said that I thought the presidential campaign of 1940 was the last one that *Time* even tried to report fairly. I was then the National Affairs editor. But in 1944 and 1948 I was managing editor, and in 1952 I was editor. Why couldn't I have seen that there was fair play in reporting those campaigns? I can only say that I did what I could—which wasn't enough; that Luce had the final authority when he chose to exercise it; and that I might have taken politics more seriously than I did. Also, in spite of all their efforts, in each of those elections until 1952 *Time* and the Republican party were the losers. In 1952, when it sniffed victory in the air at long last, there was no holding *Time*. The distortions, suppressions and slanting of its political "news" seemed to me to pass the bounds of politics and to commit an offense against the ethics of journalism. The climax was a cover story on Adlai Stevenson, the Democratic candidate, which was a clumsy but malign and murderously meant attack. As editor, I had taken over the editing of the cover stories, so I was able to scotch this particular snake—but Luce was appealed to, and that was the last political story I was allowed to edit. At that point I decided to resign.

I waited, however, until the rancors of the campaign had died away and Luce had returned to the office after a well-earned vacation trip. When I told him I was going to resign, he suggested that we both think it over, and eventually offered me two alternative propositions: to make a long, leisurely, educational journey to the Far East (in his phrase, I was "innocent of Asiatic experience"), or go to England and look into the possibilities of starting a special British edition of *Time* there. Why did I listen to him? Why didn't I stick to my resolve and quit, then and there? I should have known that if I didn't I would only be postponing a step long overdue. That seems clear enough now, but it didn't then. Anyone who stays in the same place for more than twenty years is likely to lose the sense of where he is. Imperceptibly to me, during my years on *Time* I had gradually shed most of my original repugnance for it; or would it be more accurate to say that I had grown a thicker skin? I had become so used to *Time*'s ways, curt, snide, conceited as they were, that I hardly noticed them any longer—as I suppose a worker in a glue factory after a while becomes impervious to the smell of glue. If I had been more perceptive (i.e., honest) I would have seen that it wasn't only *Time*'s dirty politics I disliked but the tone, the smell, the personality of *Time* itself. Nevertheless I had been immersed in its atmosphere so long that I was reluctant to leave it. So I listened to Luce.

If I went to Asia, I thought, in some way I should have to pay for the trip later, by writing articles or doing further jobs. The British mission, on the other hand, was clean-cut; I could go, investigate and report, and that would be that. Early in the new year of 1953, I went to London.

My investigations were finished and my report ready in four months. A budget expert was sent from New York to look over my facts and figures—and although the estimated costs were considerably higher than the agreed budget, he returned to New York enthusiastic about the scheme and its feasibility. By that time, so was I. My plan for "*Time*-in-Britain" was simple but had some drastic differences from *Time*-in-New York. The magazine was to be divided into three parts: (1) News, in departments like *Time*'s, but with no political slant, and written (I hoped) in better and clearer English; (2) Views, which would contain signed articles of opinion; (3) Reviews, also signed, of theater, books, art, etc.

Early in June I took my report to Rome to give to Luce. His wife was then Ambassador to Italy and he was spending a good deal of time there. He seemed sympathetic, he was even guardedly encouraging; but he warned me that he didn't have the final say—that would be up to the combined heads of his cooler colleagues in New York. He would put in his word, of course. By this time it was understood—by me, at any rate—that if *Time*-in-Britain came into being, I was to be its editor. I returned to London and waited for the decision.

Some time in August it came: a long cable, about 200 words, saying no. It was not signed by Luce but by the president, the business head of the company. Luckily I was staying then with a friend who worked in *Time*'s London office. I say "luckily," because he prevented me from sending the first seven versions of the cable I wrote in reply. The eighth, which in fact was his suggestion, I sent: "Why did you keep me standing on tiptoe so long if you weren't going to kiss me?"

On the Bridge

A few weeks later I returned to New York to wind up my twenty-four-year affair with *Time*. I had found London a blessed relief from New York and had decided to try living there for a while. On one of my last nights in New York, Luce and I had a farewell dinner together. An old friend of mine, an even older *Time* hand than myself, made me promise to give him an account of that dinner. Some months later, in a letter, I did:

"But alas, I took no notes; alas, I had had several drinks. I wish, for my sake as well as yours, that there might have been a tape recording of the momentous meeting. There wasn't, and the poor old world is poorer than ever.

"Well, I'll tell you what I *do* remember. First, I was twenty minutes late (I'd been giving my departing secretary drinks and had cut the timetable too fine). He was waiting for me at the Links Club; I think we were the only people there, except for the waiter and the doorman—and I suppose a cook. He made me have some oysters and a large cocktail; he had already, he pointed out (only sign of temper) had both. And he waited to hear what I had to say. As I could see that I was going to have to make the conversational pace, I started slow and cautious-like, chatting of this and that. It gradually became evident during the ensuing meal (which lasted till about 10:15) that if anybody was going to say anything to fit the occasion it would have to be me.

"We reminisced. (If this sounds impossibly antiphonal, you know what I mean. The *decani* tended to become a monologue, but the *cantoris* got in their licks whenever possible.) Somewhere in the course of the—I almost said conversation, but you will understand—the discourse, I decided that I might as well get a few things said. These, as I remember them, are the few things. 'Harry,' I said, 'now that you've got America, how do you like it?' Of course you want to know what his reply was; so do I. There must have been a reply, or at least an answering spate of words, but what it was I cannot tell you. Anyhow I regard that as one of the few blows landed during the entire bout. As a dead-game sport, I can now admit that he jarred me once; he said (or words to this effect), 'By what right do you put me on the moral defensive?'

"I remember bringing one haymaker right up from the floor: I

273

told him that he was kidding himself about the power of the press; the press had no power of *accomplishment,* though it did have a negative power—to debase taste, harm individuals, etc. That should have laid him out, but it never fazed him. What an iron jaw! The only other punishing punch of mine I can remember I clumsily blocked myself. I reminded him of a series of meetings I had once engineered between him and a little gang of subversives which ended with Harry's answering the question 'Under what circumstances would you make *Time* a political instrument?' His answer was: 'If I thought the Republic was in danger.' Which at the time we thought unexceptionable. But on this last-supper occasion I pointed out (I *hope* I did, at least; I can't be sure) that as a Republican he had come to the point of believing that the Republic was in danger whenever the Republicans weren't running it.

"Well, that's about it, or all I can recall of it. Except that I did feel that one of us ought to say something about the final severance of an association that had lasted 24 years—and as he obviously wouldn't say anything, I did. I'm sure it wasn't graceful, and I'm sure anyone else could have said it better. I hope it wasn't fulsome; I don't think it was. I just said, as I remember, that in some ways it was a wrench to leave an organization you'd given so much of your life to, or words to that effect, and that I was sorry to be saying goodbye. He seemed to agree that that might well be so. Anyhow, we shook hands on the sidewalk, and—parted friends. Eh? What did you say?"

I thought that might have been our final meeting, but it wasn't. Five years later chance brought us face to face in New York. I asked him to dinner; he turned the tables on me as usual by having me instead, and we spent a pleasant evening in his apartment talking over old times, like two ex-cronies who weren't saying all they knew but who shared some deep memories. I felt again some of my old fondness for this grizzled tycoon whose hard-shell opinions hadn't become any softer. He was a little put out because I hadn't reached sixty yet, as he had, but I mollified him by promising that I soon would. And though we raised our voices, it was not from temper but because we had both become rather hard of hearing.

Part Three

Part Three

THE GENIE
IN THE BOTTLE

THEY SAY THAT IF YOU WANT A CHILD TO DISLIKE SOMETHING, give
him too much of it. It didn't work like that with me and whiskey.
My parents got me drunk twice before I was ten, and I have not
taken against whiskey yet.

Both times, they thought they were saving my life, or at least
helping to prolong it. The first time, when I was nine, I stepped
off a pier into fifteen feet of Lake Michigan water, and swallowed
a bellyful before I was hauled out. I was on my way to dancing
school, which I hated; perhaps, in an absent-minded way, I was
exemplifying the death wish. I was wrapped in blankets, rushed
home, and given enough whiskey to make me dizzy.

The second time, soon after, was in North Carolina; a lot of us
children were playing on the mountainside above the house, and
someone started a rattlesnake scare. We all broke for home, me
well in the lead, when I caught my foot in a wild grapevine, which
threw me, and I came in last. I was yelling bloody murder and
holding my nose, which I thought was broken; as I was the last one
in, the others all pointed at me and said I'd been bitten by a rattlesnake. My mother started to heat a lancet and got out the whiskey
bottle. She had a tourniquet on my leg and was just about to stab
me when I managed to convince her that I hadn't even seen a snake.
But by that time the whiskey was down my throat.

Eight years later I was a freshman at Princeton; Kaiser Bill had
been given his comeuppance, the world was safe for democracy
and freshmen, and I believed every word of it. I went to Trenton
with some pals, and smelt my first bar. Those were the days
when they had a fragrant jar of rock-and-rye on the counter, which
everybody thought was good for colds—and maybe it was. One of
my friends was such a man of the world that he always downed a
cocktail in one gulp, or at the most two. I felt this would be for-

ever beyond me, because the stuff tasted so awful I had to sip it, and even then it was hard to choke down. Once you managed to swallow it, however, you soon began to get what you had paid for: first a slight numbness, then a sensation of increasing buoyancy, then the coming-forth of the cooped-up personality; before you knew it, shy Dr. Jekyll withered away like a dying balloon, and there was swaggering Mr. Hyde.

One pleasing feature of this transmogrification was that not only did you like everybody around you but everybody else liked you. As you came through the looking glass, they greeted you like a long-lost friend, pounded you on the back, yelled with laughter at your amazing wit, and told you that you were the damndest fellow they'd ever laid eyes on. It was a precarious pinnacle, and when your foot slipped you went whirling down in an avalanche, to wake next morning, sick and shaky, wondering whether you were going to die, and not even glad to find yourself safe in your own bed or grateful to the unremembered friend who must have guided you there.

Those hangovers! While they lasted it seemed as if they would never end. No pinnacle in the world was worth that cureless suffering—conscience and stomach and memory and head throbbing in syncopated misery together. You would never touch another drop as long as you lived; that was so obvious you didn't think about it, in fact you couldn't without being sick. When I first read Lamb's gloomy sentence, "In the daytime I stumble upon dark mountains," I recognized a fellow sufferer; that was exactly how I felt myself, once I was able to get to my feet.

Learning to hold your liquor is a hard lesson, requiring persistence in drinking as well as patience in suffering the effects of drink. I persisted; I suffered, and by slow degrees I learned. I hadn't learned much before the great wet blanket of Prohibition settled down on America, in January 1919. Prohibition was an added inducement to drinking, which immediately became unlawful and chancy, and sometimes dangerous. I took Prohibition as a part of growing up, half wonderful and half awful. It also drew my attention to my parents' attitude toward drink. My father's position was clear enough: whatever was illegal was wrong. Even at my wedding he would not join in toasting the bride, for he knew the champagne must be bootleg. But Mother's point of view was different: there was something about drinking that frightened her—"horrified and repelled" would perhaps not be too strong. In theory she was no teetotaler, but in practice she very nearly was, and with Mother, the way she acted was the thing to watch. It was her half-denied feeling that drinking was immoral or led to immorality; and her feeling colored mine. In those early days drinking had two great attractions for me: it was illegal, and it was a sin.

I don't know how much blindness and death were directly caused by bootleg liquor during Prohibition's thirteen years; probably not nearly so much as rumor reported. If you could afford to pay the high prices and were lucky enough to find the right speakeasies and the right bootleggers, the stuff you got might be raw but it was seldom actually poisonous. As they couldn't very well advertise, except by word of mouth, the problem of finding the right speakeasies and bootleggers was considerable, at first. Later on, as both sides got better acquainted, it wasn't so bad.

But we were always collecting new speakeasies; our wallets bulged with cards initialed by Joe or Mac or Hymie. Without this countersigned admission ticket it was almost impossible to get in anywhere; even with it you often had to argue with the hard eye glaring at you through a barred wicket in the door. And sometimes you showed the wrong card or to the question, "Who sent you?" gave a name that brought the answer, "Never heard of him!"—and the wicket banged shut.

The only people who escaped the general condition were the bootleggers themselves and the very rich, who had well-stocked cellars or the foresight to stock them. Some of the rich also had daughters for whom they gave parties, and these were red-letter affairs, for the drinks were not only good but free. Not always; sometimes the host was mean or cautious, or took a dim view of a lot of young drunks messing up the place. Then it was fruit punch with no "stick" in it. Somehow we generally got the word in advance when a party would be dry. In that case, the thing to do was to take a flask. But once I went with some friends to a dance in Philadelphia at the Bellevue-Stratford; we discovered, too late, that it was a dry party, and none of us had a flask. A bellboy said he could get us a bottle of Benedictine but it would cost $25. We said O.K. The bottle he brought looked genuine enough, but all it contained was sweet syrup of figs.

When the host was generous, or foolhardy, I usually drank as much as I could, and often disgraced myself. During one Tennis Week at Newport I met a pretty, red-headed girl on a picnic and took her to a dance that night at the Clambake Club. When we arrived she went to powder her nose; I found that the bar was serving champagne. The next thing I remember is lying flat on my back on the ground, clutching the grass because the earth was whirling and I didn't want to be hurled off into interstellar space. Afterwards I wrote several letters of apology; the one to the girl said that my conduct was inexcusable and that we would never meet again, as I would soon be leaving the country forever.

It was always a risky business to feel, as I usually felt at some point in a drinking evening, that I was in complete control of a very fine fellow. That was almost bound to lead to a not-so-fine fellow out of control. In spite of my landslide lapses, however, for which I paid at least partly in shame and suffering, I find it hard to regret having been a drinker. Drink brought me into situations and introduced me to people I would never have found otherwise.

My friendship with Schuyler Jackson dated from these early drinking days, though it was based on some chemistry more mysterious than alcohol's. As an undergraduate at Princeton, I spent many an evening sitting in Schuyler's study while he read aloud to me. It was almost always poetry: Ralph Hodgson, Flecker, Housman, de la Mare, Edward Thomas, Synge, Hardy, Yeats, Milton, Wordsworth, Blake. Yeats was far and away his favorite. These evenings were accompanied by drink, when there was anything to drink. At one period we could only get straight alcohol, which we mixed with grape juice or, when that became too sickening, with plain water. It didn't mix with anything very well, and had a delayed effect that was stronger than anything we were accustomed to. It landed me in trouble with the proctor several times, but for some reason Schuyler had better luck. He didn't get bawling drunk like the rest of us, but he was sometimes dangerous; a frenzy of anger would come over him, and he would attack anybody who got in his way. I remember one snowy night when I tried to see him home from my room. He wouldn't let me come near him, so I followed him. Every now and then he would stagger and fall down, but when I ran up and tried to help him he would swing at me. It wasn't a playful swing, either.

One afternoon we had been drinking alcohol-and-water in his room. I was supposed to go to dinner with a classmate who ran the Théâtre Intime, to discuss the next program of plays. This classmate lived at home with his family, in a very correct house with a butler. By dinnertime I was in no state to discuss anything, but I said goodbye to Schuyler and went along. Luckily no one was at dinner but my classmate and me—and the butler. Even so the conversation was one-sided, as I couldn't speak. Halfway through there was a low roaring sound from the hall, and Schuyler appeared in the doorway on his hands and knees. I saw immediately that he thought he was disguised as a Hyrcanian tiger, and had come to rescue me. I got up without a word and went off with him.

We drank bootleg liquor all through college and for ten years after. Toward the end of Prohibition the safest and cheapest stuff in my neighborhood was applejack, which was distilled hard cider, and sold for about $10 a gallon jug. Its taste was raw and fiery, and it was indigestible as well as intoxicating. I remember a dance at the Princeton Inn where applejack punch was served that knocked out the whole community. It was "a good party," as we said in those days: next morning only a corporal's guard of commuters showed up for the 7:56.

In my young married days, dinner parties were always a problem. Unless you knew your hosts well enough to count on them, dinner might be dry or nowhere near wet enough. If you were in any doubt, you "laid a foundation" before you went. When we gave our first dinner party in Princeton, the two couples we had asked, not knowing us very well, arrived with a foundation well and truly laid. For the same reason I produced a more than adequate supply of cocktails. One of the men fell asleep at the dinner table, and after dinner, when we all went on to a dance, the other one drove his car into every whitewashed boulder bordering our

40-foot driveway and grazed one of the trees at the entrance. Arrived at the party, this same man—a most respectable newspaper executive—dancing with my wife, tripped and fell heavily to the floor with her. For the rest of the evening he stood stiffly and respectably at the side of the room, occasionally putting down his glass on a table he thought was there but wasn't.

Edmund Wilson once told me that he had tried drinking while he wrote, with only limited success. It was all right, he said, if you took a swallow and then wrote it out before taking another; but you must not allow yourself a second until you had wrung everything possible out of the first. And when you stood up from the table, it was all over. At one time I practiced a less serious form of writing in drink. My family were away for the summer, and my job at *Time* kept me in the city except at weekends, but most evenings I hadn't enough to do to keep me busy at the office. I took to visiting bars by myself, and writing poems while I drank. Often I hadn't intended to write anything, but after the second or third drink a line of a poem would come into my head and that would set me off. Some evenings, when I got melancholy enough without getting too drunk, I would write three or four poems at a sitting.

Drinking on the job was a different thing entirely. It was frowned on, with good reason. But cocktails at lunch were allowable, and drinks after work were the regular thing. For a time I reached a point of dangerous compromise. While I was managing editor of *Time*, Sunday was my longest and hardest day, when I had to deal with the great bulk of the copy for the issue that went to press on Monday night. By dinnertime Sunday night I was pretty tired. I always had dinner alone that night, carrying a stack of copy along with me to edit, and drank two dry Martinis beforehand. After dinner I worked until my desk was clear; that usually took me until one in the morning or a bit later. By that time a pile of Monday morning newspapers had been put on my desk. I tucked the papers under my arm and went off to Toots Shor's, a brassy restaurant that catered to the Broadway and radio crowd, and stayed open till all hours. I usually sat at the same table and had the same waiter, who didn't need to be told my order: a double Scotch and Saratoga Vichy. Then I started on the papers, tearing out items of fresh news or paragraphs that had some bearing on current and future stories. By the time I'd finished my third or fourth double Scotch I had also finished the newspapers and it was getting on toward three or four in the morning.

At that point I felt fine, but I didn't feel fine on Monday. To set an example, I always got to the office around nine, no matter how late I'd been up the night before. This meant that by the time my week was finished, on Monday night, I was nearly finished too. We had Tuesdays and Wednesdays off, but on Tuesdays I was no good to myself or anybody else, and couldn't have been very pleasant to live with. After a while I realized that if I wanted to do a decent job, I ought to stop drinking. But I didn't want to stop. I knew it was a vicious circle: I got very tired and drank to get over feeling tired, and the drink made me even tireder. For what seemed like a long time, perhaps a year and a half, I went on the wagon. I think I began then to realize that I was fundamentally dissatisfied with the job and couldn't have gone on doing it indefinitely without some sort of drug to keep me quiet.

There have been moments, before and since that time of abstinence, when I was afraid I couldn't do without drink. I have a horror of addiction to drugs—among which I include the lowly aspirin pill—but I am unable to think of alcohol as a drug. I know it has its addicts, but I've decided I'm not one, because I can give it up when I have to, or want to. But I know I drink "more than is good for me"; I am not a "social drinker" (though I've filled in that expected answer on more than one questionnaire) and I have no qualms whatever about drinking alone.

None whatever? That's not true. I swallow at least one qualm in every glass I drink, in company or not, since I was brought up to believe that drinking is morally wrong or at least morally dangerous, and I've never succeeded in completely living down what I was taught as a child. So perhaps I get more out of a drink than most people.

When I was young I drank for excitement, adventure, "for the hell of it." Each time was like a journey of exploration into unknown country, where the landscape was heightened beyond the colors and shapes of the sober daylight world. I could travel light in those days: it took only a few drinks to get me there.

As a young married man, a suburbanite and a commuter, I learned to drink with my neighbors and contemporaries "socially" —to lubricate our mutual stiffness, apathy and boredom into an evening's semblance of hearty good fellowship. With my pals at the office I drank for the same reasons and to the same effect. As the pressures of the job accumulated I found a further reason: I "needed a drink" to keep me going.

And finally I drank as an anodyne, to drug mental strain and emotional suffering, or the fear of it, and to make sure that I wouldn't lie awake with my painful thoughts. I can remember the night this phase began. It was in Paris, in midsummer of 1949; we were halfway in our ill-fated trip through Europe. I knew, but wouldn't yet admit, that something was dreadfully wrong with Julie. The three older boys were out on the town for the evening; the youngest was asleep; Julie was pretending to be, so as not to worry me; and I sat in our hotel sitting room, trying not to think. After a while I went out to a nearby zinc bar. They had no whiskey, but there were several brands of cognac.

"How much?"

"The whole bottle?"

"Yes."

"But monsieur would have to pay by the number of drinks in the bottle!"

"All right, I'll pay."

That was the first night. Until she died, six months later, I never went to bed sober. I waited for the first drink until after she had kissed me good night; then I went downstairs and drank with anyone who would keep me company, or by myself. Did it do any good? I don't suppose so. But it was something to look forward to, in a time when there was nothing to hope for, and at least I usually fell asleep as soon as I got to bed. Did it keep me from suffering, or make the suffering less? I don't suppose it did that either; it may even have postponed or extended the facing of a fact that seemed impossible and unbearable to face. But at the time, as the only anodyne I knew, I was grateful for it.

Counsels of perfection have always attracted me, though I never get close enough to be singed. G. K. Chesterton said that drink is a sacrament, only to be taken when you are in a state of grace; you should never drink to cheer yourself up. It is a good precept, and I have sometimes obeyed it, but it never really moved me like Housman's wish that a man could be drunk forever.

I think of drink now as if it were a genie in a bottle, and the genie is powerful; you must treat him with respect and use the proper forms; but that's not the way it appeared to me when I was young. In those days drink was a purer magic—not so much a spirit you could summon up at will as a sacred grove you could sometimes find. And when you had found it you didn't try to make things happen, you let them happen to you. They did happen, and even if you couldn't remember afterwards quite what they were, you were always somehow the larger for it. That is as near as I can come to saying that Dionysus is a god.

THE SERPENT,
THE DOVE

HOW IS IT POSSIBLE TO TALK STRAIGHT or think straight about sex? Someone has said: "The problem of sex is the problem of a broken unity." And that must be so. Our nature knows itself fragmentary and longs to be whole; we suffer all our lives from this half-knowledge and this longing. *Non posse non peccare;* there is no remedy. According to the Church, in marriage a man and his wife "are no more twain, but one flesh." The brief act of love seems to achieve such a union, however imperfectly; a truer and lasting unity is forever denied us. A man, like a woman, was created incomplete.

All those acts and feelings that we huddle together under the name of "love" are groping attempts to mend this irreparably sundered unity; and this love is colored, stained, illuminated, sometimes blacked out, by sex—our own or the mixing of our own with another's. The relation between sex and love is at best ambiguous. Often we cannot really tell which is which or where one begins and the other leaves off. But although we do not comprehend the nature of either, we feel the power of both; and instinctively we regard "love" as white magic, "sex" as black. Love and sex are mysteries; which is the major mystery and which the minor?

Our fear of sex has placed a powerful taboo on it which we cannot reason away, which we can only placate worshipfully, as in poetry, or blaspheme against, in jokes and swear-words. We fear its deepness and darkness: as deep as the unconscious, as dark as our dreams.

A baby's sexual curiosity is greedy but unfocused—it wants its own genital organs, its mother's breast, anything it can taste, touch or handle. Later we begin to particularize and compare. Little boys and little girls are equally fascinated to discover the oddity of the other sex's private parts. I had sisters and no brothers, and we must have shared this common curiosity, but I have no recollection of it. The first sexual scene I can remember is "playing doctor" in the Michigan woods with our Cleveland cousins. I might have been six; some of the others were older and some younger than that, and we were boys and girls together. We knew that what we were doing was "not nice," but it was fun; and some of the fun came from the knowledge that we would certainly be spanked if we were caught. The game consisted of the "doctor" (we took turns being that) making the rounds of his patients and putting a twig thermometer in their little bare behinds.

I remember that game as delightful, but the first (and I think the only) time I saw my father naked, I was disgusted and appalled. I was still curious, however, about my mother's body. She once caught me, as she thought, spying on her, though I don't think I was. It was in our unfinished house in the mountains of North Carolina: the floors of the attic had not yet been laid, so you could climb over the rafters, looking down into all the upstairs rooms. I was doing this, at least as much for the climb as the view, when

I looked down and saw Mother in the bathtub. She was standing up, with her back to me, so the view was not very revealing; I just thought she looked awfully big and white. She must have heard me if she didn't see me, and called to me sharply to get down from there, immediately. And I was made to feel very much ashamed of myself, a peeping Tommy.

Before I was adolescent, sex began to horrify and fascinate me. Everything I learned about it from my playmates and from older boys—much of this, of course, wildly false rumor passed along as gospel truth—convinced me that it was ineradicably dirty, a conviction further strengthened by my mother's practice and precept: that it was something to be anxious and shamefaced about.

I remember a chauffeur we had when we were little, a sly, unpleasant young man, who seemed to delight in troubling our innocence. When he was driving one of my sisters and me he would try to teach us a popular song, *When I Get You Alone Tonight*, to which he had put even more suggestive words—threatening to show you

> *How your father and your mother*
> *Made your little baby brother*
> *When I get you alone tonight.*

And once, in a Cincinnati barbershop, the barber who was cutting my hair regaled a friend who had dropped in to see him with a grossly detailed account of how he had seduced a girl the night before. After fifty years I can still remember that it was on the screened back porch of her house, that he "did it" twice, and that he seemed proud of having fooled her into believing that he was a Pullman porter, just passing through town. He sounded to me like a gloating murderer boasting of his crime. I held my breath and felt sick.

When I was twelve my father finally got around to telling me about the birds and the bees—and that was literally as far as he went; he gave me a book, *What Every Young Boy Should Know*, so that I could read the rest of it. I found my father's "little talk" very embarrassing, not only because of the subject but because I

287

had to pretend it was all news to me; whereas I privately thought I already knew every wicked bit of it, and probably a good deal more than he did. But the book did put a new idea in my mind; it informed me that masturbation was a hideously dangerous practice, usually leading to madness. From this I drew the inevitable conclusion that I would die in an asylum.

Such were my instructors in sex and such the lessons I learned. (Why can't they leave this kind of thing to hard-headed, warm-hearted women?) I learned that sex was not only sinful and disgusting but horribly dangerous and often resulting in disease, blindness, insanity and death. The bishop who gave a Commencement address at Shattuck urged us to keep ourselves morally clean, and ended by reciting a narrative in verse: it was all about a young man who had caught syphilis and then married. The last line went (in a dreadful whisper):

For the child that she bore him was blind.

A few years later, at Princeton, I had to listen to a lecture on venereal disease. The lecturer showed lantern slides of infected tissue and of more recognizable parts of the body. Several boys fainted and were carried out.

I hated to think of grownups, and particularly those I loved, in a sexual connection; sex seemed to me to require deeds of such darkness and shame that I shrank from imagining anyone sharing the experience. My first experiments on myself, as a small boy, were uncomfortable, but once I had discovered the pleasure in them, my own private parts drew me like a magnet. Sex became for me the most secret, delicious and vicious of all sins. In fact, it became Sin.

When the first signals of adolescence appeared in my body I was horrified; I thought them abnormal stigmata, and felt as if I were going through a long-drawn-out nightmare. The dream book my father had given me was no help whatever; it told me nothing, in plain enough words for me to understand, about what was taking place in me. I was so sure that there was something dreadfully wrong that at last, in desperation, I went to my father. I suppose he must have tried to reassure me, but either because I didn't regard him as an authority on the subject or because he thought I didn't, he took me to see a doctor in Trenton. The doctor was so old that his head shook and his voice quavered, but he kept a straight face; and when *he* told me that what was happening to me was perfectly normal, I believed him.

That was a great load off my mind, but I still knew that sex was sinful, even if I weren't yet required to pay the penalty. Then, when I was sixteen, I fell in love with Julie. It was a severe attack of puppy love, but it lasted; three years later it had become incurable. I was much too shy to do anything about it. In her presence all I could do was stammer, turn red or, if I met her unexpectedly, shake all over. I wanted to kiss her (although the idea also terrified me) but hadn't the least idea of how to go about it. Her older brother, who gave me friendly and sophisticated advice, said the thing to do was to wait for a good chance and then throw my arms around her and give her a kiss. I did, and she slapped my face. Not knowing the answer to that, I relapsed into feeling guilty.

How to reconcile sex with love? I had learned (I don't go so far as to say I'd been taught; perhaps I misunderstood the teaching) that the two were irreconcilable. When we were sophomores my friend Jack Wainwright, a noble and eccentric soul, shocked me deeply by maintaining that if you were in love with a girl you naturally wanted to go to bed with her. This struck me at the time as a wicked heresy. Applied to my own case, it would mean— well, what would it mean? I simply refused to answer the question; I said it was the wrong question.

The following summer, Jack and I were in Paris together, both for the first time. Like the young Wordsworth in an earlier, revolutionary France, I felt

> *Bliss was it in that dawn to be alive;*
> *But to be young was very heaven.*

One of our classmates, a hard, saturnine boy like a handsome wolf, sniffed the Paris air at dusk and said, "Whore dust!" A crude blasphemy which partly expressed a sense of delight, wonder, awe.

Jack had arrived several days before me, and he undertook to guide me. We were lost continually, but it didn't matter; everywhere we went and everything that happened was wonderful. The first night we naturally drank champagne, and before the late evening was over, our heads roaring with the glorious stuff, it seemed equally natural that we had picked up a melancholy tart. Not two, one.

Her melancholy may have come from *chagrin d'amour*, and Jack was sure she had some secret sorrow that we must discover and set right. I think she was just drunk. We could only talk to her in pidgin French, but she managed to make us understand that she wanted to go home. In the taxi, supported gallantly by our combined arms, she fell deeply asleep. She roused herself to recognize her doorway and produce a key, and we helped her upstairs; in her small flat, crowded with dusty furniture, she undressed sketchily, fell into the enormous bed, and was immediately asleep again.

Jack and I looked at each other with owlish suspicion. By our champagne-buzzing logic, we had now reached the stage of protecting not only her but each other. We solemnly agreed not to take off our underclothes—Jack was wearing long woollens and I had cotton shorts. I think we shook hands. Then we climbed into bed, one on each side of our hostess, now lightly snoring.

As soon as the light was out I discovered that I had no intention whatever of keeping our pact. I whispered into her sleeping ear: "*Attends qu'il dort!*" Moving by cautious centimeters, I inched as close to her as I could. But at the slightest stir Jack shot up in bed, growling "Tom!" I thought dizzily I would just have to wait him out; in spite of myself I soon fell sound asleep. She slept like a log all night. Jack swore next morning that he hadn't closed his eyes.

I am aware, now, that Paris was wasted on me. At the time I had the smugly virtuous feeling that I was touching pitch—and what lovely pitch—without being defiled. The all-important thing was to preserve your virginity, because by the code I had been taught virgin should marry virgin. I preserved mine not from any Galahad-like strength but from fear of disease, fear of guilt. This attitude was mulish and quite incomprehensible to the straightforward girls of Paris. To one, who did her modest best to persuade me, patting her bare haunch *("C'est ferme, hein?")*, I lied that I was engaged; she said with wide eyes: "But I'll never tell your fiancée!"

It was grimy London, not summery Paris, that saw my downfall. By then I had carried my long-hoarded virginity for 22 years. Talking the matter over with another young American who was in the same situation, we agreed that it was high time. We were sharing a compartment and a bottle of whiskey on a train from Cambridge to London. He had "an address"; we went there, were received by an unenthusiastic woman who seemed to me middle-aged, and took turns. It was almost as bad as waiting to see the dentist. I don't think any of us enjoyed it a bit, but he and I were so relieved to have got it over with that we celebrated by getting whoopingly and joyfully drunk.

We had known enough to take all the prescribed precautions, before and after; nevertheless, with my limited knowledge and exaggerated fears, I lived for some days in guilt, remorse and expectation of punishment. After a while, when neither the police nor any symptom of disease had appeared, I began to breathe more easily, and tried to put the whole thing out of my mind. Weeks later, and back in America again, I had been playing squash with a friend; in the showers he jovially called my attention to a brown mark on my shoulder, and said, "Looks to me like syph!" This was a well-established form of humor in my youth, and I knew that was the way he meant it, but my heart nearly stopped beating.

As soon as I got home I looked myself all over carefully; there were several more brown spots, none of which I had noticed before. Yes, it must be syphilis. My reason, not yet panicked, told me that was very unlikely, and pointed out that I could make quite sure by going to a doctor. But that would have meant confessing my sin (I was afraid the doctor would consider it a sin too, and feel it his duty to tell my parents). I couldn't face that. At least, not yet. And while I was still vacillating my family took me off with them to the mountains of North Carolina. No doctors there.

On the train a further horror occurred to me. Or rather, it recurred; I had thought of it immediately, with the first shock, but had managed to suppress it. Now it came back to haunt all my waking hours: *I must have infected everyone I had kissed.* My parents, my sisters, my old governess—worst of all, if there could be any worst, the girl I loved. (It had been a farewell kiss and before this horrible revelation; I had told her I was tired of asking her to marry me and would not see her again; if she ever changed her mind, she could send me word.) I tried to remember how many were on the list. It amounted to thirteen.

We were in the mountains for three weeks. The brown spots on my body didn't increase in size or number, and no other signs appeared. But with every day, I thought, the disease would be getting a firmer grip on my body—not to mention all the other bodies that didn't know they had been infected. By now I had panicked to such an extent that I could see no way out, and told myself that the only honorable thing for me to do was to kill myself. I went for long walks, going round and round the dreadful circle and trying to nerve myself for suicide.

When my parents went to Asheville for a day's shopping, I tagged along, gave them the slip and sought out a doctor. The one I found seemed a poor specimen but he happened to specialize in venereal disease. He looked at my brown spots and told me that I had one of two things: a very rare and harmless skin disease—or syphilis. I didn't know enough to ask him for a blood test, and he didn't suggest it.

One further turn of the screw was still to come. In a few days we returned to Princeton. I went straight to an undergraduate friend of mine, told him the story, was taken by him to a doctor and given a blood test. It would be twenty-four hours before I knew the result. Driving home, I passed Julie on the street and she waved at me as if she wanted me to stop. I pretended not to notice. But a few minutes after I got home the telephone rang. She wanted to see me. As she opened the door she said shyly, "I guess you know why I wanted you to come." This time, in spite of my friend's smiling assurances that I couldn't have infected anybody just by kissing them, I managed to avoid kissing her on the lips. I got away as soon as I could, and went to visit friends for the weekend. There, next day, a telegram arrived from the doctor, giving me a clean bill of health.

In the story of the Garden of Eden, God put a curse upon the serpent, condemning it to crawl on its belly and eat dust all the days of its life, and also linking it forever in enmity with the seed of Eve: "it shall bruise thy head, and thou shalt bruise his heel."

I felt my inclusion in the Old Testament curse, for the serpent of sex dogged my footsteps and bruised my heel. The nightmare panics, the imagined horrors, the clandestine misery that resulted from my sexual education could hardly have been worse if I had been brought up in a savage tribe, in abject fear of a devil-god. And yet my upbringing had been supposedly enlightened, supposedly Christian, supposedly civilized. I thought it was all these, and though I blamed my parents for many shortcomings it never occurred to me to hold them responsible—or in fact anyone but myself—for misinforming me, or not informing me truly, about these dark facts of life. And how could they? They themselves had known no better. They were only passing on to us the tribal taboos they had been taught. There seemed nothing odd, and there was certainly nothing unique, in the way I was brought up; those beliefs and standards were common to my generation and background.

The one effective charm against the black magic of sex, we were also given to believe, was the complementary and rescuing mystery of love. Only love could deliver us from the body of this little death; love alone could transform us from helplessly rutting animals to the semblance of self-respecting human beings. How the charm worked, and whether it really worked, were questions I couldn't answer clearly. I thought I could see the evidences of this redeeming love in other lives (they were plain to be seen in my mother's case, and even plainer to me in Julie's) but in my own I could not be sure. The "love" I had felt for them and for a few others varied in nature and degree, not only with the person but with our emotional weather. Could I truthfully say that my feeling toward the one I had loved most in the world had been constant and invariable, that it looked on tempests and was never shaken? No, I couldn't. Yet, travesty of the truth though my love might be, it was truth, not a lie, that was being travestied.

I had learned, as anyone who has the luck learns, that "the act of love" is rightly named, although its name can also be taken in vain. I recognized that side of the coin in Hogarth's pictures of desire and possession: the idiot stare of lust in *Before*, the animal blankness *After;* if he had been Goya instead of Hogarth, he might have called the cartoons "Is that all?" As a sexual being, the seed of Eve, I shared the serpent's curse and the lifelong mixed pleasure of its company—for pleasure it surely was, as well as curse. I had been taught that love and sex were distinct, and that only the marriage bed could excuse their coming together. There were occasions when I wanted to separate them, when it seemed simply a question of having your cake and eating it; but at those times too— or perhaps particularly then—I felt the broken unity of human beings, and wished that the act of sex might be also, and inseparably, an act of love.

I doubt whether we learn much from our own mistakes. For one thing, we are not apt to recognize them as mistakes after they have become habitual, or until it is too late to remedy them. What we think we learn from are the much more visible mistakes of others. Looking back over my early education, for which my parents were responsible, I could make one sure criticism: that in trying to protect me, they had wrapped me in fear. The only clear idea I had about my own sons' education was not to repeat the obvious mistakes that were made in mine. My father had waited until I was twelve before he told me anything whatever about sex—and then he told me nothing helpful. I determined to do better.

When my oldest son was three, I made a clean breast to him of everything I knew on the subject. It took me the best part of an hour. He listened with a glazed expression. I doubt if he understood one word; he certainly forgot it all immediately. Some years later, and probably bit by bit, in answer to his questions, his mother quietly gave him all the information he wanted. Having made such a mess of it, I let her instruct the three others too. So I didn't even do as much of a job as my father.

"YOU FRENCH?"

ONE UNSEASONABLY HOT MAY MORNING in the forties I landed in New York at a North River pier. With my fellow passengers I lined up to wait my turn for a customs inspector and, when he had passed my three suitcases, queued again to wait my turn for a porter. In spite of the large signs, prominently displayed, proclaiming that there should be no tipping, I knew enough to give my porter a dollar. But I had forgotten that his duties ended at the top of the luggage escalator, and that at the bottom I had to collect my bags and hand them over—with another dollar—to one of the seedy nondescripts hanging about the pier entrance, who would then carry them all of ten feet to a taxi. This last bit of racketeering seemed to me, for some reason, one too many; I seized my suitcases and flung myself and them across the pavement and into the nearest cab.

Momentarily I had upset the system, and the system resented it. As we drove off, hard words followed me. The taxi driver turned his head and said, mildly,

"What seems to be the trouble?"

I told him. I tried to say, as briefly and pungently as I could, what I thought of the welcoming gauntlet an incoming passenger had to run, and of the whole inefficient and damnable system. I paused for breath. The taxi driver said,

"You French?"

Can I really claim to be a good American? I was brought up to believe that Americans can be divided into three classes: good, bad and expatriate. No American citizen who lives out of the country, unless his job demands it, can be considered a good American. Rather to my surprise but not at all against my grain I find myself living in London, but I have no job there, so I haven't that excuse; I simply prefer London to the other cities I know, and I like living in a city.

I know other Americans who feel the same way—though in their case their favorite place to live may be Paris or Rome or Florence —but they have an excuse: their job keeps them there. If it didn't, they would get another job that did. Of the hundreds of thousands of Americans who live abroad, a great many don't regard themselves as exiles but as Americans who are luckier than most. And a few, a very few, like Ernest Hemingway, Jacob Epstein, T. S. Eliot and Bernard Berenson, have made such resounding names for themselves that they are not thought of as expatriates, although Hemingway and Eliot certainly are, and so were Epstein and Berenson.

The government of the United States continues to tax me but will no longer let me vote. If I can live wherever I want to, that seems to me a fair exchange. And as Frank Kent used to say, a contribution to the party war chest is a more effective way of exercising your franchise than marking a ballot. Should I still be allowed to have an opinion about American politics, or to take an interest in U.S. domestic affairs? At any rate, since there's no law against it as yet, I do. And what seems to be the trouble? (There's that taxi driver again.)

First of all, I object to being disqualified as an observer of the American scene. I can't help being an observer of that scene, and an inveterately interested one; and when my friends in the United States tell me, "Ah, you're out of touch." I retort, "But perhaps in focus!" You do get a larger view from a distance, though you lose the details. These are figures of speech, I know, and can only suggest the argument, not define its terms. There is an argument, or at any rate a difference of opinion, between me and my country —or the people who I think have run away with the country.

In the summer of 1956 I spent a day in Libertyville, Illinois, at Adlai Stevenson's farm. He had just been nominated, for the second time, as the Democratic candidate for the presidency, and his campaign was about to get under way. Half a dozen advisers had come to plan the campaign strategy, and the meeting went on almost all day. I was there simply as a friend; but at one point Stevenson asked me, "What do *you* think?"

I said, "I think you should declare war on Ohio."

He laughed; the others stared, and then went on with their serious discussion. And Ohio won again, as expected.

I don't mind being considered a bad Ohioan or a renegade Middlewesterner; and besides, anyone, from Lincoln down, is allowed to change his state with impunity. It's only when you're thought to have cut the umbilical cord that binds you to your native land that your Americanism comes in question. But can you cut the cord?

It seems to me a difficult thing for an American—and for me impossible—to change his nationality, whatever his name and address happen to be. If I never saw the United States again I would never cease to know it as my country; that consciousness goes deeper than loyalty or patriotism—two words that have been dirtied by an ugly kind of American—it is in my blood. I was born and bred there, I hope to return there often, I expect to be buried there. Meantime, as an American who is lucky enough to be able to choose, I think I have a right to travel and live where I like. I shouldn't like to be compelled to live anywhere. I would hate to have to live in Russia, or China, or Hungary, or under any dictatorship. But I shouldn't like to be compelled—by a job or by a law—to live in the United States either. For this is not my day in America. This day belongs to the "100 percenters," the new-rich Texans, the Madison Avenue boys, the professional patriots, the organization men, the hard-eyed herdsmen of political Yahoos, the dogs that eat dogs. If they have really taken over America, and taken it over for keeps, then I think the American experiment has failed. The dinosaur, its tiny brain still dreaming of paradisal forests, is plodding witlessly towards the asphalt lake.

I don't think, however, that the American experiment has utterly failed. Nevertheless, unless I have completely misunderstood its purpose, neither can I see that it has anywhere near succeeded. I should like to think that the majority of Americans are also dissatisfied and disappointed by what we have so far accomplished as a nation. But I don't. Much as I'd like to, I can see little evidence for the hopeful assumption that there are still so many rugged individuals and independent cusses in the United States that they really form a crypto-majority. It looks to me more as if they were a formless, scattered and dominated minority. If it were not so, how could half the country, however shamefacedly, have followed a cynical thug like McCarthy? From fear, yes—fear of Russia? Fear of fear itself. And fear will always find an object. How could an American be proud of his country, how could he help being ashamed, when the voice of McCarthy was heard throughout the world, and was allowed to be heard, as the voice of America? Demagogues, the constant parasites on democracy, come and go, but the rabble whose fears and hatreds they foment are always there to be roused. "McCarthyism" is not dead; it existed long before McCarthy and will long survive him, under different names and other auspices. Like the hysteria it feeds on, it lies, a quiescent but malignant growth, under the thin American skin.

What has become of the American idea, the hope of raising a standard to which all just men could repair? Has it really petered out into a "dream," or worse, into a nervously advertised and jealously guarded "way of life"? I believe that the American experiment was intended as a conscious revolution in human affairs; that the new nation was to be not only an anthology of the best in Europe, it was to evolve a way of living, for all comers, so superior to Europe's ways that the new republic might some day become unique among the nations—a promised land that would honor its promise to any decent applicant.

What has become of that enormous invitation, and the faith it was based on? From the skeptical or European point of view the invitation and its subsequent withdrawal were alike regulated by economic demand. Once America badly needed cheap labor, and rationalized its need by declaring a limitless capacity for making new American silk purses out of any old European sows' ears. The need fulfilled, the United States will now accept only a strictly limited quantity, grading its quotas by an arbitrary assessment of quality—northern and western Europeans are better stuff than southern Europeans, and Orientals almost unusable. The factory of liberty has stockpiled all the raw material it can handle.

America's faith in its own experiment has been further weakened by a growing preoccupation with self-protection—it used to be called "isolationism" and is now "security": both are fancy synonyms for "the fear of being robbed." It is a preoccupation, most Americans say, that has been forced on them by the threat of Russian aggression. But no Communist threat existed when America began to build up its tariff walls and dam immigration to a trickle: these were protective devices against the whole untrustworthy and envious world. The United States has become an exclusive society. Our demagogues now orate about *preserving* America's liberties, not attaining them. Security is the present goal of the American experiment.

In short, the experiment is over. There are still a few loose ends to be tied up—such as making the economy depression-proof, teaching college boys and girls to read and write, raising the Negroes (and their oppressors, the white trash of both North and South) up from third-class to second-class citizens—but America is a huge success, the greatest success that ever came down the pike. All "good Americans" think so, anyhow, no matter what the rest of the world says. For the result of the American experiment is democracy. As every American schoolboy knows, the United States not only invented democracy but has patented it, and owns the world-wide copyright.

"Democracy" is a word rapidly becoming peculiar to America, and almost meaningless elsewhere. (The Communist "people's democracies" are helping to complete the general confusion.) I think the British, who themselves use the word sparingly though they practice the thing itself more thoroughly than we do, are often puzzled by what Americans mean by democracy. What they mean is American democracy, and that means the American way of life. When Americans get wrought up, as they have been lately, their religious zeal for this central article of faith tends to get out of hand. Then those who do not conform 100 per cent to the tenets of Americanism, "loyalty to the American way of life," and who for any reason are reluctant to "stand up and be counted" on the demand of any rascally patrioteer, are tagged as bad Americans, probably traitors and possibly Communist spies.

A few years ago a retired American general announced to an approving civilian dinner party that any American citizen who refused to jump to his feet, whenever called on, and swear allegiance to the Constitution, should be shot. No one at that particular table, luckily, was packing a shooting iron.

Every morning, in every public school, every American school child recites a Shinto prayer—i.e., pledges allegiance to the flag. The flag is regarded not as a symbol, as in other countries, but as a sacred object in itself; its desecration is blasphemy, and to allow a fold of it to touch the ground is pollution. In like manner, the Constitution has replaced the Bible as an object of veneration. The Constitution too is regarded as a sacred object, a more-than-human document, almost literally inspired.

To make the world safe for American democracy the world will have to be, by one means or another, converted to it. So far, America has drawn back from the implications of this logical extreme. Even Russia seems to have temporarily abandoned its equally logical theory of world-wide revolution. But in each case the logic is there, waiting—and others see it, if we don't. Americans did not like the Germans calling themselves, with blood-curdling sincerity, "the master race." Nor did anybody else. And yet Americans wonder why the United States, with all its generous and well-meaning strength, is so widely disliked and distrusted. The outspoken German claim to be the master race was based on the fancied purity of their blood-lines. The tacit American claim is based on the fancied moral superiority of America.

If you ask the bystanders, you will of course get an un-American (i.e., wrong) view. No responsible American has ever quite said so, but the present aim of America seems to be the moral domination of the world. Americans hate and fear—or say they hate and fear—any sort of world domination, by anybody. It is fear of Communist domination that steers American policy. But suppose that American might could make American right everywhere predominant? Would Americans really hate and fear that worldwide domination? Some Americans, not so long ago, were dreaming of a *Pax Americana*, clamping the volcanic surface of the world together. And such an enforced peace, in that dreamy American view, was to be brought about and maintained by a judicious greasing of palms (tactics) and a show of bombs and intercontinental missiles (strategy).

I do not believe that America is pre-eminent in every respect, or even that it is the real leader of the Western world. It is acknowledged to be the richest and claims to be the most powerful country on earth; but I think the grimly emerging fact is that the West has no real leader. The East has its herdsmen and suffers the brutal discipline of the herd. If Eisenhower and Macmillan and Khruschev and Mao * are really in charge of our affairs, then God help us all. The world is going to hell, and has been ever since its record began to be kept. Even so, even if the worst happens, as I think it usually does, I believe that some day in the future there will be another America, because the idea behind the American experiment is too tough to die.

The most pathetic fallacy of our barbarous and backward age is that man is in control of his fate. We cling desperately to this sentimental notion, though its true fanatics are mainly to be found among the Communists. Even their fanaticism cannot stand up forever against the evidence. Men once, at certain times and in some places, knew more and better; they knew that "history" is an ambiguous account of man's superficial disasters and recoveries, and that the only fragments of his real record are to be found in the capriciously preserved or capriciously destroyed works of his art. And that human life, whether it be a mystery, tragedy, dream or fungoid disease, is private and personal—in a slave state as in a free republic, in Russia as in America. The only thing I can do about fate is to bow to it as politely as I can, and all I can hope to do about my own life, which has some untraceable connections with others' lives, is to try to find out who I am. One thing I know about myself is that I am an American—whatever that means.

Being born an American may be luckier, much luckier, than be-

---

* These names will give place to other names.

ing born a Chinese or a Portuguese or a "citizen" of the Dominican Republic, but it cannot free you from the human condition. We're all in that together, separately and alone.

Can I honestly say that I believe in God? Most uncertainly. (I do certainly believe in angels.) But I am not a "naturally Christian soul." If there are such people, and I like to think so, the ones I've encountered, almost without exception, have not followed their bent into the Christian Church. Most of the really religious people I have known have been either agnostics or what the Church calls heretics.

In spite of my background I am not a religious person—not as much as Nicodemus, I think, although I sympathize with his anxious curiosity about religion. The God I was first introduced to was a Protestant God, a stern stickler for proper behavior ("The Lord is in his holy temple, let all the earth keep silence before him"), a relentless layer-down of the Ten Commandments and a pitiless punisher of the guilty—in a word, Jehovah. It never occurred to me not to believe in *Him*. But the only person he seemed to be fond of, as far as I could see, was his only Son, our Lord; and I couldn't understand a love that could abandon Jesus to his dreadful fate, any more than I could understand Abraham's willingness to sacrifice Isaac with his own hand. The doctrine of the Trinity was always a puzzle to me rather than a mystery; I could never get the relations of the three Persons straight, and the Holy Ghost, although for some reason there was an unspecified sin against him which was the very worst thing anybody could do, seemed to me a poor third.

I don't remember when it was that doubts about religion first entered my mind. I think it was at boarding school, when I began to read H. G. Wells. By the time I had reached *God, the Invisible King* and *Soul of a Bishop* and the one about Job, I was a fledgling Wellsian agnostic and humanist. But never an atheist; my doubts were all of Christianity and the Church. When I was allegedly grown up, and trying to define my belief, this was the best I could do: "I think of God (who includes death) as representing a notion so final that it makes all human values irrelevant. But the dialect in which this modern 'God' is being phrased is mathematical and physical rather than religious—a phrasing which amounts to a begging of the traditional questions. 'God' is being increasingly split into two parts: a Christly pseudo-human figure, more and more anthropomorphic, and an unknown, undefined, shadowy omnipotence, further and further removed from human affairs. As the Christ-figure grows more tangible, 'God' grows less so; and the upshot, it seems to me, is that the modern religious-minded man 'takes God' on despair (rather than on faith) and tries to forget the notion, or soothes his irritation with its difficulties by making the Christ-figure more human, more familiar, more contemptibly 'one of ourselves.' "

At college I found myself in the awkward position of being a nonbeliever who nevertheless had to conform or cause a scandal. As the son of the bishop whose diocese included Princeton, I had to do more than conform; I was expected to be an active member of my Church's undergraduate society. For three years I was the lay reader in charge of the mission at "the Basin," Princeton's only white slum. "The Basin" was a hamlet of tumbledown houses and shacks strung along a disused canal. The men loafed or fished in the canal; the women supported them—according to rumor, mostly by disreputable means. It was Prohibition, not our mission, that put the Basin on its feet; the men became bootleggers and began to provide for their families at last.

The mission church at the Basin was a rickety wooden shed, with a rusty iron stove and some benches. On Wednesday evenings, with whatever friends I could dragoon to help me, and a bucket of ice cream and some cookies, we held a party in the church (drawing a curtain across the altar). One of us played the guitar, another a banjo, another a fiddle, I beat the drums, and we all sang songs. The small audience, mostly women and children, were attentive but not enthusiastic. The only applause I can remember was when a man softly struck his palms together, once, and said, "That's all right." On Sunday nights, with an even smaller congregation, I held a service. I had a harder time persuading friends to come with me on Sunday nights, to act as a choir, but they were necessary, as none of the Basin people would open their mouths. Nothing was ever said about it, but it was an understood thing that if they didn't get their party on Wednesday, nobody at all would come to church on Sunday.

As a lay reader I was supposed to read my sermons from an authorized book, but I felt hypocritical enough already, and thought I might ease my conscience by talking in my own words, saying only as much as I actually believed. I supposed the simplest text must be the Lord's Prayer, the inimitable model for all prayer, which had come down to us as the very words of Christ himself. So I started to explain the Lord's Prayer to my Basin people. I didn't get very far. The second Sunday night, on the second phrase, "who art in Heaven," I realized I didn't know what I was talking about. And that was the end of my preaching. As soon as I was out of college and on my own, I stopped going to church.

But the Lord's Prayer continued to haunt me. Though as far as I could see it contained no dogmatic statements of theology—at least it said nothing about the Trinity, nor about God's omnipotence, nor about Christ himself being God—its simplicities went down into unknown depths. The Lord's Prayer had obviously not been a big enough or clear enough statement of belief for the Church; it contained tremendous implications but no exact answers to all the theological questions the Church wanted answered. Hence the Creeds: "I believe in God the Father Almighty, Maker of heaven and earth, And of all things visible and invisible."

Was all that implied in the simple phrase, "Our Father"? Perhaps it was. In relation to our feeble, brief and precarious lives, a longer duration and greater power might seem absolute and eternal. We were simply incapable of seeing or thinking very far into the infinite-finite universe of which, we learned with pain and increasing dismay, we were a smaller and smaller fragment. The Christian Creed was an attempt to reassure the quailing human mind that the Church, at least, understood all that could possibly be known about the real nature of the universe, which it called God, and had put down its findings in compact theological shorthand.

But the shorthand of theology was incomprehensible to me, and the Church's explanations of it equally so—or else so formal or so superficial that they seemed to have lost the original meaning. The Church itself must have forgotten what it once knew. That was no doubt the reason for the schism of Protestantism and all its subsequent fissions—and for the extreme, singular attempts of individual men like Tolstoy to find some lost key to the locked-up secret truth. But what oddly twisted keys they found, or invented! Whatever deep wisdom it might have been that the Church had forgotten, I felt sure it must have been something wiser and wider than Tolstoy's formula—or Gurdjieff's.

For twelve years or so after we left the Gurdjieff group, I was not a member of any church or sect. Julie, who was a naturally religious person, returned to the Church, and tried to bring up our four sons as Christians. At a crisis in my life, when I was forty-two, I too went back to the Church; but not as Julie had done, because it was home to her. I didn't know where else to go, and felt that I had to go somewhere to get out of the hopeless tunnel I was in.

I became an Anglo-Catholic. I went to Mass and Confession; I genuflected and crossed myself and repeated thousands of prayers. My only hope was that by "walking through the act" often enough and long enough I might come to believe in it. And when, on the door of a church in London, I saw a warning sign, "THIEVES infest this church," I tried to tell myself, "Yes, I have come to the right place." If it were true that outcasts and sinners infest the Church, instead of avoiding it, I too might have learned to feel at home there. But the company of saints is too hot for me, and the odors of sanctity too reminiscent of my childhood.

Do I know, after living more than 58 years, who I am? No, I don't. I had hoped that in telling my story I might find out. But in this case I couldn't bring myself to follow Orage's rule of thumb about telling yourself the story over and over. Perhaps in our dreams that is what we do—reiterating with almost idiot persistence, with endless cunning and patience, the dramatized but unresolved problems of our lives, a lifelong conversation with ourselves whose shadowy meaning we only partly realize and whose very terms we do not understand. In our waking lives we try to suppress the shadows and to see ourselves clearly, "as we are"—but I think in a way we see better in the dark, even though we do not recognize what we see as ourselves.

As a child I was told what to believe, and believed it. What I was told included what I should believe about myself. Though later I learned to be skeptical of my instructors and of many things they had taught me, for some reason it never occurred to me that they might have given me, or helped to give me, a wrong idea of myself. Not until I was past middle age did I begin to think, seriously, that the self I thought I knew might not be the real one. The notion came to me first in the form of a joke. I was reading a book by C. G. Jung in which he told of a gloomily pious churchwarden who, when he was fifty-five (just my age at the time) sat up in bed one night and said to his wife; "Now at last I've got it! As a matter of fact I'm just a plain rascal."

A joke? Not to the churchwarden; it was a revelation. And did I really want to be visited by the same sort of flash of recognition? Suppose I too turned out to be a rascal? A hard question. Do we really want to know who we are? Part of us does, part of us doesn't; but once the question is raised, it is even harder to suppress. All my life I had given myself gloomy answers; perhaps they were also wrong answers. Could a rascal then be happy to be a rascal? He certainly couldn't be happy as a churchwarden.

Yes, I want to know who I am. I have picked up a hint here and there, and I have my suspicions; but no certain knowledge. And I haven't allowed myself much time, it's pretty late in the game. Also I don't know any very satisfactory method of finding myself out. I have heard the tone of my voice in Confession, and that whining humility is phony. Dutch uncles seem more useful. One of them has told me that there are certain notions I simply can't swallow without getting pains in the stomach, and, having had an ulcer, I think I see that connection. So far, however, my "researches" are hit-or-miss, and a relaxed attitude seems more favorable to results— such as they are—than earnestness.

Some of my findings are quite funny; at least I think so. Most of us develop the habit of a besetting phrase, and I've been trying to catch mine. It's much easier to notice other people's, and often a temptation to point them out, though you won't be thanked for it. One of my friends has a beauty: "This, that and the other, whatever it may be." I'm not sure, but I'm afraid mine's quite a common one: "I'm afraid. . . ."

I've also made a list of the things I mutter to myself when I'm alone. Here are a few:

"Don't *tell* me!"

"Can you tie that?"

"Son-of-a-bitch."

"O God, what's going on there?"

"How do you like that?"

"Well, God *damn* it. D'you suppose I've lost it?"

"Abandoned me."

"*Ab*-so-lutely hopeless, the whole bloody thing."

For the last few years I have kept a diary (or a noctary) of my dreams. If I weren't so lazy, or for some stubborner reason so averse to remembering them, the record would have many fewer blank pages. It may be (Dr. Jung might say, "it must be") that all the evidence I need is there, in my own handwriting. That's a tantalizing possibility. But I can't understand my own dreams, or what I keep trying, passionately or angrily or brokenheartedly or happily, to tell myself in them. All I can be sure of is that I am there, in ingenious guises and disguises; and I strongly suspect that if only I could recognize myself and see what I was up to, I should see my life with the lid off. Then at last I would know who I am. Sometimes I think that the nearest we get to being alive is when we're asleep.

I have already had a longer life than a great many get—not to mention my better luck in many lesser ways. You might think that anyone of average intelligence and with my advantages would be able to say where he had been and what he had learned in fifty-eight years—even if he didn't know exactly who he was. No, I can't even say that, with any confidence. The list of my accomplishments would read like anyone else's, though it might be shorter than many: can drive a car, shave himself, type (with two fingers), read without moving his lips (though the tendency has to be consciously suppressed), dress himself as quickly as an actor. The list of things I have forgotten would be longer: a little Latin and less Greek, my first sight of a mountain, and of the sea, childhood, early love. That list could go on indefinitely.

As for things I can't do, such as talk in any language but my own, and mend or assemble anything whatever, they would fill hundreds of dull pages. I know, though I am largely unaware of what they are, that I have become barnacled with crotchets, prejudices and habits. I make occasional desperate attempts to be neat, but my desk always gets cluttered and untidy, and I feel uneasily that it is a sign of a disorderly mind.

Is there any hope that in my remaining years I will pull myself together, keep my desk clear, really learn French and Spanish, breathe properly when I swim, become a graceful and witty speaker, recover my forehand drive, write one good poem, love anyone unselfishly, make up for lost time and fulfill the unkept promise, whatever it was, of my life? I have just enough sense to know that there isn't any hope of my accomplishing any of these things. And yet I live hopefully; I am glad—more than glad, thankful, full of thanks—to be alive.

My life has been a good deal like this book. I set out to become a first-rate man, or at any rate a good one, and instead turned into —me. In this book I meant to write the truth, even more of it than was decent, about my life; and I discovered that I didn't know the truth and that there were a good many things I didn't want to tell. This record is incomplete—partial in both senses of the word. As it stands, probably, it has neither given me away nor made my case, whichever you like, any more than a newspaper succeeds in telling you what actually happened to the human race yesterday. A better journalist might have made this book more of a journal. And I have told almost nothing about my personal weather, which, like everyone's, is continuous, ever-changing and unrememberable. Like everyone's, that weather has at times been shockingly bad, "unbearable" or at any rate extremely painful, at other times hopeful, halcyon, unspeakably pleasant.

I have left out almost all the "small things" that fill the days of a man's life, those 25,000-odd days (the Biblical threescore and ten) of which I have now used up nearly 22,000. If I had really tried to describe myself, wouldn't I have confessed that my besetting phrase isn't a phrase at all but an incoherent sound, the same nervous clearing of the throat that I thought so annoying, ludicrous—and, in retrospect, endearing—in my mother? Why haven't I given some indication of the extent to which tennis (and, for fifteen years, its bastard little brother, squash rackets) has both lightened and darkened my life?

In short, I have failed to do what I set out to do. I thought I could paint a self-portrait, warts and all—and found I couldn't. (Why didn't you catch him shaving, or asleep, or when he thought he wasn't being watched? Ah, if only I could have.) So the book has turned out as it has—me again.

This is not a satisfactory conclusion, nor in fact a conclusion at all. I neither can nor want to imagine the ending of my own story —which, like the story itself, I shall have lived through with mixed emotions and no clear understanding. My world, my family, my nature have not taught me clarity. To my pent-up way of thinking, which has no more sense nor reason in it than a dream, in every good man there is a rascal, in every rascal a good man, struggling to get out. I can only be sure that in us, in me, something is struggling.